MARKET FRIENDLY
OR
FAMILY FRIENDLY?

MARKET FRIENDLY
OR
FAMILY FRIENDLY?
THE STATE AND GENDER
INEQUALITY IN OLD AGE

MADONNA HARRINGTON MEYER
AND PAMELA HERD

A Volume in the American Sociological Association's
Rose Series in Sociology

Russell Sage Foundation • New York

Library of Congress Cataloging-in-Publication Data

Harrington Meyer, Madonna, 1959-
    Market friendly or family friendly? : the state and gender
inequality in old age / Madonna Harrington Meyer, Pamela Herd.
        p. cm. — (Rose series in sociology)
    Includes bibliographical references and index.
    ISBN 978-0-87154-598-5 (alk. paper)
    1. Older women—United States. 2. Older women—United
States—Social conditions. 3. Sex role—United States. 4. United
States—Social policy. I. Herd, Pamela. II. Title. III. Series.

    HQ1064.U5H26 2007
    362.6'5610820973—dc22
                                                              2007008382

Text design by Suzanne Nichols.

RUSSELL SAGE FOUNDATION
112 East 64th Street, New York, New York 10021
10 9 8 7 6 5 4 3 2 1

Previous Volumes in the Series

Forthcoming Titles

Pension Puzzles: Social Security and the Great Debate
Melissa Hardy and Lawrence Hazelrigg

The Production of Demographic Knowledge: States, Societies, and Census Taking in Comparative and Historical Perspective
Rebecca Emigh, Dylan Riley, and Patricia Ahmed

Race, Place, and Crime: Structural Inequality, Criminal Inequality
Ruth D. Peterson and Lauren J. Krivo

Repressive Injustice: Political and Social Processes in the Massive Incarceration of African Americans
Pamela E. Oliver and James E. Yocum

Re-Working Silicon Valley: Politics, Power and the Informational Labor Process
Seán Ó Riain and Chris Benner

Who Counts as Kin: How Americans Define the Family
Brian Powell, Lala Carr Steelman, Catherine Bolzendahl, Danielle Fettes, and Claudi Giest

The Rose Series in Sociology

T he American Sociological Association's Rose Series in Sociology publishes books that integrate knowledge and address controversies from a sociological perspective. Books in the Rose Series are at the forefront of sociological knowledge. They are lively and often involve timely and fundamental issues on significant social concerns. The series is intended for broad dissemination throughout sociology, across social science and other professional communities, and to policy audiences. The series was established in 1967 by a bequest to ASA from Arnold and Caroline Rose to support innovations in scholarly publishing.

DOUGLAS L. ANDERTON
DAN CLAWSON
NAOMI GERSTEL
JOYA MISRA
RANDALL G. STOKES
ROBERT ZUSSMAN

EDITORS

to our mothers
Anne and Michele
and our daughters
Ellen and Maureen and . . .

Contents

= About the Authors =

Madonna Harrington Meyer is professor of sociology, director of the Gerontology Center, and senior research associate at the Center for Policy Research at Syracuse University.

Pamela Herd is assistant professor of public affairs and sociology and a research associate at the Institute for Research on Poverty at the University of Wisconsin, Madison.

Acknowledgments

W e are deeply thankful for the assistance of many readers along the way. We thank Paula England for her initial encouragement that we do a book. We thank all of the editors in the Russell Sage Editorial group both for the helpful suggestions we received at their workshop and for their patience and guidance over the last three year: Naomi Gerstel, Joya Misra, Douglas L. Anderton, Dan Clawson, Randall G. Stokes, and Robert Zussman. We also want to thank our anonymous reviewers for important suggestions and criticisms. In particular, we thank our editors at the Russell Sage Foundation, Suzanne Nichols and Matthew Callan.

Several people read the entire manuscript, and for their comments we thank Jill Quadagno, Wendy Parker, Liat Ben-Moshe, and Martha Bonney.

We thank our friends and families, both for their interest in the work and their understanding when we had to work. Special thanks to Samuel, Maureen, Ellen, and Jeffrey Meyer. And special thanks to Don Moynihan.

Chapter 1

Disappearing Problems?
Gender Inequality in Old Age

*When we were on the commission we had a lot of people looking at the current
distribution of retirees and elderly widows and . . . at the low benefits they get.
The issue is, how do you deal with that? Well, that is a disappearing problem . . .
That is not going to be happening in the future. That is not the long run.*
> Tom Saving, Public Trustee for Social Security, and member of
> the President's Commission on Social Security, on how proposed
> Social Security reform might affect older women, speaking at
> The University of Texas at Austin, April 21, 2005.

W E HAVE witnessed an incredible decline in poverty among older
Americans in recent decades. In the 1950s, 36 percent of those
sixty-five and older were poor (U.S. Census Bureau 2004).
Today, only 10 percent are poor. This rate is below the 11 percent for
adults between eighteen and sixty-four and well below the 18 percent for
children (He et al. 2005).

Conventional wisdom is that older people—all older people—are
doing well. Variation between older women and older men, however, is
pronounced. As figure 1.1 shows, older women are nearly twice as likely
to be poor. Higher poverty rates, coupled with the tendency to outlive
men by an average of five years, means that 70 percent of all poor older
people are women (He et al. 2005). Equally important is the degree of
variation among older women by race. The pockets of poverty are most
pronounced for older Hispanic and black women: 22 percent of Hispanic and 27 percent of black women are poor in old age. Older black
women are two and a half times as likely as older white women, and five
times as likely as older white men, to be poor.

Much of the overall improvement in economic and health security
among older people has been linked to the post–World War II economic
boom, increasing levels of education, expansions in employer-provided
benefits, and, in particular, Social Security and Medicare benefits (Estes
2001; Engelhardt and Gruber 2004; Hacker 2002). Improvements in the
economic and health status of older women in particular have been linked

1

Figure 1.1   People Sixty-Five and Older in Poverty, 2003

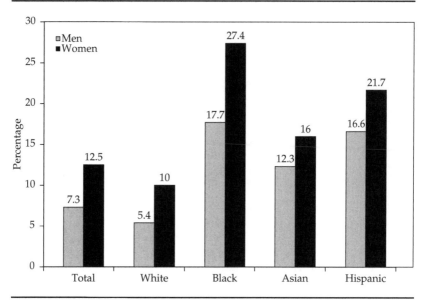

Source: U.S. Census Bureau 2004, table POV01.
Note: Hispanic includes all races. Civilian noninstitutionalized population.

to improved education, greater presence in the labor force, and more equitable wages (Smeeding, Estes, and Glasse 1999). Despite these improvements, inequality among the aged is pronounced. It may even be growing.
Why has it been so persistent? What is the state's role in shaping it?

Our answer to these interrelated questions is straightforward. Times
have changed, but the situation for many older—and younger—women
has not. The problem is that many of the gains made in the family, the
labor market, and the welfare state have been offset by losses in the same
realms. Fewer women are marrying and more are raising children on
their own (Hartmann, Rose, and Lovell 2006). Our social policies fail to
recognize our social trends; couples who are not married, whether gay
or straight, operate without much of a safety net. Moreover, increases at
the top, in the numbers of women doctors and lawyers, for example,
have been offset by lower real wages and limited protections for women
at the bottom of the labor market (England 2006). Furthermore, we
have not adapted the welfare state to make it more responsive to these
changing dynamics. The policy agenda is instead dominated by efforts
to decrease the role of government by constraining welfare costs and
outsourcing social provision to private corporations. Some argue that
strengthening markets will ultimately lead to increased well-being among

older people. Others maintain that, to the extent that social policies are being privatized and downsized, the welfare state may in fact be introducing new risks (Hacker 2006, 2002; Estes 2001; Katz Olson 2003; Gilbert 2002).

What is the role of the state in shaping inequality in old age? The answer depends on whom you ask. In recent decades, a growing share of congressional and administrative leaders have supported a series of proposals aimed at retrenching social welfare, privatizing benefits, and using social policies to bolster markets (Hacker 2006, 2002; Yergin and Stanislaw 1998). Indeed, we are in the midst of an era in which the role of the state is being redefined by corporate leaders, conservative policy makers, and think tanks (Gilbert 2002). The pro-market economic philosophy is that welfare state benefits should be reduced and privatized in ways that maximize individual choice, risk, and responsibility. We refer to the policies favored by the coalition of conservative and traditional liberal ideologies as market-friendly welfare policies.[1]

The contrasting philosophy, that welfare state benefits should offset the harsh realities of the market, reduce inequality, and redistribute risk and resources, is now championed mainly by feminists, sociologists, advocates for vulnerable populations, and a small group of liberal policy makers (Hacker 2002; Yergin and Stanislaw 1998; Estes 2001). They emphasize collective, rather than individual, risk and responsibility. We refer to the policies favored by this coalition as family-friendly welfare policies.[2]

In the middle are a growing group of mostly liberal policy makers and academics who favor what is now dubbed a third way. These policies focus on human capital development such as education and training programs that get people into the labor market, and wage and tax incentives that keep them there (Myles and Quadagno 2000; Reich 1999). They emphasize the commodification of all labor, suggesting that "most people should find their 'welfare' *in the market* most of the time" (Myles and Quadagno 2000, 162, emphasis in original). This approach, similar to market-friendly approaches, neglects the incredible amounts of unpaid care work that mostly women perform, and fails to prioritize social supports that facilitate the juggling of unpaid and paid work. From this perspective, it is hard to distinguish market-friendly from third-way policy. Thus, we generally do not address third-way compromises here. They have little relevance for old age policy in the United States, which has long been more heavily commodified than European policy designs.[3]

Our purpose in writing this book is to analyze the impact of the current tendency to retrench or privatize the old age welfare state and to explore the possibilities of the more redistributive modifications needed to address recent sociodemographic trends. Our concern is that our failure to implement responsive changes, coupled with our growing willingness to retrench and privatize, may well prompt inequality in old age to increase.

We begin by exploring the causes and consequences of inequality in old age linked to gender, race, class, and marital status. We trace efforts to retrench the welfare state, making it more responsive to markets than families, and suggest that this trend may further entrench inequality. Then we lay out a slate of old age policy reforms that respond to socio-demographic trends. We evaluate policy reforms with one criterion in mind: the degree to which they reduce inequality in old age. The evidence suggests that if we do nothing, gender inequality will be very similar in thirty to forty years. If we continue to adopt market-friendly welfare policies, however, gender inequality in thirty to forty years may well be measurably worse.

Gender Inequality

One fact about old age remains stubbornly true. Being an older woman is a substantially different experience than being an older man (Quadagno 1999; Moody 2002; Sahyoun et al. 2001). Although longer life expectancy is clearly a boon, it is problematic for those who face more of the hardships without adequate resources. Women live longer than men. Figure 1.2 shows life expectancy by gender and race in 2002. For all races, women outlive men by more than five years. Black women outlive black men by nearly seven years. Figure 1.3 shows the impact of women's longer life expectancy on the sex ratio. At age sixty-five to sixty-nine, there are about eighty-six men per 100 women. That rate drops quickly. By age ninety and older, there are only thirty-four men for every 100 women. After age 100, women outnumber men four to one.

Given that older women outnumber older men in a fairly dramatic way, it is no surprise that they are less likely than older men to be married. Figure 1.4 shows that older women are only about half as likely to be married. Although older men and women are nearly equally likely to be divorced or never married, older men are much more likely to be married and older women are much more likely to be widowed. In the sixty-five to seventy-four age bracket, 78 percent of the men and only 56 percent of the women are married. Among those seventy-five and older, 70 percent of the men and just 31 percent of the women are married. As figure 1.5 shows, older women are thus more than twice as likely as older men to live alone. In fact, 75 percent of all older people who live alone are women (He et al. 2005). Although living alone has its merits, those who do live alone enjoy neither the benefits of two sources of income nor the economies of scale inherent in living together. Indeed, those who live alone are more than four times as likely to be poor as those who live in couples.

Figure 1.2   Life Expectancy, 2002

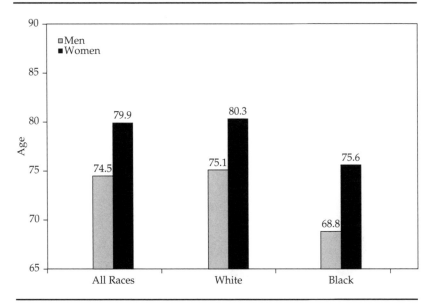

Source: National Center for Health Statistics, 2004, table A.

Figure 1.3   Number of Men per 100 Women, 2000

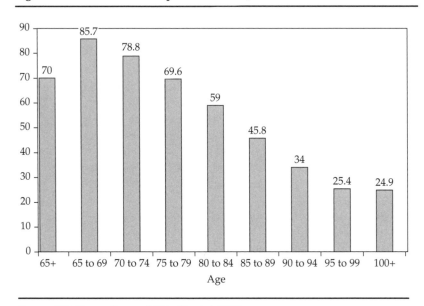

Sources: U.S. Census Bureau 2005a; He et al. 2005.

Figure 1.4   Marital Status of Those Sixty-Five and Older, 2003

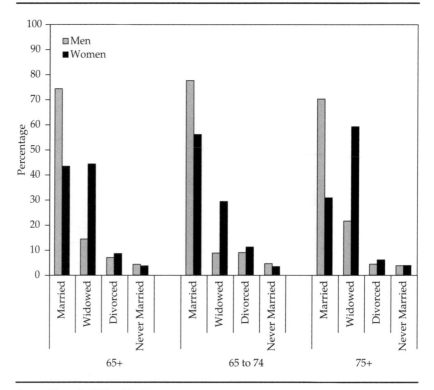

Source: He et al. 2005, table 6-1.
Note: Civilian noninstitutionalized population.

Older women have fewer financial resources than older men, no matter how you measure them. As we show in chapter 4, women's old age income streams are significantly smaller than men's. Throughout the life course, women earn substantially less than men, and black and Hispanic women earn substantially less than white women (Padavic and Reskin 2002; Blau, Simpson, and Anderson 1998). In old age, the picture is no different. Women's average Social Security benefits are 75 percent of men's (Lee and Shaw 2003). They are only 60 percent as likely as men to receive a private pension and when they do receive one the average size is about half that of men's (McDonnell 2005). Women's lower old age income is linked to lower wages and higher responsibility for care work throughout the life course. Women retain primary responsibility for the care of children and disabled and frail adults, though men have become more involved (Hooyman and Gonyea 1995; Padavic and Reskin 2002). Although care work can be emotionally rewarding, it often takes a toll

Figure 1.5   Living Arrangements of People Sixty-Five and Older, 2003

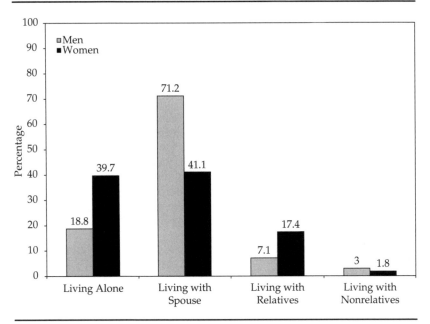

Source: U.S. Census Bureau 2005b, table 6-3.
Note: Civilian noninstitutionalized population.

on care workers in terms of economic, physical, emotional, and social health. Fully 60 percent of adult women will provide care for a frail relative at some point, truncating their wages, pensions, and savings in the process (Katz Olson 2003).

Older women's health is only slightly worse than older men's, but the consequences of poor health are more pronounced for women because they live longer and have fewer resources (He et al. 2005; Himes 2001). Moreover, the exclusion of long-term care coverage in Medicare makes it more difficult for them to obtain formal health care. Obtaining informal care is also more difficult for them because they are so much less likely to have a spouse as their caregiver. Older women are twice as likely as older men to need a caregiver and twice as likely to be one (Hooyman and Gonyea 1995; National Alliance for Caregiving and AARP 2004). Two-thirds of all older people receiving long-term care in the community are women and three-fourths of those receiving care in nursing homes are (He et al. 2005; Estes 2001). We have summarized these gender differences in old age in table 1.1. The discrepancies noted in this chart have persisted for decades; as we shall see, many are likely to persist for decades more.

Table 1.1   Gender Differences

- Older women are nearly twice as likely to be poor.
- 70 percent of all poor older persons are women.
- Women live more than five years longer than men.
- Older women are only 50 percent as likely to be married.
- Older women account for 75 percent of all older people living alone.
- Older women are only 60 percent as likely as older men to be employed.
- Older women's average public pensions are just 75 percent of older men's.
- Older women are only 60 percent as likely to receive private pensions.
- Older women's private pensions are just 50 percent of men's.
- Older women report worse overall health.
- Older women have more chronic conditions than older men.
- Older women report more functional limitations.
- Older women are twice as likely as older men to need a caregiver.
- Women are twice as likely as men to be a caregiver.
- Older women make up 65 percent of the community-based long-term care population.
- Older women comprise 75 percent of the nursing home population.

Source: Authors' compilation.

Inequality Linked to Race, Class, and Marital Status

Considerable inequality between men and women is matched by considerable inequality among women. Thus a comprehensive discussion of inequality in old age requires careful attention to inequality due to race, class, and marital status. As figure 1.1 shows, Asians, Hispanics, and blacks are substantially more likely than whites to be poor in old age due to a broad array of economic and social factors. Education levels vary dramatically among the aged by race. Fully 76 percent of older whites have at least a high school degree, versus only 52 percent of older blacks and 36 percent of older Hispanics (He et al. 2005). Across the life course, whites have higher average earnings and lower unemployment rates than blacks and Hispanics. By old age, family incomes are dramatically different. Among families with a household head between sixty-five and sixty-nine, median household incomes of blacks and Hispanics are 57 percent those of whites (He et al. 2005). Lower incomes lead to lower asset accumulation, and older blacks, Hispanics, and Asians are significantly less likely than older whites to own their own homes. In 2001, for example, 83 percent of whites versus 66 percent of blacks, 65 percent of Hispanics, and 63 percent of Asians were homeowners (He et al. 2005).

Older whites, Asians, and Hispanics are much more likely than older blacks to be married. Marital rates for black women, as shown in figure 1.6, are significantly lower than for other groups. Among those age

Figure 1.6   Married and Widowed Women Sixty-Five and Older, 2003

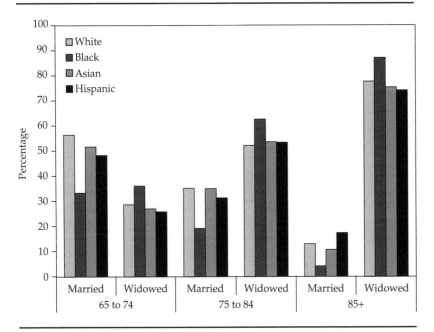

Source: He et al. 2005, table 6-2.
Note: Hispanic all races. Civilian noninstitutionalized population. Married spouse present and widowed.

sixty-five to seventy-four, 57 percent of white women—versus 52 percent of Asian, 48 percent of Hispanic, and just 33 percent of black women—are married. By age eighty-five and older, 17 percent of Hispanic, 13 percent of white, 11 percent of Asian, and 4 percent of black women are married. Partly as a result of lower marital rates, black women are by far the least likely to live with a spouse. Among women sixty-five and older, 42 percent of Asian, 41 percent of white, 40 percent of Hispanic, and 25 percent of black women live with a spouse (see figure 1.7). In the process, black women have less access to multiple income streams and to the economies of scale that come with cohabitation. Along with fewer resources, older blacks and Hispanics have worse health. They tend, as we explain in chapter 5, to be sicker throughout old age and to not live as long as their white and Asian counterparts. The intersection of gender, race, class, and marital status becomes clear in figure 1.8. Among older women who are black or Hispanic, and single and living alone, poverty rates are 40 percent.

Figure 1.7   Living Arrangements of Women Sixty-Five and Older, 2003

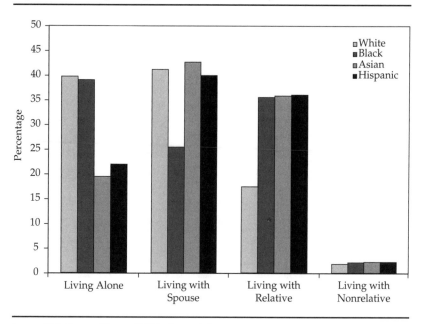

Source: U.S. Census Bureau 2005b, figure 6-4.
Note: Hispanic all races. Civilian noninstitutionalized persons.

Responding to Inequality

Given the existing degree of inequality, the United States could be entertaining, and even implementing, a series of policy changes that would reduce inequality in old age. We are not. In part, inaction is linked to an optimistic political argument that the problem of gender inequality in old age is a disappearing problem (Blau, Brinton, and Grusky 2006; Johnson 1999). Many scholars and policy makers argue that though women who are old today are worse off than older men, their daughters will not be because women's rising education and employment rates may diminish gender inequality with each successive generation. Tom Saving, public trustee for Social Security and member of the President's Commission on Social Security, agreed with this sentiment when he told a University of Texas at Austin audience that the problem of low benefits for older women is a disappearing problem. The result of this optimism is that gender inequality among future generations of older women is receiving relatively little attention in current welfare state debates. Indeed, very few of the debates on the reform of Social Security have even mentioned the impact on spouse and widow programs through which most older women gain benefits.

Figure 1.8   Those Sixty-Five and Older Below the Poverty Line, 2003

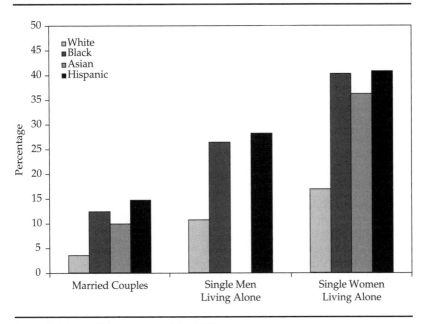

Source: DeNavas-Walt, Proctor, and Lee 2005.
Note: Civilian noninstitutionalized persons.

There is some basis to this optimistic perspective. We have witnessed impressive changes in the last several decades, including a significant movement of women into the labor force, a retreat from marriage, numerous expansions and retrenchments of the U.S. welfare state, and a notable decline in poverty among the older Americans. Nonetheless, the scenario for women born in the 1950s, 1960s, and 1970s may look a lot like that of their predecessors because many of the improvements for women have stalled out (England 2006; Hartmann, Rose, and Lovell 2006; McCall 2001). The sources of old age inequality include gender and race discrimination in the labor force, unequal responsibility for care work, and an increasingly outdated benefit structure in our old age welfare programs (Padavic and Reskin 2002; England 2006; Herd 2005b). Indeed, we are in the midst of large demographic and social changes, and yet the policy changes that would make old age welfare programs more responsive are generally not even on the table for discussion (Hacker 2002).

The second, and more complex, political argument hampering the development of a more responsive welfare state is the growing acceptance of the ideology that welfare policies must be market friendly. The basic premise of this market-friendly economic position is that the government should do less and not more. Emphasis on a market-friendly ideology represents a shift in thinking among those who have long criticized welfare spending. Throughout the 1970s, 1980s, and 1990s, the main tactic for reducing welfare spending was to restrict eligibility, tighten means tests, and minimize benefits. Pro-market politicians and economists argued that tax-and-spend government is too burdensome on businesses. During those decades, welfare state debates in the United States shifted away from questions about how we might best expand social benefits to how we might best restrict them (Aaron and Reischauer 1995; Pauly et al. 1991; Yergin and Stanislaw 1998). Such efforts were modestly successful when targeted at poverty-based programs, but created public outcries when aimed at universal social insurance programs such as Social Security and Medicare (Herd 2005a).

By the mid-1990s, opponents of welfare spending changed their tactics and began to emphasize market-friendly policies. Many corporate leaders, politicians, policy makers, and scholars argue that our existing welfare state programs are too costly and therefore unsustainable. Instead of retrenching benefits, however, they now emphasize privatizing them (Herd 2005a). They demand that the government get out of the retirement business and let the market respond to consumer choices and demands for resources such as old age income, health care, and long-term care (Hacker 2002; Pauly et al. 1991). Individuals should be able to make their own choices about what pension or health care plans to buy into, and the government should neither provide nor restrict those choices. From this perspective, the litmus test for welfare state policies is that they should be market friendly in that they mimic, or even buttress, goods and services provided through the market (Quadagno 1999).

Thus the national policy agenda has been redefined by politicians and policy makers who want to constrain or privatize rather than retool universal old age welfare programs. Instead of redistributive universal benefits, they favor programs that emphasize individual choice, risk, and responsibility (Hacker 2006, 2002; Yergin and Stanislaw 1998). In contrast to those who rather unsuccessfully opposed welfare expansion throughout the 1970s and 1980s by demanding a return to means-tested programs targeted at the neediest of the poor, current opponents demand that we replace public welfare programs with privatized programs that place the market center stage (Herd 2005a). These recent efforts may be more successful in part because they are subtle, confusing, and appear initially to be expansions rather than contractions (Hacker 2002, 2006; Pierson 2001; Quadagno 1999).

They may also be more successful because, with the increase in support of market-friendly welfare policy, calls for family-friendly welfare policies that would alleviate old age inequality by expanding redistributive and universal coverage for older people have subsided to a whisper (Myles and Quadagno 2000). Serious policy proposals aimed at expanding welfare state benefits to offset the inequalities created by the market, socialize risk and responsibility for care work, and provide a safety net below which no one would fall, are difficult to pinpoint on the political landscape (Hacker 2002; Yergin and Stanislaw 1998; Estes 2001; Myles and Quadagno 2000). The feminist sociological perspective of using welfare state benefits to reduce inequality is not well represented outside of academia and liberal policy organizations.

Critics of market-friendly welfare policies suggest that the free-market economic approach emphasizes individual risk and responsibility and undermines the philosophy of social risk and collective responsibility. They point out the ironies in the market-friendly approach. Pro-market policy makers criticize high welfare costs but propose solutions that will in fact raise costs (Herd 2005a). Pro-market policy makers criticize government involvement but propose solutions that in fact increase governmental regulatory involvement (Herd and Kingson 2005). Their most serious concern, though, is that market-friendly proposals under-mine redistributive features in ways that few Americans seem to under-stand (Harrington Meyer 1996; Herd 2005a). Instead of shifting benefits from the well off to the most vulnerable, market-friendly programs are more likely to benefit the well off than the poor. Moreover, advocates of family-friendly welfare policies are concerned that the failure to develop and implement responsive new welfare policies, coupled with a grow-ing willingness to retrench and privatize existing programs, may well cause inequality in old age to increase.

From the family-friendly perspective, the U.S. welfare state has failed to expand in ways that would reduce gender and race inequality, and has retrenched in ways that have entrenched inequality in old age. The few programs that embrace redistributive and universal features have been tinkered with, or may soon be tinkered with, in ways that increas-ingly privatize costs and risks rather than socializing them across the broader population. To be clear, the stakes are high. Our two universal old age programs, Social Security and Medicare, have been proven to reduce poverty and inequality. Pro-market economic policies intend to redefine these programs with privatized programs that have, thus far, proved unsuccessful at reducing poverty, inequality, costs, or govern-ment involvement (Korpi and Palme 1998; Engelhardt and Gruber 2004; Moon with Herd 2002).

Here we contrast the market-friendly welfare agenda of retrenchment and privatization with a family-friendly welfare agenda of social expan-sion, intervention, and insurance. This family-friendly approach builds on work by feminist sociologists such as Joan Acker (2006), Carroll Estes (2001), Nancy Hooyman and Judith Gonyea (1995), Jill Quadagno (1999, 2005), Angela O'Rand and John Henretta (1999), Walter Korpi and Joakim

Palme (1998), and others who take a life course perspective and emphasize a universal social welfare agenda as the best method for reducing old age inequality. Rather than cuts, supporters of family-friendly welfare proposals lay out specific policy proposals aimed at improving the redistributive impact of universal old age programs, thereby reducing old age inequality. On the heels of European scholars such as Korpi and Palme (1998), supporters of family-friendly policies suggest that universal benefits are the most efficient and effective method of improving the physical and fiscal health of marginalized older Americans. From this perspective, our failure to adjust or expand the welfare state has less to do with cost and more to do with redirecting social resources to the market.

Overview

As we assess economic and health instability in old age, we explore variation between older men and older women and among women with respect to race, class, and marital status. Although many scholars emphasize the intersection of gender, race, and class, we stress that it is important to also take marital status into account both because it shapes income and health so dramatically and because the United States has a long-standing tradition of distributing welfare benefits on that basis (Harrington Meyer 1996; McCall 2001; Lorber 2005; England 2006; Herd 2005b). Benefits linked to marital status have provided a vital safety net for women whose retired worker benefits would otherwise be meager. Critics of the benefits, however, point out that marital rates are down, particularly for black women. Moreover, cohabiting partners, whether homosexual or heterosexual, remain unrecognized by most federal and state welfare programs (Harrington Meyer, Wolf, and Himes 2006). Coverage provided by this safety net is thus growing increasingly spotty and may in fact be contributing to, rather than reducing, old age inequality.

Chapter 2 lays out two competing positions on the state's role in shaping old age inequality. Since the late 1970s, the dominant political ideology guiding welfare state development has been a market-friendly approach, which draws on neoconservative and traditional liberal theory and seeks to minimize government supports and regulations while maximizing individual choice, risk, and responsibility. The contrasting family-friendly approach, which draws on feminist life course theory, argues that a universal and redistributive welfare state is needed to lessen the inequalities created by the market and other social institutions. Supporters of family-friendly policies seek social provision aimed at reducing inequality linked to gender, race, class, and marital status.

In the latter half of the chapter, we apply these competing philosophies about the role of the state to three main debates surrounding how social resources should be allocated. First, we address their respective positions on whether welfare benefits should redistribute risk and resources from the well off to the most vulnerable. Should benefits be directly linked to contributions, or be progressive so that those with a lifetime of lower contributions receive a higher replacement rate? The redistributive impact of welfare policies is profoundly shaped by whether benefits are linked to income, employment, marital status, citizenship, or residency. Second, if we do redistribute, should benefits be targeted or universal? Historically, many European counterparts have favored universal benefits, which reduce gender and race inequity, and the United States has favored targeted programs, which tend to increase inequality (Gilbert 2002; Skocpol 1991; Grogan and Patashnik 2003). The tension between the efficiencies of targeting versus the costlier effectiveness of universalism is persistent in policy debates. Third, should benefits be gender neutral or gender targeted? Benefits can be designed to reward either women who embrace the stereotypical male breadwinner role or those who embrace the stereotypical female caregiver role. A consensus is emerging, however, that suggests this is a false dichotomy. The trick is to address gender inequality for various combinations of these roles while simultaneously addressing inequality by race and marital status. Finally, we summarize how privatization has reshaped welfare state debates and redefined the role of the state.

In chapter 3, we set the stage for our discussion of old age inequality by reviewing the factors that have shaped women's financial security over their life courses. We review the literature on inequality in the labor force and in families. We assess the market-friendly perspective that gender and race inequality in various forms of income are linked to weaker education, experience, or ties to the labor force. We also assess the family-friendly perspective that even when women, and particularly minority women, have equal human capital and work records, they tend to have worse outcomes. We find that even though there have been many gains, including rising labor force participation, a shrinking wage gap, and somewhat more equitable division of labor at home, those advances have been offset by losses in the same areas. Gender inequalities remain pervasive across the life course. Moreover, inequalities among women linked to race, class, and marital status contribute to growing inequality in old age. Decreasing rates of marriage, coupled with rising rates of single parenting, mean that more women are juggling paid and unpaid work on their own. A central consequence has been increasing inequality among women throughout the life course. The outlook for future generations of women is not much different than the realities of today—some will accumulate advantages throughout their lives and fare particularly well in old age, and others will accumulate disadvantages and enter old age with relatively few resources.

Chapter 4 explores women's economic resources in old age. We assess gender, race, class, and marital status differences in retirement income, including Social Security, Supplemental Security Income (SSI), private pensions, and savings. We show how demographic trends, particularly the retreat from marriage and the rise in single motherhood, interact with changing policies to increase women's economic vulnerability in retirement. Social Security is the most important source of income for older women. Its progressive benefit structure does a lot to reduce inequality in old age. In fact, for people in the bottom fifth of the earnings distribution, the ratio of benefits to taxes is almost three times as high as it is for those in the top fifth (CBO 2006). Poverty among the elderly would be four times higher if they did not have Social Security (Porter, Larin, and Primus 1999). Still, the program could be made more responsive to changing families. Its retired worker benefits best reward those with long histories of high earnings and its spouse and widow benefits best reward those with long marriages and no work history. Increasing numbers of women, particularly black women, do not fit either mold and they pay a hefty price. To a much lesser extent, SSI plays a role in poor women's income security in old age. Like other income and asset tested programs, SSI generally fails to provide much protection to the poor. In contrast to the large growth in Social Security since its inception, SSI coverage of the aged has shrunk dramatically. Strict asset guidelines that have been in place since the 1980s, coupled with penalties for wages or cohabitation, mean that many poor are ineligible and many who are eligible find it burdensome to apply.

We then explore inequality in private sources of income, particularly pensions and savings. Pensions are both a primary source of private retirement savings and a strong determinant of income security in old age. We show how both the chances of having a private pension and the size of that pension are linked to gender, race, class, and marital status. We also enumerate some of the adverse effects of the shift from defined benefit to defined contribution plans, particularly for poor and less educated women. Although some argue that the portability of defined contribution plans will be beneficial for women, we suggest that the size of women's pensions will continue to be smaller than men's, given occupational segregation and interruptions for child care. We also explore how women's ability to accrue savings and assets is affected by work experiences, race, marital status, and children. As important as they are, women are decidedly less likely than men to establish independent sources of private savings for retirement. Blacks and Hispanics are even less likely than whites to accrue assets such as homes. Ultimately, we show how reliance on market-friendly solutions leads to market-based forms of inequality. Other than Social Security, few family-friendly income benefits are available to soften the blunt forces of the market.

Inequality is therefore growing and will likely continue to grow for future cohorts.

In chapter 5, we turn to health inequality. Too often, assessments of inequality in old age emphasize economic considerations without paying careful attention to the impact of health inequalities. We begin by taking stock of gender, race, and class inequalities in old age health. We then assess the main sources of old age health insurance, Medicare, supplemental insurance, and Medicaid, focusing on their strengths and weaknesses in addressing health inequality. As costs for these programs spiral out of control, the emphasis in Washington is increasingly on cost cutting and cost shifting. We focus on the ways in which cost containment has lead to retrenchments that are increasing inequality in old age. For example, we show how the 1997 Omnibus Reconciliation Act has had pronounced consequences for Medicare recipients, hitting older women, blacks, Hispanics, and the poor hardest. The premiums for Part B have already risen sharply and are expected to continue in an upward direction. Because of the cost-cutting initiative, Medicare beneficiaries' out-of-pocket costs will rise by 94 percent between 1998 and 2025. These expenditures, which usurped 19 percent of older people's incomes in 1998, will usurp 29 percent by 2025 (Moon with Herd 2002).

We then turn our attention to privatization. Although not commonly recognized, the privatization of Medicare has already begun. Many beneficiaries are already in health maintenance organizations (HMOs), which has led to very predictable patient skimming. Congress has also recently shifted more money toward HMOs in the hope that more older Americans will participate in them—despite the fact that they have raised, not lowered, costs. Moreover, the new Medicare prescription drug policy provides coverage not by giving the benefits to the aged through Medicare, but by subsidizing insurance companies to encourage them to offer drug-only insurance packages to older people. Efforts to implement such market-friendly plans prevail even though they have led to higher costs. The market-friendly impetus to act as informed consumers has proven difficult for older people, as Robert Pear reported in the *New York Times,* both because reliable information about the dozens of plan choices is hard to obtain and because decisions must be based on predictions about future health ("Investigators Find Medicare Drug Plans Often Give Incomplete and Incorrect Data," July 11, 2006, p 1). This sort of privatization undermines the universal and redistributive features of the Medicare system and further entrenches gender, race, class, and marital status inequality in old age.

Chapter 6 traces recent market-friendly proposals to retrench and privatize old age welfare state programs. Despite dramatic demographic and social changes, including the decline in marriage, the increase in divorce, greater life expectancy, and women's increased participation in the labor force, our main old age programs are unchanged. The reason is that the policy proposals now on the public agenda are focused not on making our old age programs more responsive to changing families, but on making them more responsive to changing markets. To the extent that market-friendly policies are implemented, they will entrench rather than alleviate gender inequality in old age.

With respect to Social Security, we trace efforts to undermine and preserve this universal entitlement. In contrast to the notion of a fiscal crisis, we point to evidence that modest repairs are all that are needed. We then explore the impact of various proposals on inequality in old age. The bottom line is that recent market-friendly policy proposals do not address the shortcomings of the existing policies. Rather than reducing inequality, we show how these proposals will exacerbate the income problems women face in old age. With respect to health care issues in old age, we argue that the rhetoric of fiscal crisis is correct. Medicare is on the cusp of bankruptcy. Medicaid costs now dominate most state budgets. Efforts to privatize have thus far generally reduced protection and raised costs. We explore the impact of various cost containment proposals, including reducing payments to providers and suppliers, reducing service use, increasing beneficiary cost sharing, raising the beneficiary age, and raising taxes. We then concentrate our analysis on the implications of privatization within Medicare. All of these proposals will reshape access to care and are likely to increase inequality in old age.

In chapter 7, we assess family-friendly social policy alternatives aimed at moving us further toward universality and at reducing inequality in old age. Given that the sources of inequality have not changed substantially, the problem of gender inequality in old age is not a disappearing problem. Thus, Social Security and Medicare will remain enormously important to ensure women's income security in old age. We assess proposals aimed at making these programs more responsive. We also assess family-friendly reform proposals that attend to inequality throughout the life course. The purpose of these programs would be to enable women to reach old age with greater economic, physical, and political strength.

With regard to Social Security, we assess several reform proposals that would address the ways in which Social Security fails women. Most prominent reforms currently on the table disregard the difficulties families have balancing paid and unpaid work. We use a Social Security policy simulation that allows us to see how changes to eligibility and benefit amounts would affect women who retire between 2020 and 2030. We examine the impact of reforms common in Scandinavian welfare states, where poverty rates among older women are the lowest in the world. We find that these reforms, particularly minimum benefits and credits for raising children, would shore up economic security for all, regardless of marital status. We also find that disentangling benefits from marital status is key to reducing inequality, given both that the decline in marital rates is so much more pronounced for blacks and that the federal government continues to refuse to recognize either gay or straight cohabitating couples.

With regard to Medicare, the evidence suggests that minor revisions will not do. In contrast to market-friendly proposals that may work to increase inequality, family-friendly policy proposals call for a single-payer national health insurance program for all ages. From this perspective, the reduction of health inequality in old age is best accomplished by a national health insurance program that is progressively financed, focused on prevention rather than profit, and that is, at least in principle, already quite popular with the majority of Americans. Despite claims that we can not afford a single-payer system, failure to implement universal health insurance has little to do with cost. In fact, a single universal health care system would likely save us money. Given that a move to national health insurance for all ages may not be politically feasible, we also assess a slate of reform measures that will make Medicare more cost effective and more responsive to the changing needs of older Americans.

Finally, because inequality in old age is mainly the cumulative effect of life-long inequality, we turn our attention to programs that might help families balance paid and unpaid work throughout the life course. When we position the United States in the context of European nations, our welfare programs for those in the earlier stages of the life course are quite limited. We lay out the case for the two universal programs that we think would have the greatest egalitarian impact on younger families: universal day care (or PreK) and paid family leave. We then review the strengths and weaknesses of the poverty-based benefits currently in place to provide various levels of support to families: Earned Income Tax Credit (EITC), Temporary Assistance for Needy Families (TANF), and Medicaid. We find that these programs (with the possible exception of the EITC) are politically unpopular, at risk of budgetary cuts, and do too little to help families juggle paid and unpaid work and prepare for the economic and health hardships associated with old age.

The United States is riding a wave of market-friendly welfare revision and our intent is to analyze the implications of this wave. If we continue to emphasize market-friendly rather than family-friendly social policies, the evidence suggests that those with ample resources may be fine, those without may not. Decades of work by social activists to implement family-friendly policies that spread the costs and risks of dependency across the entire population and offset the inequalities that accumulate over the life course may be replaced by market-friendly policies that emphasize individual choice, risk, and responsibility. Such policies are likely to make inequality among the elderly more, rather than less, pronounced (Wray 2005).

It is ironic that policy makers are retrenching and devolving even our universal programs at a time when the vast majority of Americans think we are doing too little for older people. Between 70 and 90 percent of poll respondents report that they would be willing to pay higher taxes to keep universal old age benefits and that they favor universal health insurance for all (AARP 2005; Pew Research Center 2005; Public Agenda 2005; Quadagno 2005; Street and Sittig Cossman 2006; Century Fund 1998). It is not middle-class, working class, or poor people in the United States who favor privatization or devolution or retrenchment. The proponents of market-friendly policies include many conservative politicians, corporate leaders, lobbyists, health insurers, pharmaceutical companies, and other fairly well-off individuals who stand to gain from these policies— who prioritize individual gain over the collective good (Quadagno 2005; Hacker 2006). In stark contrast, the proponents of family-friendly policies prioritize reduced inequality. They favor policies that correspond with family demographics in the twenty-first rather than the nineteenth century; redistribute resources through universal programs in ways that constrain rather than escalate gender, race, class, and marital status inequality; and spread the costs and risks of old age dependency across families rather than concentrating them within families.

Chapter 2

Market Friendly or Family Friendly? The Role of the State

It is more respectable than it was a few decades ago to defend near-complete laissez-faire.

Milton Friedman, in 1994 at the Hoover Institute, excerpt from the 50th Anniversary edition of Hayek's *Road to Serfdom*.

WHAT IS the role of the state in shaping old age inequality? Welfare programs may be arranged in ways that add new sources of inequality, replicate market and social forms of inequality, or reduce inequality. Although the overall financial and health outlook for the aged is the best it has been in our nation's history, inequality on both measures is widespread. At present, policy proposals that might reduce it and make the old age welfare state more responsive to changing social and demographic trends have been pushed off the national agenda by market-friendly proposals that aim to constrain and privatize social benefits and may, in the process, increase old age inequality.

Scholars and policy makers have long debated the proper role of the state in shaping inequality. Proponents of a market-friendly welfare state, which has gained popularity in recent decades, suggest that inequality is a natural and even necessary component of a capitalist economy (Hacker 2002; Yergin and Stanislaw 1998; Quadagno 1987). We do not need a large welfare state aimed at reducing that inequality. Rather, government regulations and supports should be kept to a minimum and be devised in ways that are market friendly (Aaron and Reischauer 1995; Pauly et al. 1991). Individual choice, risk, and responsibility should be maximized. Cato Institute's David Boaz explains that when people are held individually responsible for their welfare, they are more responsible acting in their self-interest (Wray 2005).

By contrast, proponents of a family-friendly welfare state suggest that inequality is indeed a common product of a capitalist economy, thus we need a well-developed welfare state to lessen those inequalities, protect families from the insecurities of the market, and help families balance the

Table 2.1   Market-Friendly Versus Family-Friendly Welfare State Policies

Market friendly
  Retrenchment and containment
    -Reduce welfare expenditures, corporate and personal taxes.
    -Emphasize free market.
  Privatization
    -Eliminate or reduce government regulation and provision.
    -Outsource provision to free market.
  Individualism
    -Emphasize individual choice, risk, and responsibility.

Family friendly
  Expansion and revision
    -Implement programs that help families balance paid and unpaid work.
    -Make programs more responsive to sociodemographic changes.
  Public provision
    -Reduce inequalities generated in the market and other institutions
    -Increase public oversight.
  Universal and redistributive
    -Spread the risk and repercussions of market instability.

Source: Authors' compilation.

demands of work and home. They point out that the emphasis on individual choice, risk, and responsibility overlooks the degree to which both economic and health inequalities are shaped over the life course by structural inequalities in education, employment, families, and other social institutions. They suggest that cumulative disadvantages across the life course create conditions wherein certain groups—notably women, blacks, Hispanics, and the unmarried—are particularly disadvantaged in old age (Collins 1991; Misra 1998, 2002; McCall 2001; Acker 2006). Thus individual choices and actions are shaped by historical, political, and economic factors—with different consequences for some than for others.

    Whether poverty and ill-health in a land of plenty are worthy of state intervention is fundamentally a moral question, the answer to which depends entirely on what ideological perspectives are embraced in social and political arenas. In this chapter, we consider two ideological perspectives that are central to current welfare state debates. We contrast the market-friendly and family-friendly positions on the role of the state in shaping old age inequality (see table 2.1). We then turn to the welfare state debates that have dominated the literature for years but have found new and different life in the wake of efforts to privatize public welfare. First, should welfare benefits be flat, or should they redistribute resources from the well off to the most vulnerable? This debate, historically earmarked as adequacy versus equity, is revived under efforts to privatize precisely because privatized benefits do not redistribute risk and resources. We spotlight the importance of adequacy, suggesting that the main aim of welfare programs is to redistribute in ways that minimize rather than maximize inequality. Second, assuming that at least some redistribution is wanted, we address the advantages and disadvantages of distributing benefits on the basis of universal versus targeted principles. Because targeted programs tend to be so unpopular, universal benefits are essential to reducing inequality and standing up to ongoing political threats. Third, we attend to the debate over whether benefits should be distributed in ways that are gender neutral versus gender accommodative. It is increasingly important that we find ways to do both. Finally, we explore how privatization cuts across all of these debates, posing new sets of possibilities and problems in the old age welfare state.

The Role of the State

The Great Depression, and the apparent pitfalls associated with relatively unrestrained free markets, ushered in an era in which government was seen as a friend rather than a foe of both society and the economy. From the 1930s through the 1970s, Keynesian economics prevailed and provided the rationale for ever-expanding social welfare programs (Quadagno 1987; Yergin and Stanislaw 1998; Hacker 2002). The logic for increasing welfare was that it would even out the instabilities of the business cycle, stabilize consumer demands, and anchor solidarity and loyalty among citizens. Wealthy nation states expected to convert economic surpluses into an ever-expanding collection of social benefits for citizens. Throughout Europe, governments grew, centralized, and strengthened the regulation and provision of services that had once been located entirely in the private domain. The United States followed suit. Indeed, the modern U.S. welfare state emerged from the depths of the Great Depression and continued to expand through the 1970s. Universal programs such as Social Security, Medicare, and unemployment insurance, as well as poverty-based programs such as Medicaid, AFDC, WIC, and Section 8 Housing, all emerged during this era to provide protections against the instabilities of capitalist economies (Katz 1986; Hacker 2002). By the late 1970s, however, stagflation, national debt, government waste, rising corporate and personal taxes, and the birth of numerous technologies prompted the beginnings of a return to a free-market, even pro-market, agenda (Quadagno 1987; Yergin and Stanislaw 1998).

Market-Friendly Welfare Policies

Since the late 1970s, one of the dominant political ideologies shaping welfare state debates has been the notion that too much government intervention is destructive to economies and societies as a whole (Yergin and

Stanislaw 1998; Gilbert 2002). Growing impatience with big government was driven in part by an economic downturn in the United States. That impatience was fueled when the economic and social collapse of the Soviet Union seemed to further vindicate free market proponents. The United States joined its European counterparts in shifting from an era in which states provided extensive social benefits and exercised considerable regulatory control over markets to one of governmental downsizing, decentralization, privatization, and deregulation (Yergin and Stanislaw 1998; Estes 2001; Hacker 2002).

Weary of expensive welfare programs and restrictive government regulations, conservative and libertarian economists and policy makers argued that big government hamstrung free markets, interfering with growth and profits (Myles 1996; Quadagno 1987; Myles and Quadagno 2000; Wray 2005). Social welfare provisions such as Medicare and Medicaid came to be seen as federal meddling "because markets have intrinsic virtues such as efficiency and consistency with the principles of personal autonomy and freedom" (Aaron and Reischauer, 1995, pg. 2). Politicians began to echo economic warnings that big government was too costly, interfered with corporate profits, and undermined individual responsibility and effort (Quadagno 1987; Yergin and Stanislaw 1998). Welfare programs were reframed, from being part of the solution to the inequalities generated by free markets, into a problem that the free market could best correct (Gilbert 2002). Proponents of market-friendly welfare policies aimed to reduce government expenditures on social welfare, taking corporate and personal taxes down with them. Americans elected officials at the federal and state level who promised to downsize, deregulate, and decentralize government. Twentieth-century progressive thinking gave way to a traditional free-market liberalism that reframed public debates (Friedman 2002; Hayek 1994; Hayek, Kresge, and Wenar 1994). Pro-market economic theory embraced by conservative politicians and voters supported a reduced role for the state, a free market, and maximum individual choice, risk, and responsibility.

By the 1990s, many government leaders and voters had accepted much of free-market thinking, promising to decrease federal government, privatize social services and benefits, and increase individual responsibility. Milton Friedman, one of the architects of the free-market libertarian economic agenda, celebrated their success in reframing public debates: "Talk is about the free markets and private property, and it is more acceptable than it was a few decades ago to defend near-complete laissez-faire" (1994, pg. 16). Similarly, Fred L. Smith Jr., president of the Competitive Enterprise Institute, signaled the success of the individualistic and competitive social and economic agenda when he said, "I am elated that the forces of collectivism have suffered great setbacks during the last 50 years." (Friedman, 1994, pg. 20)

In many ways, free-market proponents have been very effective in achieving their goals. Government officials have reduced or contained many welfare expenditures and orchestrated a massive deregulation and privatization of services once provided by the government (Hacker 2002; Yergin and Stanislaw 1998). Indeed, social spending has fallen from 20 percent of GDP in 1975 to 17 percent, and corporate taxes have fallen from 3.5 percent of tax revenues in 1962 to 2.5 percent (Hacker 2002; Walker 2006). Most sectors, from airlines to telecommunications, have seen a dramatic reduction in government regulation, and proponents emphasize the positive impact of that change. Deregulation and privatization have led to more consumer choice, more competitive pricing, and, some would argue, improved standards of living (Yergin and Stanislaw 1998).

In the past twenty years, the U.S. government has turned over the provision of a wide variety of services to the private sector, everything from power and water supplies to trash pickup (Hacker 2002). It has increasingly done the same with social welfare (Quadagno 1999). Ironically, though free-market theory dictates a reduced role for government, in many ways government has increased its role—but rather than supporting people, it is supporting corporations (Hacker 2002). Government officials are shifting many of welfare responsibilities to the private market through private companies and improving corporate profits at the same time. Jill Quadagno (1999) describes the shift to a capital investment state wherein public benefits coincide with the interests of the private sector, transferring risk and responsibility to individuals and their families. Efforts to use social welfare expenditures to push beneficiaries into market programs are nowhere as pronounced as with the recent efforts to grow Medicare Advantage HMOs and PPOs (Herd 2005a). As we discuss in chapter 5, efforts to use public welfare spending to expand HMO markets have been sweeping. Yet Medicare is paying more, not less, per enrollee in the program, even though the stated intent was cost savings. Government spending to encourage the growth of Medicare HMOs represents a substantial shift toward privatization in the welfare state and marks a growing commitment to market-friendly welfare policies.

Proponents of market-friendly policies contend that a smaller government with more restricted budgetary and regulatory capacity will interfere less in the private market. Less burdened by federal taxes and regulations, corporations may be more competitive, raising wages and expanding fringe benefits and enabling workers to support themselves and their families with little support from a welfare state (Wray 2005; Gilbert 2002). The premise is that what is good for Wall Street is good for Main Street. Conservative economic theorists have generally not favored welfare programs that address inequality linked to gender or race discrimination, for example, because they argue that these inequalities will generally disappear in the competitiveness of a free market

(England 2006; England and Folbre 2005). They have generally opposed programs or regulations that address gender and race inequality in wages because they attribute differences in pay to differences in human capital development such as less education, less experience, and less training (England 2006).

Government policies that offset gender, race, and class inequality are believed to create market inefficiencies (Acemoglu and Angrist 2001). Indeed, proponents of market-friendly policies warn that welfare in general is costly, encourages lazy dependence on the state, and undermines individual choice, risk, and responsibility (Murray 1984; Katz 1986; Hacker 2002; Wray 2005). Protective employment policies directed at women are bad for business—and also bad for women because they tend to make employers less likely to hire women (Jacobs and Gerson 2004). The market-friendly approach to welfare provision is subtly underpinned by notions of filial responsibility (England and Folbre 1999; Folbre 1994; England 2006). It is expected, though rarely stated explicitly, that the care and feeding of all those who are unable to care for or feed themselves will be performed by family members (Acker 2006; Folbre 1994; Katz 1986). In a free-market scenario that emphasizes individual choice, risk, and responsibility, welfare programs that would help families balance paid work with the unpaid work of caring for children and disabled or older adults are generally opposed.

From a market-friendly perspective, a healthy free market negates the need for a well-developed welfare state. Although this economic scenario might work in theory, it has not proved effective empirically.

> The move to the market may bring a higher standard of living, better services, and more choice. But it also brings new insecurities—about unemployment, about the durability of jobs and the stress of the workplace, about the loss of protection from the vicissitudes of life, about the environment, about the unraveling of the safety net, about health care and what happens in old age. (Yergin and Stanislaw 1998, 404)

Throughout this volume we address these new insecurities. The market-friendly thrust raises concerns for several reasons. First, to the extent that the United States constrains and privatizes welfare benefits, universal, and redistributive features of the old age welfare state will be undermined. As a result, older people and their families may face growing inequalities. Second, privatizing and retrenching welfare programs will transfer even more responsibility for unpaid care work for children and disabled and older adults to families. Third, preoccupation with market-friendly policy initiatives interferes with serious consideration of policy proposals that would make existing universal old age benefits more responsive to changing demographics and social trends. Fourth, privatization, which is actually the outsourcing of social provision from government agencies to private companies, redefines recipients from beneficiaries to consumers, which has thus far been fairly problematic, particularly for those with fewer resources. Finally, privatization removes social debates and decisions from the social arena, pushing them out of sight and out of reach (Estes 2001; Gilbert 2002; Herd 2005a; Acker 2006; Yergin and Stanislaw 1998). As a result, privatization impedes social research. It is substantially more difficult to conduct analyses of the impact of social policies provided through private, for-profit firms (Weir 1998). Ultimately, because it truncates the capacity of welfare programs to redistribute risk and resources from the well off to the most vulnerable, privatization concentrates risk and responsibility on individuals and their families rather than spreading it across society more generally.

Efforts to downsize public benefits for older people and their families have come at a time when corporations are also downsizing benefits for employees and their families. Corporate America has made it clear that it will not pick up the slack if welfare programs are dismantled. Already, companies have eliminated or reduced many employee income and health benefits. Employers are shifting pension coverage from defined benefit to defined contribution plans, reducing their expenses and risk by shifting portions of each back to employees. Similarly, employers are reducing expenses and risk by cutting employee and retiree health benefits. Indeed, the proportion of workers with employer-provided insurance has diminished dramatically over the last few decades. Those who continue to have these benefits, generally full-time and more highly paid employees, face growing cost-sharing and shrinking coverage. If government and corporate benefits are shrinking simultaneously, what are typical families to do? According to proponents of market-friendly welfare policies, they are to act as individual consumers, exercising individual responsibility and choice, which will drive market competition and improve system efficiency (Pauly et al. 1991).

Acting as consumers will be challenging for future cohorts of retirees whose retirement income will have been shaped by stagnating wages and growing income inequality. Although wages have risen dramatically for some, for others the past thirty years have been about declining real wages. Since the late 1980s, overall income and wealth inequality have risen. Families in the highest fifth of the earnings brackets now make thirteen times what those in the bottom fifth make each year, up from a factor of seven in the 1960s (Fields 2003; U.S. Census Bureau 2004; Eitzen and Baca Zinn 2003; Danziger and Gottschalk 1994). Market-friendly welfare supporters see little problem with income inequality per se, but generally want overall standards of living to improve for each generation. Meanwhile, real wages are actually falling at the very bottom of the distribution and median wages have been flat since the 1960s (Waldfogel and Mayer 1999; Hoynes, Page, and Stevens 2005).

Family-Friendly Welfare Policies

The counter to market-friendly welfare policies are family-friendly welfare policies. Proponents of family-friendly policies—who include feminists, sociologists, liberal think tanks, and activist groups that represent vulnerable populations—argue that we need a well-developed welfare state to offset the harsh inequalities of the market. The aim is to provide public rather than private benefits that help families balance paid and unpaid work. Supporters favor universal and redistributive social insurance programs that take into account major sociodemographic changes already well under way. Proponents of family-friendly policies stress the many ways that discrimination on the basis of gender, race, class, and marital status limits resources, opportunities, and full participation in social, political, and economic life (Herd and Harrington Meyer 2002; Estes 2001). To redress these inequalities, they advocate welfare programs that will protect individuals and their families from the harshness of profit-driven corporations and offset poverty and inequality generated in social institutions. In contrast to the individualistic notions of market-friendly policies, family-friendly policies are based on collective notions and emphasize the need to spread risk and insecurity across families rather than concentrating them within families. The ideology rests on collective solidarity, rather than individual competition (Orloff 1996, 1993; Quadagno 1999; Harrington Meyer 1996; Estes 2001; Acker 2006).

Some scholars suggest that the family-friendly perspective has been nearly silenced, relegated to a shrinking pool of left-wing academics (Friedman 1994; Yergin and Stanislaw 1998). Indeed, in the existing climate, few elected officials dare to speak of a protective or redistributive role for the government (Hacker 2002). Among scholars and among voting citizens, however, the debate over the proper role of the state and the market in social provision remains vigorous. Feminist sociologists note how the conservative emphasis on individual choice, risk, and responsibility overlooks the degree to which corporations and other institutions constrain individual agency. They caution that in the rush to minimize government and maximize corporate profits we risk growing inequality along the lines of gender, race, class, and marital status. Indeed, they suggest that instead of reducing inequality, social policies created under an agenda of free-market liberalism are likely to reinforce, or even magnify, inequalities created by the market (Acker 2006; Quadagno 1999; Estes 2001; Herd 2005b). The central concern is that the types of social policies possible under a market-friendly agenda are fundamentally different—and less effective at reducing inequality and poverty—than those under a family-friendly agenda.

Family-friendly advocates favor welfare state policies that will help families balance paid and unpaid work, but are divided about how best to accomplish this goal. Some favor a gender-neutral approach, others a gender-accommodative approach. Historically, liberal feminists have focused on removing barriers to fair competition, so that women and men share equal responsibility for and rewards from the home, the labor market, and the political arena (Lorber 2005; Jacobs and Gerson 2004; Tong 1998; Bergmann 1982, Brenner 1987; Reskin and Hartmann 1987, Pascall 1986). They have generally been concerned with integrating higher paying and higher prestige occupations, reducing the gender gap in wages, and demanding equal opportunity. This perspective integrates more readily with a market-friendly agenda because of its emphasis on individual rather than collective action. Because their aim is for women to compete fairly with men on the current playing field, supporters of more gender-neutral policies have not supported expansive paid maternity, family leaves, or child allowances (Jacobs and Gerson 2004; Hewlett 1986). They suggest these benefits link women even more closely to unpaid care work, entrenching the gendered division of labor, and subverting the goal of an equal division of labor in both the paid and unpaid arena (Morgan and Zippel 2003; Mandel and Semyonov 2006, 2006; Bergmann 1982; Brenner 1987; Jacobs and Gerson 2004; Hewlett 1986; Harrington Meyer 1996; Misra 2002). In short, they may drive women away from paid employment and toward unpaid care work. In addition, the presence of these benefits may make hiring women more costly, prompting employers to discriminate against women in hiring, wages, and promotions. They are largely correct on both counts. Women in countries with more established child care benefits do the majority of unpaid domestic labor. In countries with the most generous family benefits, such as Sweden, most women are hired in fairly traditionally female jobs in government or public service agencies, rather than in more male-dominated jobs in private company settings (Morgan and Zippel 2003; Mandel and Semyonov 2006; Hewlett 1986; Gornick and Jacobs 1998).

By contrast, socialist feminists have historically been much more likely to favor welfare policies that help women balance work and family, even if in the process women were further entrenched in a traditional division of labor (Lorber 2005; Tong 1998; Nakano Glenn 2005; Fraser 2005). Socialist feminists favor welfare policies that rewrite the rules to reward women for both the paid and unpaid work they are doing (Lorber 2005; Nakano Glenn 2005; Fraser 2005; Hewlett 1986; Pascall 1986; Herd and Harrington Meyer 2002; Harrington Meyer 1990; Quadagno 1988). Socialist feminists are critical of the tendency to devalue unpaid care work precisely because women do so much of it (Pascall 1986; Quadagno 1988; Moen, Robison, and Fields 1994; Bianchi, Milkie, and Sayer 2000). Indeed, women perform the majority of care work for children, people with disabilities, and the aged (Cancian and Oliker 2000; Hochschild 1997; DeVault 1987; Hooyman and Gonyea 1995, Bianchi, Milkie, and Sayer. 2000; Bianchi, Robinson, and Milkie 2006). Instead of regarding welfare benefits such as paid parental leaves, health insurance, child care credits, child allowances, and flex time as benefits to women, feminist sociologists regard them as vital benefits to children (Korpi 2000). Aided by such programs, women are somewhat freed up from unpaid domestic labor. They are thus better able to compete with men in the workplace, if they so choose. They are also, however, somewhat more freed up from paid work. Thus if they prefer, they may concentrate more fully on unpaid work (Herd and Harrington Meyer 2002). In short, they have a much greater range of options and bear less of the costs associated with care work (Korpi 2000; O'Rand and Henretta 1999; Sainsbury 1999).

Although feminists who favor gender-neutral approaches strive to free women from unpaid work and make them more available for paid work, their counterparts who favor gender-accommodative approaches strive to free both men and women from the demands of paid work to have more time for families, leisure, or social activism (Korpi 2000; Sainsbury 1999; Orloff 1993; Misra 2002). Europeans, despite considerable variation across countries, have more fully embraced a feminist socialist agenda and have shorter work weeks, less overtime, and more vacation time, sick leave, and paid absences. They thus work fewer hours and are less likely than their U.S. counterparts to be on call for their jobs around the clock (Padavic and Reskin 2002; Hochschild 1997; Leete and Schor 1994). They also generally have a smaller gender gap in wages, fewer poor older women, and more women in elected office (Siaroff 2000; Smeeding and Sandström 2005). Supporters of family-friendly welfare programs favor policies that shore up women's economic situation without making them reliant on husbands or forcing them to choose between paid and unpaid work to the degree that the choice is forced in the United States (Edin and Lein 1997; Zimmerman 1993; Siaroff 2000; Sainsbury 1999; Leira 1992; Korpi 2000; Herd and Harrington Meyer 2002).

In addition to expanding welfare provision in ways that help families juggle work and home life, proponents of family-friendly policies call for a retooling of existing programs to make them more responsive to sociodemographic changes. In the past four decades, we have undergone major sociodemographic changes, including unprecedented increases in women's labor force participation, divorce rates, cohabitation, and single parenting (Padavic and Reskin 2002). Our social policies have not kept pace and proponents of family-friendly welfare policies campaign for revisions that will make welfare programs more responsive to current family forms (Orloff 1993, 1996; Estes 2001; Harrington Meyer, Wolf, and Himes 2006; Acker 2006). This lapse in responsiveness is quite apparent in the current debates about Social Security. As we will show, declining marital rates, especially among black women, mean that a growing proportion of older women will reach old age ineligible for spouse and widow benefits. Although the implications of these shifts are far reaching, they are not being addressed in welfare debates or policy initiatives. Proponents of family-friendly policies emphasize how persistent organizing features of social life in the United States, notably gender, race, class, and marital status, continue to generate significant income and health inequality across the life course (Acker 2006; Orloff 1996; O'Rand and Henretta 1999; McCall 2001; Lorber 2005; Padavic and Reskin 2001; Hooyman and Gonyea 1995; Estes 2001). The family-friendly perspective suggests that we need a public, universal, redistributive welfare state to offset inequalities created by the market and other social institutions.

Discriminatory practices and outdated benefit structures play a central role in shaping economic and health inequality for older women today and will continue to do so for their daughters and granddaughters (Estes 2001; Calasanti and Slevin 2001; Harrington Meyer 1996; Quadagno 2001; Hooyman and Gonyea 1995). There is little question that many of the difficulties associated with old age fall disproportionately on women. Remember that women live longer, are sicker along the way, have fewer economic resources, and both perform and require the bulk of long-term care. Women are more directly affected by the old age policies currently in effect—and by our failure to implement any that are more responsive. Thus the story of inequality in old age is first a story of gender inequality in old age. But it is also a story of inequality linked to race and ethnicity, class, and marital status. Advocates of family-friendly policies pay careful attention to multiple layers of accumulating inequality, highlighting the more severe forms of disadvantage found at the intersection of gender, race, class, and marital status (Baca Zinn and Thornton Dill 2005; Misra 2002; Lorber 2005; Tong 1998). Indeed, among older, single black women, poverty rates exceed 40 percent and health outcomes are significantly lower than for any other group (U.S. Census Bureau 2005a; He et al. 2005; Himes 2001).

For supporters of family-friendly policies, the emphasis on life course ramifications is pivotal because it highlights the cumulative effects of various forms of inequality at different stages of life (Elder 1985, 1998; Pavalko, Elder, and Clipp 1993; Harrington Meyer and Pavalko 1996; Settersten 1999, 2003; Moen, Robison, and Fields 1994; Moen and Wethington 1999). For example, when women take time out from work to raise children, the immediate consequence is loss of salary, but the long-term consequence is reduced access to public pensions, private pensions, savings, and fringe benefits (Padavic and Reskin 2002; Harrington Meyer 1996; Hooyman and Gonyea 1995; Estes 2001; Harrington Meyer and Pavalko 1996; Dannefer 2003; O'Rand and Henretta 1999; Pavalko and Smith 1999; Settersten 1999, 2003). People take different pathways through their life courses, facing different societal and institutional pressures and expectations, and experiencing different fortune or misfortune linked to gender, race, and class cleavages (O'Rand and Henretta 1999; Settersten 1999, 2003). Thus a lifetime of performing unpaid care work, often in concert with paid work, leaves many older women at a much greater disadvantage than men (O'Rand and Henretta 1999; Pavalko and Smith 1999; Hondagneu-Sotelo 2000; Hooyman and Gonyea 1995). Similarly, a lifetime of performing lower-waged domestic or agricultural work leaves many older black and Hispanic women at a much greater disadvantage than their white counterparts.

Family-friendly policies recognize that those who arrange their lives to fit the rules for work or benefit programs tend to be more financially secure in old age (Katz Olson 2003; Harrington Meyer 1996; Estes 2001). Working continuously in highly paid employment with excellent fringe benefits, including health insurance and a private pension plan, is one way to maximize financial security in old age. Another is to be married to a highly paid employee with excellent fringe benefits, as long as the marriage does not end in divorce. Many women who juggle paid work and unpaid care work, however, find that they pay the price in old age; often in relatively low-wage jobs without fringe benefits, they fail to meet the requirements for a private pension, employer-based health insurance, or maximum Social Security benefits (Katz Olson 2003; Estes 2001; Harrington Meyer, Wolf, and Himes 2006). Cumulative advantage is not randomly distributed. The capacity to arrange one's life so as to maximize benefits under current benefit structures varies by gender, race, and class precisely because the benefit rules were created to be maximally beneficial to certain groups (Harrington Meyer 1996, 2000; Quadagno 1984; Estes 2001; Orloff 1993; Sainsbury 1993).

If the social, political, and economic institutional factors that constrain women's choices and shape the outcomes of various types of choices are socially created, they can be recreated (O'Rand and Henretta 1999; Estes 2001; Padavic and Reskin 2002; Hooyman and Gonyea 1995; Acker 1988, 1990: Quadagno 1988; Minkler 1986). Advocates of family-friendly policies point out that the rules can be rewritten so that they represent and respond more to vulnerable populations, reducing inequality linked to gender, race, class, and marital status (Lorber 2005; Tong 1998; Kennelly 1999; McCall 2001). By way of example, many women care for frail older relatives, and even find the work fulfilling and rewarding, but few chose to pay a price so dear with respect to income, private and public pensions, or health (Bengston, Parrott and Burgess 1996; Minkler 1986; Katz Olson 2003; Padavic and Reskin 2002; Harrington Meyer 2000; Herd and Harrington Meyer 2002). Given a highly restricted range of options, they may choose to forfeit long-term economic security to provide much needed care work to a spouse or parent. Given a fuller range of options, most would certainly prefer to perform care work as they secure a more stable financial outlook for their own future. Supporters of family-friendly policies highlight the potential role of the state in lessening inequalities generated by a capitalist economy and recognize the potential for welfare policies to expand the slate of options available to families. Rather than concentrate risk and responsibility on individuals and their families, the aim of supporters of family-friendly policies is to develop universal social insurance policies that spread the risk and socialize the impact of market ups and downs. They favor universal policies because they are more effective at reducing inequality and because they build social solidarity rather than competitive individualism (Estes 2001; Korpi and Palme 1998; Skocpol 1992; Quadagno 1994; Orloff 1996).

Under the existing set of rules, some fare very well and others do not. It is critical to identify the forces behind current attempts to privatize, devolve, and dismantle various welfare programs and to pay careful attention to the underlying power dynamics that shape social inequality and social policy. Lower incomes and disproportionate responsibility for care work inhibit women's clout in the economic market and in the political arena. Those with greater incomes and little responsibility for unpaid work generally have greater clout in economic and political arenas, but may be less likely to support policy changes that would produce more egalitarian results (Hernes 1987; Lister 1997). Indeed, those faring well under the current system may have few incentives to change it, while those faring poorly may have few resources with which to demand change (Estes 2001; Padavic and Reskin 2002; Hooyman and Gonyea 1995; Acker 1988, 1990: Quadagno 1988, 2001; Minkler 1986). In our final chapter, we assess a slate of policy proposals that cover the life course and are consistent with the family-friendly objectives of implementing programs aimed at helping families juggle work and family, responding to important sociodemographic trends, reducing inequality generated in the market and other social institutions, and spreading rather than concentrating the burdens of risk and responsibility.

Welfare State Debates

From the market-friendly perspective, then, welfare states should be small. Because they regard the welfare state as an impediment to the free market, pro-market conservatives call for a lean government with spare regulatory and support functions (Hacker 2002). They seek to maximize individual choice, risk, and responsibility. When the government does provide social benefits, it should do so in ways that coincide with trends in the private sector (Quadagno 1999, 2001). Over time, consumer competition will create efficient and effective benefits. By contrast, from the family-friendly perspective, the market already constrains individual choice, risk, and responsibility too severely. The last thing advocates for vulnerable populations want is a greater foray into privatized benefits, precisely because they are likely to increase inequality in old age. Instead, family-friendly advocates favor national, compulsory, universal benefits that redistribute resources to the most vulnerable groups and spread risks for market instability across all age groups. They want to take privatization off the table and refocus the national debates on reforms that will make existing universal programs for the aged more responsive to social and demographic changes and decrease rather than increase inequality among the aged.

Regardless of political perspective, it is important to recognize welfare state policies as systems of distribution and stratification with a wide range of effects (Acker 1988, Esping-Andersen 1990; Korpi and Palme 1998; Ruggie 1984; Skocpol and Armenta 1986; Walzer 1988; Harrington Meyer 1996; Quadagno 1999; Misra 2002). Some programs reduce inequality. Others replicate or even magnify it. The impact of welfare state programs depends to a large extent on the features that define distribution in any given policy. In this section, we address three underlying tensions that shape social policies and, in turn, shape the effects of those policies.

Flat Versus Redistributive

Welfare states may distribute benefits on the basis of contributions or redistribute from the wealthiest to the poorest. In other words, they may replicate and highlight inequalities born in the labor force and in the unequal division of labor in families, or they may be used to intervene and reduce some of that inequality. In reading the papers regarding the origins of Social Security at the National Archives, we were struck by how often legislators and policy makers debated the question of adequacy or equity (Harrington Meyer 1996). It's not that their attention to the poor was surprising; it is our lack of attention to the poor in current debates that is surprising (Myles and Quadagno 2000).

In a system based on equity, both the funding mechanism and the benefit formula are flat. Taxes are collected through a flat tax and benefits are to be paid out in the same proportion they were paid in. In a system based on adequacy, both the funding mechanism and the benefit formula are progressive, so that higher earners pay in at a higher proportion and receive benefits at a lower proportion than do lower earners. Social Security is a mix. Social Security is taxed by a flat tax, but because that tax has an annual ceiling, it is in fact regressive. In other words, lower-income people pay a higher proportion of their income to Social Security. We could remove the Social Security tax ceiling and create a truly flat tax. We could also switch to a progressive structure, such as an income tax, that emphasizes adequacy. Benefits paid through Social

Security are already redistributed progressively. Lower-income benefi-ciaries receive a higher return on their contributions than those with a lifetime of higher earnings do. Legislators in the 1930s, realizing that a flat benefit ratio would not provide adequate income to older people with a lifetime of low earnings, deliberately implemented a redistribu-tive benefit formula to rectify that shortcoming (Harrington Meyer 1996).

The importance of adequacy seems to have slipped off the national radar (Myles and Quadagno 2000). In thousands of pages of debate over the privatization of Social Security, few even mention that priva-tization would weaken the redistributive features of Social Security. Such a move would be particularly harmful for older women, blacks and Hispanics, and anyone else with lower lifetime earnings. Atten-tion to adequacy should be pivotal in policy debates; from our perspec-tive, progressive redistribution should be a central tenet of welfare state policy.

Targeted Versus Universal

Early welfare programs were nearly always social assistance programs based on means-testing or targeting. The intent was to provide a bit of relief for a bit of time, and only then to the most needy and deserving (Harrington 1984; Katz 1986). Unlike Europe, the United States has maintained a steady diet of means-tested, poverty-based programs, notably TANF, Medicaid, SSI, food stamps, and WIC. Proponents of these programs argue that they are less expensive and more efficient in that they target resources only to the very poor (Murray 1984; Gilder 1981). They discourage dependency on the welfare state because bene-fits are small and temporary; thus they encourage self-reliance. Critics of targeted programs argue that these benefits are politically divisive because they pit taxpaying contributors against highly stigmatized wel-fare recipients. Means-tested welfare programs are politically unpopu-lar and therefore politically vulnerable (Katz 1986; Gutmann 1988; Block 1987; Quadagno 2005). Furthermore, they have limited efficacy because, with the exception of the EITC, they have generally not pulled people out of poverty.

Universal programs, by contrast, are based on an ideology of social insurance. Benefits are generally more generous. Because all pay in and all receive benefits, these programs have historically been regarded as politically unifying and politically invincible (Harrington Meyer 1996; Esping-Andersen 1990; Katz 1986). The United States has only two uni-versal programs for aged and disabled citizens: Social Security and Medicare. Unlike targeted programs that emphasize gatekeeping and cost containment, universal programs boast broad eligibility, rela-tively generous benefits, and sweeping approval by voters (Estes 2001;

Quadagno 2005). They are decidedly more effective at reducing poverty because coverage is so much more comprehensive and benefits are so much more generous (Korpi and Palme 1998).

The debate over targeting versus universalism has grown more complex in recent years but these complexities have not overshadowed the basic elements of the debates (Skocpol 1991; Grogan and Patashnik 2003). Targeted programs tend to increase inequality because so many who are poor do not actually receive the benefits and because the benefits are meager and distributed on the basis of complex guidelines aimed at keeping most people off the roles (Myles and Quadagno 2000). Targeted programs do not, generally, bring people out of poverty. To be eligible, one has to be significantly below the federal poverty line, and as income and assets approach the cut-offs, benefits dry up (Katz 1986; SSA 2006). Targeted programs are less costly, in part because the benefits are small, and in part because cuts to benefits are rarely opposed. The constituents of poverty-based programs are not well represented in legislative arenas and more well-to-do constituents are not overly concerned with the welfare of these programs (Quadagno 2005; Estes 2001; Katz Olson 2003; Misra 2002; Herd and Harrington Meyer 2002). One exception to this, which we will discuss in chapter 7, is the EITC.

By contrast, universal programs tend to decrease inequality because nearly everyone receives benefits and the benefits received are relatively generous—often near or above the poverty line. In fact, the combined value of Social Security and Medicare is credited with reducing poverty among the older adults from more than 50 percent during the Great Depression to about 11 percent in 2005 (Engelhardt and Gruber 2004; Katz Olson 2003; Quadagno 2001). Universal programs are costly not only because of the magnitude of benefits but also because proposed cuts face enormous opposition by very well-organized old age constituencies. Recent attempts to privatize Social Security were met with perhaps the most pointed rebuttal the AARP has ever set forth. Despite the variety and number of other contributing factors that helped swamp these attempts, there is little question that the AARP's unified and well-funded response curbed legislative activity.

The universal versus targeted debate highlights the moral underpinnings of any welfare state discussion. Shall we, as the wealthiest nation, provide a certain set of social rights to all citizens or not? Shall we have good schools, good health care, and a guaranteed income for all? During the 1960s, 1970s, and 1980s, a great many scholars and policy makers argued that universal benefits should be expanded (Katz 1986; Piven and Cloward 1982; Block 1987; Gutmann 1988; Harrington 1984; Korpi and Palme 1998; Esping-Andersen 1990). The political agenda, however, shifted dramatically when President Reagan was elected and downsizing became the political buzzword (Piven and Cloward 1982;

Block 1987; Gutmann 1988; Estes 2001; Quadagno 2005). The debates pivoted and the emphasis shifted from expansion to cost-containment, personal responsibility, devolution, new federalism, and privatization (Estes 2001; Katz Olson 2003; Quadagno 1999, 2005). Opponents of universal programs argue that the programs are simply too big and archaic, that we can no longer afford them because of their adverse effects on labor costs, productivity, and public coffers. These opponents, though, do not favor targeting as the alternative. The debate is now about privatization (Herd 2005c). Regardless of the high degree of risks associated with them, markets are regarded as more modern and dynamic, hence the impetus to privatize (Quadagno 1999).

Gender Neutral Versus Gender Accommodative

One persistent tension that underlies debates on the distribution of welfare benefits relates to the gendered division of labor. Feminists have long debated whether welfare state benefits should be based entirely on contributions through paid work, and therefore gender neutral, or based on a mix of contributions through paid and unpaid work, and therefore gender accommodative. The American welfare system is based on an outdated male breadwinner–female homemaker model in which men make claims as paid workers or right bearers, and many women make claims as dependents or clients (Sainsbury 1994, 1999). The former tend to receive more generous and stable benefits that are considered social rights and the latter smaller and more precarious benefits that are considered social favors (Harrington Meyer 1996; Acker 1988; Ruggie 1984; Orloff 1993; Misra 2002). Supporters of gender-neutral welfare policies prefer redefining women's roles so that women compete more fairly and aptly with men and claim benefits equivalent to men's (Bergmann 1982; Brenner 1987; Hewlett 1986; Padavic and Reskin 2002). They criticize gender-sensitive polices such as paid family leaves and job sharing because, they argue, linking benefits to those duties keeps women linked to those duties. They argue that the development of gender-accommodative policies undermines efforts toward gender equity by further entrenching the gendered division of labor at home and by concentrating women in lower-paying, traditionally female occupations (Mandel and Semyonov 2006; Morgan and Zippel 2003). They favor an equal division of paid and unpaid work and a gender-neutral welfare state that generally links benefits to paid work rather than marital or parental status.

By contrast, supporters of gender-accommodative policies argue that such policies are needed to account for the unequal amounts of unpaid work that women continue to perform (Hewlett 1986; Pascall 1986; Herd and Harrington Meyer 2002; Harrington Meyer 1990; Quadagno 1988).

Rather than demanding that women and men be treated fairly on the existing playing field, those who favor gender-accommodative programs aim to change the playing field. They do not want to define such benefits as benefits for women, but as benefits for families and children. They want men and women to receive benefits from the state that help them juggle family and work. Given that women still perform the bulk of unpaid work at all stages of the life course, benefits such as paid parental leave, care work credits, or subsidized child care are indeed gender accommodative.

Review of this debate is particularly useful in calling to our attention the incredible diversity among women. Instead of looking for a single model, welfare state policies need to take into account growing diversity among women by race, class, and marital status. It is not a question of choosing gender neutral or gender accommodative, then, but of doing both. From a family-friendly perspective, the aim is to develop a slate of policies that enable women and men to better juggle work and family across the life course. The aim is to organize social provision in ways that allow families to perform unpaid care work and paid work without facing such extreme economic consequences in terms of reduced wages, health insurance coverage, public pensions, and private pensions.

Impact of Privatization on Welfare State Debates

The market-friendly approach has taken central stage in debates on the provision of welfare across the life course. Opponents of big government want to downsize the federal government by outsourcing public provision to private firms. Getting government out of the pension business is one of the battle cries for those who want to privatize Social Security (Becker 2005; Quadagno 1999; Myles and Quadagno 2000; Estes 2001: Katz Olson 2003). As we will show, the provision of both old age income and health benefits is increasingly mimicking the private market. This outsourcing of welfare programs to private providers has thus far failed to contain costs or reduce government involvement. Not only that, it has moved decisions about who shall receive what benefits out of the public eye and out of the public control (Weir 1998; Estes 2001). Perhaps most important, efforts to reduce government involvement and increase individual choice, risk, and responsibility have generated new sources of inequality and instability in old age.

Ironically, privatization cuts across all these debates. Privatized systems could be either flat or redistributive, targeted or universal, or gender neutral or gender accommodative. Once benefits are privatized, however, we as taxpayers and voting constituents have very little say with regard to any of the debates. If managed-care health facilities skim off the healthiest applicants and leave the less healthy uncovered, what can we do about it? If private pension firms restrict eligibility or default on their promises, what can we do about that? The answer, of course, is fierce federal regulation and enforcement. Such a solution is ironic given the rhetoric of policy makers eager to downsize the federal government. In the end, we can use the federal government to create simple and effective programs that provide universal coverage and a decent safety net for all; alternatively, we can pay for the private market to provide benefits through a complex web of programs that we will be hard pressed to either navigate or regulate.

Whether we will continue to attempt to privatize old age benefits is uncertain. What is certain is that providing benefits through the market is profoundly different than doing so through the welfare state. Public benefits are generally compulsory and redistribute both resources and risk. Rather than hold each individual or family entirely responsible for their own welfare, social provision spreads risk and responsibility across all families. The importance of such redistributive insurance can hardly be overstated; some families have considerable resources and relatively few hardships, others are overburdened. A family with a disabled child and a sick parent is hard pressed to be fully self-supportive. A family with all four grandparents in failing health simultaneously finds the going decidedly rough. Social benefits are most beneficial to those with fewer resources and greater hardships.

By contrast, private benefits offered by employers or the private sector are generally neither compulsive nor redistributive. They tend in fact to be most beneficial to those in higher income groups. For example, the proportion of workers covered by private pension benefits jumps from 16 percent in the lowest quintile of earners to 72 percent in the highest quintile. The picture is similar for employer health insurance. The proportion of covered workers jumps from 24 percent in the lowest quintile to 69 percent in the highest (Hacker 2002). The market-friendly emphasis on privatization and maximum individual risk, responsibility, and choice has eclipsed serious debate about redistribution, universality, and gender accommodation. We weave these distributional principles back into the debates, highlighting how various policy decisions either increase or reduce inequality in old age.

The Role of the State in Old Age Inequality

Who is responsible for taking care of older people? For the better part of a century, the U.S. answer has been the three-legged stool. A third of old age security should come from the welfare state, through universal and poverty-based benefit programs. Another third should come from the corporate sector, through employment-based benefits. The remaining third should come from older individuals themselves. Since the late 1970s and early 1980s, however, policy makers have restricted supports provided through the welfare state, employers have cut benefits provided through jobs, and many older people and their families are left wondering how they will respond to these growing insecurities (Harrington Meyer 1996, 2005; Estes 2001; Katz Olson 2003, Quadagno 2001).

Recent efforts to shift the costs of old age dependency onto the shoulders of individual families are not without precedent. Indeed, they reflect a return to pre-industrial welfare provisioning. Historically, most societies placed the burden of any sort of dependency squarely on the family. Between the mid-1800s and mid-1900s, however, modern welfare states became increasingly involved in taking responsibility for at least some basic needs of certain, if not all, citizens. Welfare states offered health insurance, income security, family benefits, and more because policy makers recognized that filial responsibility had real limits (Katz 1986; Harrington Meyer 1996). For many families, needs far outpaced resources. The aged came to be defined as the deserving poor and policy makers recognized that filial responsibility concentrated risk, privatized cost, and maximized inequality between families.

The United States was reticent in comparison with most other developed western nations, exceptionally slow to form programs, and exceptionally restrictive with the benefits offered (Quadagno 1999). Nonetheless, between the 1930s and the 1970s, the United States implemented and expanded poverty-based welfare programs, such as Medicaid and SSI, and two universal programs, Social Security and Medicare. A major point of U.S. exceptionalism, however, has been the tendency to rely on employment-based benefits encouraged through tax breaks to employers. As a result, most Americans with health insurance or a private pension obtain them through their jobs (Hacker 2002). Benefits offered by employers, however, only spread risk, share costs, and alleviate inequality for those with strong enough links to the labor force to receive the benefits (Harrington Meyer and Pavalko 1996). To the extent that they have weaker links, or are less rewarded for their efforts, women, minorities, and part-time or low-wage workers are significantly less likely to reap the rewards of employment-based benefits (Harrington Meyer and Pavalko 1996; Harrington Meyer 1996). By contrast, benefits offered by welfare states have the potential to spread risk, share costs, and reduce economic uncertainty and inequality (Korpi and Palme 1998). Particularly when universally distributed, welfare state benefits are proven effective at reducing inequality.

Although the U.S. welfare state never caught up to the level of universalism of many peer nations, it has begun dismantling in earnest. In recent years, costs for welfare state benefits and employment-based benefits alike have spiraled and containment has become a central preoccupation. Since the late 1980s, the United States has undertaken various forms of retrenchment, devolution, and privatization, neglecting reforms that would make policies more responsive to social and demographic trends (Estes 2001; Quadagno 1999, 2001: Hacker 2002; Katz Olson 2003; Harrington Meyer 2005).

At the root of dismantling efforts is the goal of shifting responsibility from welfare states to corporations, from employers to employees, from collectives to individuals (Estes 2001). The aim is to transfer responsibility from Pennsylvania Avenue or Corporate America to Wall Street or Main Street (Quadagno 1999). Rather than provide benefits through the welfare state or through employment-based programs, the goal of twenty-first-century individualist policies is to minimize both government and corporate expenditures by relying on a free market to provide services to older people. The pro-market agenda is to encourage each individual to invest for old age and then to let him or her face the consequences alone. Proponents of individualistic market solutions seem unconcerned that some people will earn too little to make such investments, that some will be displaced or downsized out of the market, or that many will have needs that far outpace their resources. Given recent fluctuations, the extent to which we will link public old age income benefits to the stock market is unclear (Myles and Quadagno 2000; Hacker 2002; Baker and Weisbrot 1999). The impact of the shift toward individualistic rather than collective solutions, though, will be quite clear. Those with adequate economic resources can weather the impact of financial, physical, and other sorts of downturns, but those with more modest resources cannot. We already have high levels of old age inequality. One sure outcome of shrinking welfare- and employment-based safety nets is even higher levels of inequality (Street and Wilmoth 2001).

Chapter 3

Accumulating Inequality
at Work and at Home

The unwritten requirement for success in corporate America is to be a corporate man.
Former women executive quoted in Crittenden (2001)

It really does raise this question for all of us, and for the country: When we work so hard to open academics and other opportunities for women, what kind of return do we expect to get for that?
Harvard University Director of Admissions
Marilyn McGrath Lewis, on learning that 60 percent
of a small email sample of Yale undergraduate
women reported that when they had children they
planned to cut back on paid work (Story 2005)

To UNDERSTAND women's lives in old age, we must understand how their earlier experiences have shaped their present circumstances. Work and family experiences in their twenties, thirties, forties, and fifties ultimately shape women's retirement experiences. In this chapter, we explore how women accumulate fewer resources than men across the life course. We note how trends in work and family among today's young women will affect tomorrow's older women. We explore inequality in paid and unpaid work, emphasizing inequality both between men and women and between different subgroups of women. We contrast the market-friendly notion that gender and race inequality in income is due to gender and race differences in human capital development and attachment to the labor force, with the family-friendly perspective that women do more and are rewarded less both at work and at home. Because gender and race discrimination are so persistent and pervasive, it is unlikely that the picture will change substantially for future cohorts of women unless more responsive social policies are implemented.

We are particularly interested in assessing the extent to which women's lives have improved over time. How different are the lives of young women today compared with those of their mothers? Consistent with the

42

feminist theory that underpins the family-friendly perspective, we find that the forces that shape gender inequality have shifted and realigned, leading to improvements in some areas of women's lives and losses in other areas (England 2006; Hartmann, Rose, and Lovell 2006). Women's work and family lives have improved in some ways but remained stagnant in others. In the workplace, younger women's experiences are certainly better than their mothers', but workplace discrimination has not disappeared. Rather, it has evolved. In families, younger women today are less likely to be married and just as likely to be responsible for raising children and caring for their parents—albeit with limited help from men or the welfare state (England 2006).

A key part of this story, however, is the extent to which the improvements in women's lives have been concentrated in particular race and class subgroups (McCall 2001). Most of the gains achieved by women over the past thirty years have occurred among well-educated, white, and married women. Over the same period, however, less-educated, black, and unmarried women have seen relatively little improvement and have even experienced some losses. Rapidly rising inequality among women is offsetting their general gains relative to men.

Inequality in the Labor Force

One of the most telling signs of women's progress in the past thirty years has been their movement into paid employment. The percentage of women working has almost doubled since 1960. Even more striking, the percentage of married mothers in paid labor during the same period has risen from 28 percent to 71 percent (U.S. Bureau of Labor Statistics 2006). Women now occupy most professions from lawyers and doctors to police officers and construction workers, though still in decidedly smaller numbers than men. Most young girls grow up thinking they can do the same kinds of work young boys dream of doing. Figure 3.1 shows that the gender gap in wages is nearly gone for women in their twenties and early thirties, though among full-time workers the gap continues to grow for women as they enter their forties (U.S. Bureau of Labor Statistics 2006). Nonetheless, women's advancements in the workplace should pay off for them in retirement. Increased earnings allow increased savings, pensions, and larger Social Security benefits, all of which are necessary for a financially secure old age.

At the same time, future projections show that younger women may not be as well off when they retire as many had hoped. Just like today, by the middle of the twenty-first century, older women will still be twice as likely to be poor as their male counterparts (Choudhury and Leonesio 1997; Smeeding, Estes, and Glasse 1999). Two interrelated issues drive women's lagging economic gains. First, they still do not work—or earn—

Figure 3.1   Wage Gap, by Age, Based on Weekly Earnings of Full-Time Wage and Salary Workers, 2006

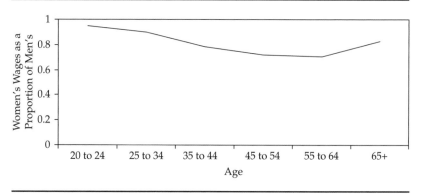

Source: U.S. Bureau of Labor Statistics 2006.

as much as men. Second, rising wage inequalities between different subgroups of women have hurt women's overall gains (McCall 2001; Blau and Kahn 1997; Fischer and Massey 2004). Well-educated white women have experienced large gains over the last thirty years, but black women and women with more limited educational attainment, who ironically have consistently participated significantly more in the labor force than their white and college educated counterparts, have at best experienced few gains and at worst fallen even further behind.

The Wage Gap

The gender wage gap among men and women engaged in full-time work illustrates both how far women have come and how far they still have to go. As figure 3.2 shows, in 1960, full-time year-round women workers made just 61 cents for every dollar men earned. In 2004, these same women earned just under 77 cents on the same dollar (Institute for Women's Policy Research 2006; U.S. Bureau of Labor Statistics 2006). If we exclude the self-employed, the wage gap falls to 80 cents on the dollar. This gap has diminished not only because women's wages have grown but because men's have stagnated and even shrunk in some cases (Blau and Kahn 1997; Waldfogel and Mayer 1999). In contrast to the promarket argument that human capital development, such as higher education, protects workers from wage gaps, researchers find that the wage gap is just as large, if not larger, among women with high educational attainment. College-educated women earn 30 percent less than college-educated men (Black et al. 2004). Although the relative gains in women's wages represent an enormous improvement, earning at best 80 percent of what men earn remains a significant hurdle for women's income

Figure 3.2   Gender-Wage Ratio for Full-Time Year-Round Workers, Median Annual Earnings

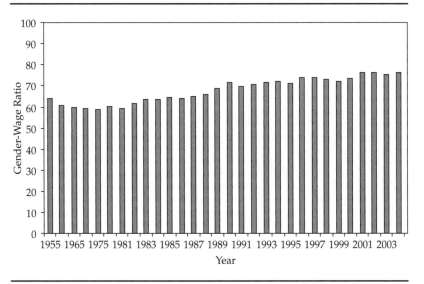

Sources: U.S. Bureau of Labor Statistics 2006; IWPR 2006.

security (Blau and Kahn 1997). To emphasize this point, studies show that the poverty rate among women would drop by 50 percent if this fissure were closed (Institute for Women's Policy Research 2000).

Most problematic, the effects of the wage gap accumulate across the life course. Hartmann and her colleagues (2006) traced the gender difference in accumulated wages over fifteen years and found that, on average, women earn just 38 percent of what men earn. In a similar project, they looked at the accumulated wage differentials for college-educated women and men. They found that for a college-educated woman age twenty-five to twenty-nine in 1984, average cumulative losses due to the wage gap were $75,585 by 1989, $273,179 by 1999, and $440,743 by 2004 (Institute for Women's Policy Research 2006). In other words, after twenty years, the average college-educated woman has earned $440,000 less than the average college-educated man. The gender gap in wages increased as these women grew older. When they were in their twenties, women's average annual full-time year-round earnings were about 75 percent of men's. By the time they were in their late forties, they earned only 62 percent. Note that these data exclude women who are not working full-time, year-round during this time; if those women were included these cumulative wage differentials would be even more pronounced.

How do we best explain the persistent gap in wages between women and men working full-time? Historically, economists focused on gender differences in human capital development, particularly gender differences in education. As women's levels of education caught up to and surpassed men's, however, economists have shifted their attention to the tendency for women to place a higher priority on family than on employment responsibilities (Becker 1981, 1985; Fuchs 1988; Goldin and Polachek 1987; Macpherson and Hirsch 1995; England and Folbre 2005). Thus, for example, women may receive a smaller return than men on their investment in college education because they subsequently focus on child rearing and homemaking. Raising children is taxing and affects women's work and consequently their earnings. Family responsibilities may limit women's education, experience, and overall productivity at work. This is part of the story, but it is not the whole story.

Another explanation for the wage gap is that women and men work in different jobs, even if they have similar education, skills, and experience (Goldin 1992; Reskin 1993; Padavic and Reskin 2002). Furthermore, the jobs that women are more likely to hold pay less. For example, women are more likely to be child care workers, with weekly median earnings of $334, whereas men are more likely to be janitors, with median weekly earnings of $405 (U.S. Bureau of Labor Statistics 2006). Occupational segregation exists at all levels. It is evident in industries, occupations, firms, public and private organizations, self-employment, specific jobs, and even in rankings within jobs (Bielby and Baron 1986; Blau, Simpson, and Anderson 1998; Reskin 1993; Reskin and Roos 1990; Wallace and Chang 1990; Wharton 1989). Occupational segregation has declined but by no means disappeared (Blau, Simpson, and Anderson 1998). In general, women have been more likely to integrate different kinds of jobs within occupations than they have been to integrate entire occupations (Blau, Simpson, and Anderson 1998). Overall, the segregation index has fallen from 61 in 1950 to 47 in 2000 (England 2006). This means that 47 percent of women would have to transfer into a male-dominated job to eliminate occupational segregation (Blau, Simpson, and Anderson 1998). Although we have seen some movement of women into higher-paying traditionally men's jobs, we have seen very little movement of men into lower-paying jobs that women have traditionally held. As Paula England (2006) points out, there is little incentive for men to move to jobs offering lower wages, fewer benefits, and less prestige.

Feminist sociologists also point out that part of the gender gap in wages is in fact attributable to the "wage penalties of motherhood" (Anderson, Binder, and Krause 2002; Budig and England 2001). Mothers earn less than women without children because of either discrimination or lost productivity, both of which are unobservable in existing data. Overall, mothers earn about 15 percent less than women without children. Even when accounting for the human capital variables that economists argue should account for wage differentials, factors such as education, work

Table 3.1   Women's Earnings as Percentage of Men's:
             Full-Time Year-Round Workers

	BA	MA	Prof.	PhD
White	69	68	82	81
Black	98	87	*	*
Hispanic	91	87	*	*

Source: Calculated based on U.S. Census Bureau 2005a, 2006a.
*Inadequate number of respondents in cell.

experience, and time out of paid labor, the wage differences between mothers and nonmothers are 5 to 7 percent.

Finally, feminist sociologists point out that discrimination may also explain part of the wage gap. There is certainly evidence that women and men with similar education and experience earn different wages. Table 3.1 shows that pursuing higher educational attainment is not protecting women from the pay gap. White women with professional degrees and masters degrees working full-time year-round earn just 81 percent and 68 percent, respectively, of what comparable white men earn. Black women working full-time year-round with master's degrees earn 87 percent of what black men earn, though black women with college degrees earn relatively equivalent wages to black men with college degrees. Court cases often conclude that these differentials are linked to discrimination. In 1998, the CoreStates Financial Corporation paid $1.5 million in back wages and salaries after the Department of Labor (DOL) found comparable women employees were paid less than men. When the DOL does management reviews, around three-quarters ultimately show pay discrimination (Burkins 1998). A 1999 review of the School of Science at MIT found that women occupied around just 5 percent of faculty positions. Women faculty received less pay, less space, fewer resources, fewer rewards, and were included less frequently on important committees than were their male colleagues (Massachusetts Institute of Technology 1999). A more recent lawsuit was filed against Wal-Mart for sex discrimination. Women in every job category were paid less than men—even women with the same seniority and higher performance ratings than the men (Green 2003). Whether these specific claims of gender discrimination would be validated with more generalizable statistics is in some question. Some argue that a 10-cent wage gap remains, even controlling for human capital variables within specific occupations. Others, however, maintain that the gap has nearly closed when controlling for these factors (Council of Economic Advisers 1998; O'Neil 2003; Rawlston and Spriggs 2001).

Feminists debate the degree of deliberateness in discrimination. Some hold that dominant groups use discrimination to preserve patterns of privilege; others argue that it is a product of unconscious thought processes (Kennelly 1999; Reskin 2000; Ridgeway 2006). Regardless, the consequences are no less real and are felt in all wage and status categories. Women represent just 4 percent of top earners in Fortune 500 companies (Catalyst 2002; Alliance for Board Diversity 2005). Fewer than 13 percent of corporate officers in Fortune 500 companies are women. Lower-paying jobs are not immune. In fact, blue-collar jobs remain incredibly resistant to any kind of desegregation (Blau, Simpson, and Anderson 1998; Padavic and Reskin 2002), as do sports. Wimbledon recently refused to pay women tennis players the same as male players. Long-time supporter John McEnroe argued in an op-ed to the *New York Times*, "the women are carrying the promotional load and bringing fans through the turnstiles. They should be paid accordingly" ("To the Men: Game, Set, Money," June 7, 1999, p. 93).

It would be foolish to imply that young women's experiences in the labor force are no different than those of their mothers. Throughout the 1970s, 1980s, and 1990s, segregation in the workplace declined and the pay gap dropped from 40 cents to somewhere between 20 and 25 cents, depending on how wages are measured (Blau, Simpson, and Anderson 1998; England 2006; Institute for Women's Policy Research 2006). Perhaps most important, young women now have an enormously different conception than did their grandmothers or mothers about what their work lives might include. Nonetheless, gender inequality in the labor force persists. To the extent that they intend to have children, young women may find that the market has not changed anywhere near enough. Workplace discrimination against women is more likely evolving than disappearing.

The Mommy Gap: "Have a Child, Experience the Wage Gap"?

As an editorial in the *New York Times* (Sylvia Hewlett, "Have a Child, and Experience the Wage Gap," May 16, 2000, p. 16) points out, having a child changes everything. The way in which gender stratification in the labor force manifests itself is changing. The most striking evidence is that while the gender wage gap has shrunk to 90 cents on the dollar for young women without children, the wage gap between mothers and nonmothers rose from 10 cents in 1980 to 18 cents in 1991 (Waldfogel 1998). Further, as figure 3.3 indicates, the portion of the wage gap accounted for by family status rose from 35 percent in 1980 to 56 percent in 1991. It appears that as young women age, and more important start to have children, they will not be able to hold on to many of the gains women appear to have made. As one former women executive said, "the unwritten requirement for success in corporate America is to be a corporate

Figure 3.3   Percentage of Pay Gap Between Men and Women, Accounted for by Family Status, Full-Time Year-Round

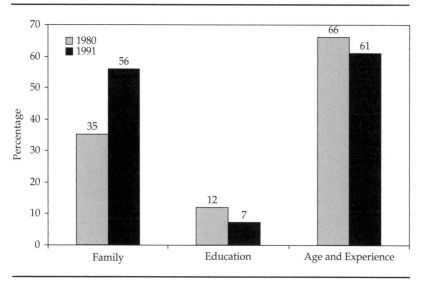

Source: Waldfogel 1998.

man" (Crittenden 2001, 29). More than anything else this means not hav-ing children.

The root of women's current predicament lies in the historic rise of industrialization and work outside the home, which was built on the premise that the worker had a wife at home to raise children and main-tain the household (Acker 1990). The workplace remains structured around this model, and women, even when they work, remain more burdened with a "second shift" of domestic responsibilities than men (Hochschild and Machung 1989). Joan Acker argues that true gender equality would require that the "rhythm and timing of work be adapted to the rhythms of life outside of work. Caring work would be just as important and well rewarded as any other . . . women and men would share equally in different kinds of work" (1990, 155). The reality, how-ever, is that the workplace largely has not changed and in some ways has become more demanding in the past thirty years (Clarkberg and Moen 2001; Schor 1991). Although men have picked up more responsibility for raising children and running the home, they do not carry an equal share (Bianchi, Milkie, and Sayer 2000; Bianchi, Robinson, and Milkie 2006). Thus, if women want to succeed, or even work consistently, they must seriously consider the impact of having children (Goldin 2006). Many jobs require forty hours or more per week, provide limited vacation and sick time, and little flexibility. To truly excel in white-collar jobs, one must meet even more stringent work demands (Crittenden 2001).

The statistics reveal a clear pattern documenting the difficulties women face balancing work and children. At any point, about 45 percent of those mothers who had a child in the last year are not actively in the workplace (Dye 2005; U.S. Census Bureau 2006a, 2006b). When mothers do reenter the labor force, they are more likely to work part time, a trend that contributes to occupational segregation (Okamato and England 1999). For example, the presence of a preschool age child increases the risk of leaving a full-time job by 127 percent for married mothers and 85 percent for unmarried mothers (Drobnic and Wittig 1997). That said, many women do reenter the labor force as their children age. About 80 percent of women whose youngest child is twelve years old are in the labor force—62 percent working full-time, 14 percent part-time, and 5 percent unemployed but looking for work (U.S. Census Bureau 2006a).

How baby boomer women have fared in the workplace exemplifies the extent to which having a child shapes women's employment opportunities. Somewhere between 13 and 17 percent of women who received college degrees between 1966 and 1979 were able to have both children and a career by middle age (Goldin 1995). Childless women were twice as likely to have a career. A study of MBAs who had reached CEO positions found that whereas 85 percent of the men had children, fewer than half of the women did (Catalyst 2002). As an associate at a prestigious law firm argued, "the only conditions under which a woman [can] succeed is if she remain[s] unmarried and certainly childless" (Crittenden 2001, 37). A government panel that attempted to explain why only one in ten government executive positions were occupied by women found that mothers, even after controlling for service length, education, and other factors, were less likely to be promoted than women without children and men with or without children (Crittenden 2001, 41).

Though there have been calls for workplaces to institute family-friendly policies, such as paid maternity leave, flexible schedules, telecommuting, and on-site day cares, few workplaces have done so. Moreover, the results have been mixed for women taking advantage of these policies in the organizations that do provide them. On the positive side, one study showed that paid maternity leave combined with child care assistance leads to new mothers' earlier return to employment (Raabe 1990; Ruhm 1998). On the negative side, there is evidence that parents are afraid to use flexible family policies because they worry about losing future pay increases and promotions (Glass and Estes 1997; Blair-Loy and Wharton 2004). That fear may be perfectly valid. Jennifer Glass (2004) found that managerial and professional women who maintained continuous flexible schedules when their children were young faced a 26 percent lower wage gain than mothers who maintained regular work hours. Evidence as to whether women's wages are negatively affected by mandatory paid leave policies is mixed (Ruhm 1998; Schone 2005).

Addressing motherhood in the labor force is tricky business. Decades of literature on occupational segregation and workplace discrimination has focused on showing that even when women act like men and do not let family interfere with work, they are often still discriminated against (Padavic and Reskin 2002; Crittenden 2001). Although most evidence supports this, it fails to capture the more expansive structural constraints that affect mothers and the few fathers who have full-time responsibility for raising children. Workplace organizations are structured in ways that often force women and anyone primarily responsible for raising children to prioritize either their job or their children. Instead of urging women to behave like men to fit into organizations for which men wrote the rules, a feminist sociological perspective entreats us to reorganize work, families, and other social institutions to make it easier for women—and men—to balance paid and unpaid work.

Inequality Among Women in the Labor Force

Gender differences in paid and unpaid work partly explain why women continue to lag behind men in the workplace. Rising inequality among women rounds out the story. Analyses of gender stratification in the labor force mask significant differences among women by race and class (Browne and Misra 2003). The expansion of employment opportunities for women has not been equally distributed. The struggle for decent jobs and wages for scores of less-educated, poor, black, and Hispanic women has only worsened as employment opportunities for well-educated women have expanded (Bowler 1999; McCall 2001). Indeed, for many women, being black, Hispanic, or poor has a more negative impact on their possibilities for promotion, high wages, and general job quality than sex (McCall 2001). This is ultimately reflected in poverty rates among black and Hispanic women that are two to three times that of white women across the life course (Proctor and Dalaker 2002).

Women's labor force experiences have long been quite different by race and ethnicity. Black women were and are more likely to work than white women. In the early twentieth century, black women were almost three times more likely to be in the labor force than white women (Goldin 1977). This differential was even more pronounced among married women—just 3 percent of white women versus 25 percent of black women were in the labor force (Goldin 1977). The rates for white women have increased over the century, but have not caught up. Currently, 62 percent of black women and 59 percent of white women work. Latino women, however, are slightly less likely to work than both blacks and whites—56 percent are employed. Among Asian women, approximately 58 percent are in the

Table 3.2   Women's Median Weekly Earnings in Current Dollars

	1979	1980	1985	1990	1995	2000	2002	2004
Black	169	185	252	308	355	429	473	505
White	194	203	281	353	415	502	547	584
Latino	157	172	230	278	305	366	397	419
Asians						547	566	613

Source: U.S. Bureau of Labor Statistics 2006.

labor force (U.S. Bureau of Labor Statistics 2006). Black women are also more likely to work full-time; eight out of ten black women versus seven out of ten white women work at least thirty-five hours a week. At the same time, however, black and Hispanic women are more likely to be unemployed than white women. In 2004, the unemployment rate for those age sixteen and over was nearly 10 percent for black women and 7 percent for Latino women, versus less than 5 percent for white women (U.S. Bureau of Labor Statistics 2006). Asian women, at 4.3 percent, are least likely to be unemployed.

As labor force participation rates between different groups have converged, however, the pay gap among different groups of women has expanded. Race inequality is pronounced and growing. As shown in table 3.2, in 1979, black women earned 13 percent less and Latino women 19 percent less than white women but in 2004, black women earned 14 percent less and Latino women 28 percent less (U.S. Bureau of Labor Statistics 2006). Asian women, however, typically earn more than white women. Even among well-educated women with strong attachments to the labor force, the wage gap between black women and white men is larger than that between white women and white men. After controlling for age, highest level of educational attainment, college major, and labor force experience, black women earned 13 percent less and white women 9 percent less than white men (Black et al. 2004).

Further, wage inequalities linked to education have been growing (McCall 2001). Between 1979 and 2003, wages grew by 33 percent for college-educated women, but only slightly for high school graduates, and not at all for those without a high school diploma (Mishel, Bernstein, and Allegretto 2005). The net effect is that the premium for completing college is growing dramatically for women. In 1980 women with a college degree earned 28 percent more than women with only high school degrees. By 2003, this difference had risen to 46 percent (Mishel, Bernstein, and Allegretto 2005). Because white and Asian women are much more likely than black and Hispanic women to complete college, they are much more likely to reap the benefits of this trend.

Although educational differences explain some of the wage differences among different groups of women, they cannot explain all of it. Occupational segregation plays a significant role. At the occupational level, black and Hispanic women are predominantly in positions that pay less and are more vulnerable to job loss (Reskin 1999). Whereas in the past black women were concentrated in domestic and agricultural labor, in recent decades they have been making inroads into professions once dominated by white women. Black women are also entering professions that white women are leaving, such as teaching and secretarial work. As the numbers of black women increase in certain jobs, the occupation is then devalued and wages drop (Sokoloff 1992; Padavic and Reskin 2002). In turn, Latino women, in particular recent immigrants, are occupying low-wage jobs that black women once occupied, particularly domestic labor employment (de la Luz Ibarra 2000; Vernez 1999).

Decreases in occupational segregation over the last twenty to thirty years have been uneven, which may have further exacerbated inequality among women. Most of the decline can be attributed to white-collar jobs. Women are more likely to be lawyers, doctors, professors, and managers, but have made few gains in the blue-collar jobs dominated by men (Blau, Simpson, and Anderson 1998). Women with less education have little more access than they did twenty years ago to higher-paying blue-collar jobs. Thus, women with college and graduate degrees have access to the highest paying work available and women with no degrees or only high school degrees do not.

In the end, higher education opens more doors and provides greater pay and benefits for white women than it does for Asian, black, and Hispanic women. Inequality among women is growing in part because white women have more successfully integrated into higher-paying and more prestigious managerial positions, whereas Asian, black, and Hispanic women are more likely to hit the "Lucite ceiling" (Sokoloff 1992). Black, Hispanic, and Asian women comprise 23 percent of women in the labor force, but hold just 15 percent of managerial positions filled by women (Catalyst 1999). Black, Asian, and Hispanic women comprise just .9, .4, and .3 percent of CEOs of Fortune 500 companies compared to 15 percent for white women in 2003 (Catalyst 2006). The parallel figures for black, Hispanic, and Asian women on Fortune 100 company boards are 2.3, .25, and .5 percent compared to 14 percent for white women (Catalyst 2006).

Decade after decade, black women have the least income throughout the life course. Regardless of education, experience, occupation, labor force attachment, and other human capital factors, black women earn the least of any demographic group (Black et al. 2004). Even when they land higher-level managerial positions, black women managers earn less than their white counterparts despite being more likely to hold college degrees (Catalyst 1999). White women managers earn $528 a week to the $514 black women earn (Catalyst 1999). Asian American and Hispanic women took in only slightly less than white women (Catalyst 1999). In old age, as we show in the chapters that follow, black women have the least Social Security, private pension, savings, and assets—and the poorest health.

Why are these differences so persistent? One explanation for racial inequality among women is that many women lack the mentoring needed to move up in the work world; thirty percent of black, Hispanic, and Asian women respondents in a survey of thirty leading U.S. companies cited this explanation (Catalyst 1999). Ultimately, though, black and Hispanic women must navigate a labor force that includes both gender and race discrimination. Scholars report that racial stereotyping has had a negative impact on black and Latino workers (Browne and Misra 2003). For example, there is evidence that employers assume that all black women are single mothers and consequently view them negatively. They assume that their family obligations will conflict with work, despite this not being true of the majority (Kennelly 1999). Numerous cases of race discrimination in the workplace have led to lawsuits. One of the most high-profile cases involved Abercrombie and Fitch, the international clothing chain targeted at teenagers. It had to pay $40 million dollars to African American, Latino, and Asian American workers who were confined to supply room jobs because they did not represent the Abercrombie image. Jennifer Lu, a student at UC-Irvine describes the Abercrombie look: "It's dominated by Caucasian, football-looking, blonde-hair, blue-eyed males; skinny, tall. You don't see any African-Americans, Asian-Americans, and that's the image that they're portraying and that they're looking for." As *60 Minutes* reported in a 2003 broadcast, Lu was actually fired from her job when a company manager visited the store, pointed to a poster of white males, and emphasized that the store needed more employees like that ("The Look of Abercrombie & Fitch," December 5). Discrimination does appear to pattern labor force participation for black, Asian, and Hispanic women.

Inequality Among Women in Paid Care Work

One of the reasons that inequality among women is so pervasive and persistent is that as highly educated, predominately white women have entered and succeeded in the work force, they look to poor, less-educated minority women, often Latinas and immigrants, to care for their children, cook their meals, and clean their houses (Hondagneu-Sotelo 2000). White and wealthier women have always relied on poorly paid, poor, black and Latina women to help fulfill their domestic duties (Rollins 1985; Romero 2002). Many older black women today were domestic laborers during their prime earning years. Although the white women they were working for seldom worked, domestic servants helped to raise a generation of white children, unable to afford the option of staying home to care for their own (Hunter 1997).

The story today is somewhat different. As well-educated and higher-paid women have increasingly succeeded in the labor force, one of the primary ways they balance conflicting work and family demands, making up for the limited participation of men in the domestic domain, is by drawing on poorer women's labor. Indeed, as Arlie Hochschild and Anne Machung (1989) noted, many middle-class families resolve domestic tensions by hiring someone to do the work they would otherwise argue about. African American women dominated this work in the past, and Latino and immigrant women follow in their footsteps today. Just as black mothers decades ago migrated North to find work, leaving their children in the South, today mothers from Mexico, Central America, the Philippines, and numerous other countries leave their children at home as they migrate to the United States to provide care for upper-class women (Anderson 2000; Parreñas 2000).

Some of these women provide paid care work in informal domestic arrangements. A growing number of undocumented—as well as documented—live-in domestic immigrants from places like the Philippines and Central America are being paid to cook, clean, and help raise U.S. children, even though they have out of economic desperation left their own children in their native countries (Hondagneu-Sotelo 2000). Such work does little to improve the economic positions of many of these women because their efforts are undermined by a lack of labor protections. In Pierrette Hondagneu-Sotelo's (2000) study of immigrant domestic laborers in Los Angeles, the average daily wage was between $35 and $50. The impact of informal domestic arrangements for women's long-term economic stability is problematic. Given that informal domestic laborers are often paid under the table, they rarely contribute to either private or public pension plans. Thus women who have performed informal paid care work through their lives typically reach old age with little in terms of savings or assets and nothing in terms of public or private pensions.

Many of the same issues play out in more formal paid care work arrangements (Romero 2002). Child care workers in day care centers and in family-run day care homes, as well as nurses' aides caring for aged and disabled in nursing homes and in home care agencies, are all disproportionately likely to be poor, less educated, black, Latino, and immigrant women (Tuominen 2003). Many of them are providing paid care work to young, aged, or disabled persons and are thus unable to be at home caring for their own children (Mink 1998). Wages for this work are generally the minimum, keeping the women at, or just above, the poverty line

(Estes 2001). Like informal paid care workers, formal paid care workers tend to reach old age with little in savings or assets. They are not likely to have received fringe benefits such as health insurance or a private pension plan. Because their pay was above board, however, they are more likely to reach old age eligible for Social Security and Medicare.

Partially relieved of child care and domestic duties, more highly educated and predominately white women are somewhat free to devote more of their energies to careers that will provide significantly higher wages and greater fringe benefits. They are more likely to reach old age with significantly greater savings and assets, greater public and private pensions, and even better health. They may never catch up with the men, who will take on substantially fewer hours of cooking, cleaning, and child care, but their economic situations in old age will eclipse those of the women who are providing these services for pay (Bianchi et al. 2000; Estes 2001; Tuominen 2003; Mink 1998; England 2006). Differential responsibility for cooking, cleaning, and child care among various groups of women fuels even greater inequalities as they reach old age.

Inequality in Families

Just as gender, race, and class stratification have evolved in the labor market, they have evolved in the family. Women may be devoting fewer hours to housework and child care than they did a few decades ago, but they are still doing much more than men. Women are still primarily responsible for raising children, cooking, cleaning, and managing the household. The difference is that they are increasingly doing so outside the context of marriage. And they pay a price. Women who have children outside of marriage are significantly more likely to be poor. Married women who stay home to raise children face difficulties finding a decent paying job should the marriage end. Although the public debate has centered on how single motherhood and divorce affects women's and children's economic well-being in their early and mid-life course, less attention has been given to how these trends will shape women's well-being in old age. The concentration of unpaid care work on women has a substantial dampening effect on women's old age income. The intersection of marriage and motherhood is, and will continue to be, a primary source of gender stratification in the twenty-first century.

Distribution of Unpaid Care Work

The primary source of gender inequality within families centers on the unequal distribution of unpaid care work. At every point in the life course, women are more likely than men to provide care—more likely to be the

Figure 3.4   Women's to Men's Time Doing Childcare

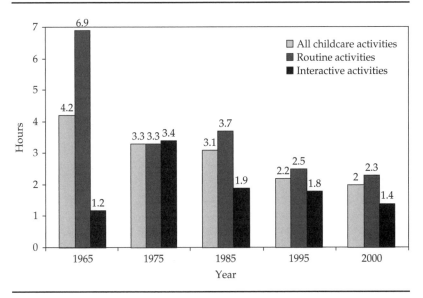

Source: Bianchi et al. 2006.

ones to change the diaper, drive for the car pool, make meals for chronically ill children, or help aging parents shower (Brines 1994; Bianchi et al. 2006; Sayer 2005; Herd and Harrington Meyer 2002). This labor is not rewarded financially, thus it has enormous implications for women's participation in the workplace and their ultimate income security. Furthermore, as figure 3.4 shows, though men are doing more childcare than ever before, they are still doing less than women. In the 1960s, women did six times as much childcare as men; today they do twice as much.

Early in the life course responsibilities include housework and child care. Hochschild and Machung's book, *Second Shift* (1989), documented the burden that middle-class career women face balancing paid work and unpaid care and household responsibilities. More recent studies continue to document women's primary responsibility for the second shift (Brines 1994; Bianchi et al. 2000, 2006; Sayer 2005). What studies reveal is not that men do not perform unpaid care work, but that women perform more of it. Time surveys estimate that men spend from 60 to 75 percent as much time on household chores as women do (Bianchi, Milkie, and Sayer 2000; Bianchi, Robinson, and Milkie 2006; Sayer 2005). Chloe Bird (1999) found that men report doing about 42 percent of all household labor, and women 68 percent. Patricia Voydanoff and Brenda Donnelly (1999) found that mothers spend about thirty-six hours a week doing household labor versus the sixteen hours fathers spend.

Men and women also tend to do very different types of household work. By and large, men do housework that is sporadic or optional, such as repairs (Cowan 1991; Sayer 2005). Some studies point to the increasing amount of time fathers are spending with children, but this is largely in play as opposed to daily parenting tasks (Arendell 1997; Bianchi et al. 2006). In fact, it is the process of having children that dramatically increases the traditional division of family labor (Cowan and Cowan 1992; Gupta 1999; Perkins and DeMeis 1996).

Care work for disabled family members can be even more taxing than that for young children. Approximately 70 to 80 percent of care for developmentally disabled people is provided within families and largely by women (Essex and Hong 2005; Hooyman and Gonyea 1995; Litt 2004; Martinson and Stone 1993). The tasks normally associated with parenting may become heightened when children have a disability. Children who use wheelchairs may need to be lifted in and out of it to go to the bathroom or to get in a car. They may need help bathing, dressing, and brushing teeth. Most children with disabilities have more appointments to attend than other children: physical therapists, speech therapists, and doctors who specialize in their particular disability. These many tasks are too specialized to itemize, but are nonetheless intense for the parents who perform them.

Historically, many disabled children were institutionalized because their needs were so intense experts did not believe families could provide care (Traustadóttir 2000). The belief that children with disabilities should be institutionalized rather than at home with families, however, has reversed over the past thirty years. Today, parents, primarily mothers, are responsible for most care. Additionally, medical advances have lengthened the life expectancy of people with disabilities (Kelly and Kropf 1995). As a result, parents of children with developmental disabilities can expect to be "perpetual parents." They are primarily responsible for care well into their own old age. The time-intensiveness of this care restricts women's activities and time across most of their life course (Brubaker and Brubaker 1993).

Families, primarily women, also do the majority of care work for the aged. Overall, families are providing close to 80 percent of all long-term care (Brody 2004; Cantor 1989). Moreover, 80 percent of those caregivers are on call seven days a week for at least three hours a day (National Alliance for Caregiving and AARP 1997, 2004; Navaie-Waliser, Spriggs, and Feldman 2002; Stone, Cafferata, and Sangl 1987). The tasks associated with caring for older people cover a broad spectrum, from handling their finances or doing errands to assisting them with bathing, dressing, eating, and getting in and out of bed. The term family, however, conceals the fact that it is women who are doing most of this work (Hooyman and Gonyea 1995). Seventy percent of spousal caregivers are wives and 60 to

80 percent of children who care for their older parents are daughters (Brody 2004; Hooyman and Gonyea 1995; Mui 1992; National Alliance for Caregiving and AARP 2004). Not only are women more likely to provide care, they also spend more time doing it than men. Compared to sons, for example, daughters do an additional ten to eighteen hours a month of care work (Allen 1994; National Alliance for Caregiving and AARP 2004; Wolf, Freedman, and Soldo 1997). In fact, daughters-in-law provide more care than sons, around thirty-seven versus twenty-seven hours per week (Chang and White-Means 1991; Abel and Nelson 1990).

Inequality Among Women in Unpaid Care Work

The distribution of unpaid care work is shaped not only by gender, but also by race and class. Low-income Americans are more likely to report higher care work responsibilities, perhaps because they are less likely to be able to outsource some of the work to paid providers (National Alliance for Caregiving and AARP 2004). Black and Hispanic caregivers also report higher levels of care responsibilities. For example, 65 percent of black care providers report visiting care recipients more than once a week versus 55 percent of whites (National Alliance for Caregiving and AARP 2004). Hispanics are more likely than whites to provide more than eight hours of care a week and also more likely to live with the care recipients (National Alliance for Caregiving and AARP 2004). Further, 48 percent of black care providers report providing medicines, injections, or pills to care recipients, but only 38 percent of white care providers report the same thing (National Alliance for Caregiving and AARP 2004). Indeed, the intensity of this care may explain, in part, why both blacks and Hispanics report financial stress associated with their care work, 22 percent and 14 percent respectively, versus 10 percent for whites.

Black, Hispanic, less-educated, and poor women bear a disproportionate load of unpaid care work. First, those with lower incomes are less likely to be able to afford to outsource their unpaid care responsibilities. Carol Stack (1974) articulated how poor black Americans developed a tight network of family and friends, in essence, to care for one another while struggling against poverty. More recent studies have documented these networks, showing how extended families and friends provide enormous amounts of informal care for each other (Barker 2002; Oliker 2000; Williams and Dilworth-Anderson 2002). In fact, one troubling outcome of welfare reform in 1996 was the fact that older siblings, many of whom were not even teenagers, were caring for their younger siblings because mothers could not afford to pay for day care (Gennetian et al. 2004). Caring for the sick and disabled also imposes heavy burdens that poor families cannot afford to shift to paid care workers. In an anecdotal, but revealing, comment, Christopher Reeve's wife spoke of how difficult caring for her husband would have been without the cadre of paid care workers who helped twenty-four hours a day, seven days a week. Second, a significant reason why poor, black, and Latino women carry such a heavy load is that these groups are far more likely to be sick. Poor people, black people, and Latinos are all more likely to have chronic conditions, such as cancer, diabetes, and heart problems, which lead to functional limitations (House 2002). Black and Hispanic caregivers also report caring for sicker friends and family members than whites (National Caregiving Alliance and AARP 2004). Third, black women are less likely to be married at all ages than are white women, and this will only grow more true with successive cohorts (Harrington Meyer, Wolf, and Himes 2006). It is hard to have a division of labor, equal or otherwise, if there is no other adult in the household to share in either child or parent care. Thus many single women perform unpaid care work for two generations with little help of any kind.

Changing Families

Gender, race, and class inequality in families is linked to dynamic changes in marital rates. From 1970 to 2005, the percentage of women married dropped from 60 percent to 52 percent, but the percentage of women divorced more than doubled, from 6 percent to 13 percent. Moreover, as figure 3.5 shows, the percentage of families headed by single mothers rose from 12 percent in 1970 to 26 percent in 2005 (U.S. Census Bureau 2006a, 2006b).

The racial, ethnic, and educational differences in marital trends are substantial and growing. In 2004, about 30 percent of all births were to single mothers, but the rate for black women was more than twice that (U.S. Census Bureau 2006a, 2006b). These births are also more likely to occur among women with less education. More than half of mothers without a high school degree but only 11 percent of those with a college degree had children outside of marriage (U.S. Census Bureau 2006a). In 2005, more than half of white and Hispanic women but fewer than a third of black women were married (U.S. Census Bureau 2006a). The trend toward never marrying, in particular, has been more heavily concentrated among black women and those without high school degrees (Goldstein and Kenney 2001). We have also witnessed a growing trend toward assortive mating, wherein highly educated people are marrying highly educated people, thereby concentrating resources and increasing inequality across the life course (Schwartz and Mare 2005).

A key reason women do not fare well outside of marriages revolves around children. Whether parents divorce or never marry in the first

Figure 3.5   Households Headed by Single Parents

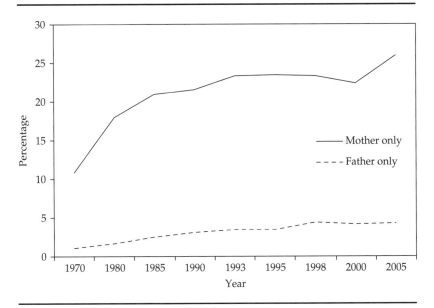

Source: U.S. Census Bureau 2006b.

place, mothers are most likely to be the custodial parent. In 2005, women comprised 84 percent of single parents (Grall 2005). Single parents are almost equally divided between those never married and those divorced or separated (Grall 2005). Custodial mothers are left with the responsibility for the majority of costs and effort associated with raising their children. More than 30 percent of children living with single mothers report that they have not even seen their father in the past year (Sorensen and Zibman 2000). Marcia Carlson (2006), using the National Longitudinal Youth Survey, estimates that between 50 and 75 percent of noncustodial fathers have little to no involvement with their children. Further, about 25 percent of single mothers are not receiving child support payments to which they were legally entitled (Sorensen and Zibman 2000; Sorensen and Hill 2004). Approximately 30 percent of those receiving payments are not receiving the full award. In sum, custodial mothers received just 60 percent of the child support due to them (Sorensen and Zibman 2000). Of course, the awards are so meager to begin with that studies show child support payments do not significantly reduce poverty among single mothers. One estimate is that 39 percent of children, as opposed to 37 percent, would have been poor if child support payments had not been made (Sorensen and Zibman 2000). In 2002, the average annual child support payment to mothers was $3,600, or $300 a month (Grall 2005). A key reason that child support payments are not the panacea to

Figure 3.6   Poverty Status of Families with Children Under 18

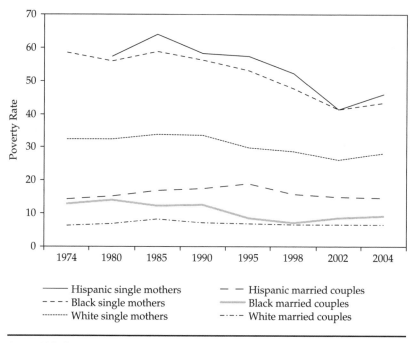

Hispanic single mothers   — — Hispanic married couples
- - - - Black single mothers   Black married couples
········· White single mothers   —·—· White married couples

Source: U.S. Census Bureau 2006b.

improving the welfare of single mothers is that many of the fathers are so poor themselves (Cancian and Meyer 2004).

Ultimately, single mothers are far more likely to be living below the poverty line than are their married counterparts. Figure 3.6 shows that roughly 10 percent of married couples, versus more than 40 percent of black and Hispanic single mothers, are poor. Divorce is problematic for women because they bear the economic brunt when marriages end (Holden and Smock 1991; Smock, Manning and Gupta 1999). By contrast, men's standard of living is little affected (Bianchi, Subaiya and Kahn 1999; Burkhauser et al. 1991; McManus and DiPrete 2001). Using data from the 1980s, Suzanne Bianchi, Lekha Subaiya, and Joan Kahn (1999) found that the income to need levels for formerly married mothers was just 56 percent that of their former husbands. Never-married mothers, however, who are disproportionately black and less educated, are even more likely to be poor than their divorced counterparts. In 2002, never-married single mothers comprised 43 percent of all single mothers but more than half of single mothers in poverty. The comparable rates for divorced mothers were 35 and 25 percent respectively (Fields

2003). This is one of the reasons why black women have poverty rates more than twice that of white women (Proctor and Dalaker 2002).

Though policy makers and welfare critics alike attribute poverty among single mothers to lack of work effort, poverty among single mothers is in fact more likely due to low, rather than lack of, wages (Seccombe 1999). In fact, single mothers are significantly more likely to work than their married counterparts. In 2004, among those mothers with a birth in the previous two years, only 55 percent of married mothers, versus some 70 percent of single mothers, were employed (Grall 2005). Among those single mothers who have a job, however, about 20 percent were still living below the poverty line (Fields 2003). Certainly, one of the cruelest ironies in the discourse around welfare reform in the 1980s and 1990s was the portrayal of the lazy black welfare queen (Seccombe 1999). Throughout U.S. history, black and poor women have consistently outworked their white and wealthier counterparts.

The decline in marriage, whether due to never marrying, cohabitation, or divorce, has led to a rise in single parenting and a concentration of unpaid care work. Together these trends may prove problematic for many women's economic security in old age and lead to increasing inequality among older women. Individuals who do not remain continuously married have much less wealth just before retirement than those with stable marriages (Holden and Kuo 1996; Wilmoth and Koso 2002). Moreover, marriages, even the best ones, ultimately do end in divorce or death. Because women continue to bear the burden of raising children and doing the housework, they rarely establish adequate independent resources to sustain them when their marriages end. The consequence is high rates of poverty among single older women and projections showing that there will be no improvement in the next thirty to forty years (Johnson and Favreault 2004). Being a single parent for any period of a woman's life leads to lower income and less wealth accumulation (Landa and Russell 1996). Marriage provides financial protection for many women for portions of their lives, but women whose marriages end and women who never marry are left to rely on their own financial resources, which have often been constrained by disproportionate responsibility for care work.

Discussion

No matter what arena we analyze, women come up short. Be it in the workplace or in the family, women do more and earn less. From a market-friendly perspective, inequality in various forms of income was historically due to gender and race differences in human capital development such as education, experience, and training. As women's education and experience started to catch up to and in many instances surpass men's, the explanation shifted. Market-friendly theorists attributed gender differences in various forms of income to gender differences in labor force attachment. If women are going to take time out to raise children, or reduce hours to attend to housework or care for a frail older relative, then perhaps they should receive fewer wages and fringe benefits. This perspective, though, fails to account for the value of the care work that women perform raising future workers and citizens. Furthermore, a central tenet of the feminist theory that underlies the family-friendly perspective is that gender and race inequality are pervasive and resilient across time and spheres. Thus improvements in one arena are often offset by shortcomings in another. In other words, there will always be a new excuse to explain why women come up short. Family-friendly supporters therefore focus not on attaining equity under the existing rules, but on rewriting the rules to reward women for the work they do.

For women, and particularly black, Hispanic, poor, and unmarried women, disadvantages tend to accumulate over the life course. Wage inequality between men and women increases with age, suggesting that the lifetime consequences of early child rearing are profound. Moreover, inequalities in early and middle life lay the foundation for inequality in old age. Pay inequities and disproportionate responsibility for unpaid and domestic responsibilities mean that older women have less in savings, pensions, and Social Security benefits. Increasing numbers of single mothers face insurmountable economic disadvantage in early life that leave them little opportunity to accumulate the kinds of resources necessary to face their own old age. Just as gender disparities in early life accumulate and translate into gender inequalities in old age, so do race and class inequities among women in early life accumulate and translate into even larger race and class inequities among women in old age.

Lack of interference through welfare state policy to help women, and families more generally, balance paid work and unpaid care work reveals how structural features both constrain women's choices and shape the outcomes of those choices. Women may well choose to stay home with young children or frail older adults, but they do not choose to bear the economic and health consequences as profoundly as they do. Supporters of family-friendly policies point out the extent to which the presence or absence of certain types of welfare policies can lessen, replicate, or even exaggerate inequalities. We have demonstrated in this chapter how juggling paid work with the unpaid work of caring for young, disabled, and frail older people shapes inequality before women reach old age. In later chapters we explore what the welfare state is—and is not—doing to lessen, replicate, or exaggerate inequalities for women across the life course.

Chapter 4

The Business of Retirement

In 2005, women are stuck with a Social Security program that is inherently flawed and biased against their needs and concerns for the future.
Congresswoman Ginny Brown-Waite (2005)

THE ECONOMIC situation of older Americans has improved considerably over the past forty years. Since the late 1960s, older people have seen their standard of living rise significantly. Their income, adjusting for inflation, has doubled in thirty years. The percentage of older people living below the poverty level fell from over 30 percent in the early 1960s to just over 10 percent today (U.S. Census Bureau 1971; DeNavas-Walt, Proctor, and Lee 2005; He et al. 2005). The implementation of universal health insurance for older people through Medicare in the 1960s, and automatic cost of living increases through Social Security in the 1970s, account for much of the improvements in older people's economic well-being.

These overall improvements are meaningful, of course, but it is not clear that older women—and particularly black, Hispanic, and single older women—are economically secure. Income inequality among the aged has been rising and is expected to continue to do so well into the twenty-first century (Smith 2003). Women are, and will continue to be, almost twice as likely to be poor as men in old age (Smeeding, Estes, and Glasse 1999). The gap between men's and women's retirement income has remained basically consistent. Men continue to have incomes that are almost twice as large as women's and poverty rates that are just half of women's. As figure 4.1 shows, the poverty gap between older men and women has remained constant since 1960 and is projected to be no different in 2020 (Smeeding, Estes, and Glasse 1999).

Although inequality among men and women has remained constant, inequality between women has increased. The gap between black and white women's incomes in retirement has remained stable at around 75 percent. Black women's chances of being poor, however, have increased from twice to three times that of older white women (DeNavas-Walt, Proctor, and Lee 2005; He et al. 2005; U.S. Census Bureau 1979, 1971). As

Figure 4.1   Poverty Rates, Age 65 and Older

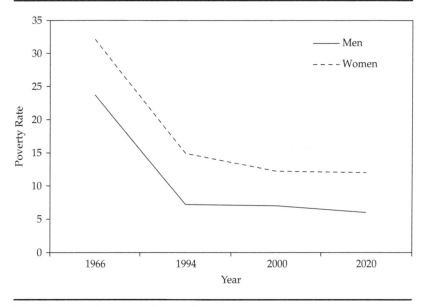

Source: Smeeding, Estes, and Glasse 1999.

figure 4.2 shows, among older women in 1970, the poverty rate was 27 percent for whites and 53 percent for blacks. In 2004, it was 10 percent for white women and 26 percent for black women (U.S. Census Bureau 1971; DeNavas-Walt, Proctor, and Lee 2005; He et al. 2005). Older Hispanic women's poverty rates have remained stable at around 25 percent since the early 1970s, meaning that the poverty gap between older white and Hispanic women has nearly doubled.

Why do older women remain so much poorer than older men, and why is inequality among women by race, class, and marital status increasing? And, perhaps most important, why is this inequality expected to persist over the next several decades? Proponents of market-friendly welfare policies suggest that these inequalities merely represent the long-term consequences of a lifetime of less human and social capital development, in part due to weaker attachment to the labor force. They favor implementing old age welfare policies that emphasize individual choice, risk, and responsibility to encourage those with weaker experiences in the labor market to be more competitive and committed. Conversely, proponents of family-friendly welfare policies point out that such individualization and privatization will lead to greater levels of inequality in old age. They argue that the problem is that our current old age income systems are outdated and should be retooled to become more responsive to sociodemographic changes. Retirement income remains

Figure 4.2   Poverty Rates Among Older Women

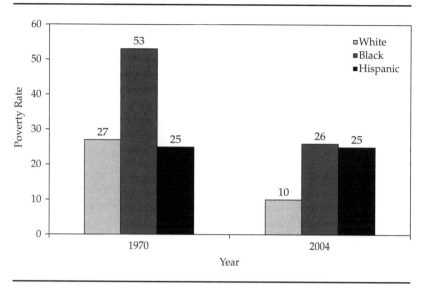

Source: He et al. 2005.

built around a breadwinner family structure. The three main streams of retirement income—Social Security, private pensions, and savings—continue to foster women's economic dependence on men. Those who fare best have remained either consistently employed or consistently married. When women, as is increasingly the case, do not fit this model, they pay a heavy economic price. Here, we review the existing types of old age income and show how continued reliance on the breadwinner model has important implications not only for gender inequality, but also for race, class, and marital status inequality among women.

Social Security

Social Security is enormously important for women. It puts food on their tables, prescriptions in their pockets, and heat in their homes. For many older women, that monthly check is the difference between poverty and insecurity and a comfortable retirement. Moreover, despite the fact it is a government program that absorbs over 40 percent of the social welfare budget, larger than any other single program, it is very popular among an American public that is sometimes uncomfortable with big government. More than eight in ten Americans favor Social Security (AARP 2005). Social Security could, however, be an even stronger program, protecting older Americans even more effectively than it already does.

Social Security is the single largest source of income for older Americans. It comprises about 40 percent of income for all those age sixty-five and older. Approximate 40 percent of the aged rely on it for 90 percent or more of their income (Social Security Administration 2004). Social Security is a particularly important source of income for older women. Although the welfare state plays almost no role in most women's financial well-being earlier in their lives, it plays an enormous role later on. Social Security contributes 60 percent of retirement income for the average woman and 100 percent for one in five (Porter, Larin, and Primus 1999). It is even more important for older minorities. Because of reduced access to private pensions and private savings, half of older Hispanics and African Americans rely on Social Security for 90 percent or more of their income (Torres-Gil, Greenstein, and Kamin 2005; Wu 2004). For black and Hispanic women it comprises almost 80 percent. The overall poverty rate among women would be four times higher if they did not have Social Security (Porter, Larin, and Primus 1999).

Social Security is more vital to women's economic well-being in old age than it is to men's. Of those lifted out of poverty by Social Security, 60 percent are women (Porter, Larin, and Primus 1999). Because women live longer, they account for 57 percent of beneficiaries (Social Security Administration 2004). Further, Social Security contributes more to women's income than to men's. Among unmarried women and men, Social Security accounts for 53 percent and 40 percent of income, respectively (Hartmann and Lee 2003). Despite this heavy reliance, older women's benefits are lower then men's. The average monthly Social Security benefit for older women in 2007 was $909. For men it was $1,183 (Social Security Administration 2007).

Social Security has played a dramatic role in improving the economic situation of older Americans. In fact, much of the dramatic decrease in poverty among the aged that has occurred over the last forty years is directly attributable to the increased size of Social Security benefits. Consequently, substantial cuts in Social Security benefits would have a deleterious impact on poverty. Even a 10 percent cut would lead to a 7.2 percent rise in poverty (Engelhardt and Gruber 2004). Because it is so much more important to the financial well-being of older women than older men, any changes to Social Security will be felt much more acutely by women. Older women, and particularly the more vulnerable, including black, Hispanic, and single older women, should be central to any reform debates. As we show, thus far they have not been.

Program Expansions and Contractions

Until recently, as table 4.1 illustrates, the history of Social Security was primarily one of liberal expansion. When the program was enacted in

Table 4.1   Selected Legislative History of Social Security

1935	Passage of the Social Security Act.
1939	Creation of spousal, survivor, parental and child benefits.
	Creation of minimum benefit.
1950	Large (77 percent) increase in benefits.
	Large expansion of coverage to previously uncovered occupations, including domestic and agricultural workers, who were predominantly African American.
1952	12.5 percent increase in benefits.
	Exclusion of 5 low earnings' years from benefit calculation.
1954	13 percent increase in benefits.
1956	Liberalized benefits for women by reducing the amount of Social Security credits needed to be eligible for benefits and by averaging their earnings over a shorter period of time than for men.
1958	7 percent increase in benefits.
1961	Widow benefit increased from 75 percent to 82 percent of deceased worker's benefit.
1962	Eligibility age reduced to 62 (for men) with a reduction in benefit. Women had been able to collect at age 62 since 1956.
1965	Widows could receive reduced benefits at age 60 instead of age 62.
	Provided benefits to divorced wives and widows if they were dependent upon the wage-earner's support and if their marriage had lasted 20 consecutive years or more.
	7 percent increase in benefits.
1967	13 percent increase in benefits.
1969	15 percent increase in benefits.
1971	10 percent increase in benefits.
1972	20 percent increase in benefits.
	Adoption of Automatic Cost of Living Adjustments.
	Provided that men's and women's benefits calculated the same way.
	Widow benefit increased from 82 percent to 100 percent of deceased worker's benefit.
1977	Increased earnings needed to receive eligibility credits.
	Reduced requirement from 20 years to 10 for eligibility for spousal and survivor benefits for divorced persons.
1981	Elimination of the minimum benefit.
1983	A gradual increase in the age of eligibility for full retirement benefits from age 65 to age 66 in 2009 and age 67 in 2027.
	Inclusion of up to 50% of Social Security benefits in the taxable income of higher income recipients and transfer of projected revenues therefrom to the Social Security trust funds. The income thresholds (adjusted gross income plus one-half of Social Security benefits) were set at $25,000 for single individuals, $32,000 for couples filing jointly, and zero for couples filing separately.
1993	Made up to 85% of Social Security benefits subject to the income tax for recipients whose income plus one-half of their benefits exceed $34,000 (single) and $44,000 (couple).

Source: Social Security Administration 2006.

1935 to provide monthly income to the aged, blind, and disabled, older people were more likely than other age groups to be poor. By the mid-1980s, however, primarily because of Social Security, poverty rates for the aged had dropped below those for other age brackets (DeNavas-Walt, Proctor, and Lee 2005; He et al. 2005). The initial legislation, which excluded agricultural and domestic workers, the self-employed, and employees of religious, charitable, and educational organizations, covered just half of all workers and relatively few women and blacks. In time, coverage was expanded. Today 95 percent of older persons are covered by Social Security (Quadagno 1984; Abramovitz 1988; Harrington Meyer and Bellas 1995; Century Foundation 1998).

Initially, only those who contributed to Social Security were eligible to receive benefits. The retirement earnings test was strict and retirees who earned more than $15 a month forfeited the entire benefit (Harrington Meyer 1996 and 2005). Expansion of the program began before the first benefits were even distributed, however. By 1939, spouses and widows were granted benefits equal respectively to 50 percent and 75 percent of their husbands' benefit. Later, the rule was made gender-neutral and men gained the right to spouse and widower benefits. As divorce became more common, the rule that spouses had to be currently married was changed to one requiring twenty years of marriage before a divorce. By 1977, this had been dropped to ten years (Social Security Administration 2006). The earnings test was also lessened over time to the point that now there are no limits on earnings for those age sixty-five and older. Earnings limits remain only for early retirees. In 2006, early retirees have their benefit reduced by $1 for every $2 they earn above $12,480 (Social Security Administration 2006).

For the first several decades of the program, cost containment was hardly an issue. Monthly FICA contributions far outweighed monthly benefit payments. By design, in the 1980s, we began accumulating a surplus that would see us through the baby boomers. This approach was quickly effective; the surplus in 2005 topped $164 billion (Social Security Administration 2005a). As the baby boomers aged, however, the ratio of workers paying into the system to beneficiaries drawing out of the system shifted from 40:1 in 1940 to just 3:1 in 2005. By 2020, the ratio is expected to hit 2:1 (Quadagno 1999).

These demographic changes prompted some questions about the future soundness of the program. The crisis language that has dominated the political landscape for a quarter of a century, claiming that Social Security will soon go bankrupt, was linked to a 1980s political agenda that aimed to downsize or dismantle federal government programs (Quadagno 1996). Even though the surplus has been large, and most acknowledge that some small changes to the program would address the remaining long-term shortfall, cost containment has driven the Social

Security reform agenda ever since (Herd and Kingson 2005). Specific policy reforms aimed at improving the fiscal solvency of the program have included decreasing the benefit-to-contribution ratio, eliminating the minimum benefit, increasing age of eligibility, extending coverage to all government employees, and raising the tax cap on earnings.

The Social Security Administration has already contained costs by decreasing the benefit-to-contribution ratio. In a series of moves that have often gone undetected by most older people, it has already recalculated benefit formulas in ways that cause each successive cohort to receive a smaller return on their contributions. Early retirees contributed for fewer years and at lower rates; more recent retirees have contributed for more years at higher rates. Benefits are indexed to cost of living increases, but the overall benefit-to-contribution ratio has declined steadily and will continue to do so (Century Foundation 1998).

Costs have also been contained by eliminating the minimum benefit (Harrington Meyer 1996, 2005). Before 1982, Social Security had a minimum monthly retired worker benefit equal to $20 a month in 1940 and $110 a month when it was eliminated in 1983 (Social Security Administration 2002). Given how small this was, about 30 percent of the poverty level, this seemed a particularly harsh cut. It also introduced an important source of gender and race inequality. Today, Social Security does have a special minimum benefit, but few older people qualify. Restoration of a minimum, set near the federal poverty line, would significantly reduce poverty and inequality in old age (Harrington Meyer 1996; Herd, 2005a, 2005b).

One of the most dramatic moves to sustain solvency of the Social Security trust funds was to raise the age for full retirement. Beginning in 2003, the age of eligibility for full benefits gradually increases from sixty-five until 2027, when it will be sixty-seven. The age for early retirement remains at sixty-two, but the penalty for taking early benefits, which most men and nearly all women take, has increased. Currently, those who take benefits before full retirement age receive 20 percent less than their full benefit for the remainder of their lives; by 2022, they will receive 30 percent less (Social Security Administration 2006).

Another approach to improving revenues has involved broadening the number of individuals eligible for the program and thus paying taxes into the program. Since its inception, Social Security has frequently broadened the eligibility base. Initially, only select workers were covered, but over time most were incorporated into the system. State and local government employees were excluded because of questions about whether the federal government could tax state governments. In the 1950s, Congress allowed states to elect voluntary coverage for their employees (Munnell 2005). In the 1980s, it extended mandatory coverage to new federal employees. Finally, in the 1990s, it extended mandatory coverage to state and local employees who had no other pension plan. Currently, about 95 percent of employees are covered, but among state and local employees, nearly 30 percent are not (Munnell 2005).

One aspect of the program that has not been changed—and that has reduced the program's revenues and progressiveness—is that higher earners are paying less than before into the system (Harrington Meyer 1996; Herd and Kingson 2005). Social Security is funded through the FICA tax, at the rate of 6.2 percent per employer and employee. Even though the tax is flat, it is in practice regressive because of a ceiling set on taxable earnings. As a result, lower-wage workers, predominantly women and blacks and Hispanics, pay a higher proportion in taxes than those with earnings above the ceiling (Social Security Administration 2006; Harrington Meyer 1996). Currently, workers pay the Social Security component of the FICA tax only up to $94,200 per year. Someone with earnings of $180,000 has finished paying the tax in July, and thus has an annual Social Security tax rate of only 3.1 percent. A person with earnings of up to $90,000 pays the tax all year, and thus has an annual rate of 6.2 percent. When the tax was first implemented in 1937, the ceiling was set at $3,000 a year. This amount meant that 90 percent of all earnings were taxed, and in fact 96 percent of covered workers paid the tax on all of their earnings (Harrington Meyer 1996). At various times during the 1950s and 1960s, the proportion of workers who paid FICA tax on all earnings dropped to as low as 65 percent. In 1991, the ceiling was reset to $53,400 and 95 percent of workers paid the tax on all earnings. By 2006, however, with the ceiling at $94,200, the tax covers only 85 percent of all earnings (Social Security Administration 2006). We would need to raise the cap to $140,000 to cover 90 percent of earnings. Proponents of this policy change argue that the cap should be restored to 90 percent and then indexed to rise automatically with earnings.

Social Security's Shortcomings

Preoccupation with the demographic changes linked to the dependency ratio has caused policy makers to overlook other demographic changes that will shape women's economic security. Social Security is increasingly outdated because its design is based on a traditional breadwinner benefit model, having been created in the late 1930s with a white male breadwinner family in mind. The program's design has changed little since then. Individuals receive benefits as workers or as the wives and widows of workers. The intent was that men make claims on the state as workers and wives make claims on the state as dependents of workers (Harrington Meyer 1996). The state simultaneously allowed men to financially support their wives and families and reinforced women's financial dependence on men. Men depended on the state and women

Table 4.2   Average Old Age Social Security Benefit

	Retired Worker	Spouse	Widow
Women			
White	807	478	911
Black	734	390	710
Men			
White	1062		
Black	878		

Source: Social Security Administration 2004.

depended on both men and the state (Abramovitz 1988; Acker 1990; Misra 1998). The result of this legacy is that Social Security best protects individuals who are either steadily employed or steadily married and not employed across the life course (Herd 2005b).

The benefits most advantageous to those with consistent employment histories are the worker benefits. Workers receive a benefit tied to their earnings history. To qualify, an individual must have at least ten earnings years. The benefit is calculated based on an individual's thirty-five highest earnings years (Social Security Administration 2006). The progressive benefit structure, with a 28 percent replacement rate for high-wage earners and a 78 percent rate for low-wage earners, means that a monthly benefit for an individual who had average earnings of $951 a month would be $852. By contrast, the monthly benefit for an individual with average monthly earnings of $3,331 would be $1,831 (Century Foundation 1998; Social Security Administration 2004; Aaron and Reischauer 1998b; He et al. 2005). Over the past twenty years, women have made significant strides in qualifying for the worker benefit. From 1960 to 2002, the percentage of female Social Security beneficiaries rose from 40 percent to 60 percent. By 2020, only about 10 percent of women who have reached the age of sixty-two will not qualify (Social Security Administration 2006; Herd 2005b, 2005a, 2006a).

Although more women are qualifying for Social Security as workers, women's worker benefits have remained at around three-quarters those of men. In 1975, men's average monthly benefits were $240, and women's were $173. We do not know what the race gap was at that time because the Social Security statistics do not report it. As table 4.2 shows, however, by 2003, differences by gender and race were substantial. The average monthly worker benefit was $807 for white women, $1,062 for white men, $734 for black women, and $878 for black men (Social Security Administration 2004). Ultimately, the problem is that most women's earnings continue to lag well behind men's. The wage gap among full-time workers stands at 76 cents on the dollar. If one includes all workers,

Figure 4.3   Basis of Entitlement for Social Security Among Women

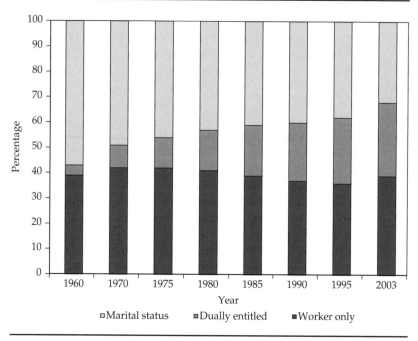

Source: Social Security Administration 2004.

full-time, part-time and part-year, it is even larger—62 cents on the dollar (Rose and Hartmann 2004). Most studies project that the size of women's Social Security worker benefits will continue to trail those of men's due to these earnings differences (Toder et al. 1999).

The relatively small size of women's worker benefits means that despite increasing numbers of women being eligible for worker benefits, the majority of women will continue to receive spouse and widow benefits. Eligibility requires that an individual be currently married to an eligible worker or, if divorced, married for at least ten years. Men have been eligible for these benefits for decades, but nearly 98 percent of the recipients are women (Social Security Administration 2004). The value of these auxiliary benefits is tied to the primary worker benefit. Spousal benefits are 50 percent and survivor benefits 100 percent of the original worker benefit. Many are optimistic about the increasing numbers of women eligible for the worker benefit, but this improvement masks a different reality. As figure 4.3 makes clear, between 1960 and 2003, though the proportion of older women eligible for the worker benefit rose from 40 percent to 60 percent, the proportion drawing on spousal and widow benefits remained at 60 percent. How is this possible? People can be eligible for both auxiliary and worker benefits as dual eligibles, but receive only the higher of the two benefits (Social Security Administration 2004; Harrington Meyer 1996). Most women, currently about 65 percent, continue to receive benefits on the basis of their marital status rather than their work status. Most projections show that this will change little into the twenty-first century (Levine, Mitchell, and Phillips 2000).

Reliance on marital status benefits poses its own problems, particularly for younger generations of women. The key point of concern is that women are marrying less and working more (Harrington Meyer, Wolf, and Himes 2006). Therefore, though worker benefits are problematic because they do not adequately address the gender gap in wages or work patterns, marital status benefits are problematic because their current structure does not accommodate women who are less likely to be married (Herd 2005b, 2005a).

Ultimately, the women who fare the best from this breadwinner benefit structure are married women in single-earner households, which comprise an ever-shrinking percentage of families in the United States (Herd 2005b). Social Security lifts out of poverty far more women who are married or have been married than women who have never married. Never-married women have no access to spousal and widow benefits (Porter, Larin, and Primus 1999). Among younger cohorts, one in three divorced women will not have marriages that last long enough to qualify (Butrica and Iams 2000). These, however, are precisely the women who have likely not had high enough earnings early in their life course to build up their Social Security benefits, pensions, and savings.

The women least likely to benefit from spouse and widow benefits, those who are single mothers during their working years, are also the fastest growing component of the population (He et al. 2005). Divorced women need a ten-year marriage to qualify, but almost 60 percent of first and second marriages that end in divorce end before the ten-year mark (He et al. 2005). In fact, only about 20 percent of currently divorced women draw on their marital status benefits (Haider, Jacknowitz, and Schoeni 2003). Never-married women, who currently make up half of single-mother households and are significantly more likely to be poor than married or even divorced mothers, cannot qualify for noncontributory family benefits (Johnson and Favreault 2004). This has large ramifications for a vulnerable group of women. After controlling for race, educational attainment, and current marital status, women currently age sixty-five to seventy-five who had raised children for at least ten years outside of a marriage were 55 percent more likely to be poor in old age than constantly married mothers (Johnson and Favreault 2004).

Moreover, married women who are employed fare considerably less well than married women who do no paid work. Imagine two couples. In one marriage, each spouse earns $30,000 a year for a combined average annual lifetime income of $60,000. The other is a single-earner household with a total income of $60,000. The woman in the single-earner household would receive $1,200 in widow benefits. The woman in the two-earner household, as a widow, would receive only $800. Her widow benefit and her worker benefit are both $800, but she receives just one of the two. This redundancy has been troublesome to many advocacy groups that represent older women and to many older women themselves (Smeeding, Estes, and Glasse 1999).

Inequality Among Women

Although this breadwinner structure reinforces gender inequality, it also has profound implications for race and class inequality among women. Remember that spousal and widow benefits are noncontributory. One need not ever be employed and make contributions to the system to receive them. This type of distribution is similar to the former Aid to Families with Dependent Children (AFDC), also created as a result of the 1935 Social Security Act, but where AFDC targeted benefits toward poor women, spousal and widow benefits increasingly tend to target white and wealthier women (Harrington Meyer 1996).

Since the program's inception, black and poor women have not fared as well as their white and wealthy counterparts. The way benefits were structured for women under the 1935 Social Security Act, and subsequent 1939 amendments, led to inequities among women in the distribution of these benefits. From the start, most blacks were excluded. Occupations dominated by African Americans, including farm work and domestic labor, were not covered under the original act. When debates about the expansion of benefits through the 1939 amendments were under way, blacks were overlooked once again. At that time, Social Security was politically unstable because it had not started distributing benefits and was generating a massive budget surplus (Harrington Meyer 1996). Policy makers immediately acted to expand the beneficiary pool. Instead of extending benefits to black workers, Congress chose to extend benefits to noncontributing wives and widows of workers. Alice Kessler-Harris (1995) argues that the reason benefits were expanded this way was that southern congressmen would have blocked the expansion to black workers. In fact, there is considerable documentation that southern politicians were worried about the impact of generous old age social benefits on the labor force participation of poorly paid black sharecroppers (Quadagno 1988). The result for many black women was that they qualified neither as workers because their occupations were excluded, nor as wives and widows because their husbands' occupations were excluded. Benefits were finally extended to these groups in the 1950s (Kessler-Harris 1995).

Given the current emphasis on market-friendly policies that will encourage people to work, that spousal and survivor benefits are more advantageous for white women than for black women is ironic. Spouse and widow benefits are most beneficial to married white women who never work because they experience no benefit redundancy (Harrington Meyer 1996). They receive 50 percent, and on widowhood 100 percent, of their husbands' benefits solely because they were married. By contrast, black women tend to work more but for less pay and lower benefits. Black married women have historically, and continue to have, higher rates of labor force participation than white women (Goldin 1977). Moreover, their salaries comprise a larger share of household income. The net effect is that they are less likely to receive auxiliary benefits and experience more benefit redundancy. Indeed, black women are 40 percent less likely to receive spousal benefits than white women (Harrington Meyer 1996).

Even when black women do receive spousal benefits, as figure 4.3 shows, the benefits are much smaller. Average spousal benefits for white women in 2003 were $478, but for black women only $390. Why? The benefit is based on spousal earnings and women tend to marry within race. White men earn more than black men, leaving white women's benefits higher than black women's. The primary rationale for the Social Security worker benefit was that the benefit be progressive but still a reflection of an individual's work history. This does not extend to spousal and widow benefits. For women with no earnings history, benefits are much higher for women married to high earning men. The wage gap between black and white men reinforces the race gap in the size of the spousal and widow benefits for women. Women married to high earners routinely end up with higher Social Security spousal and widow benefits than women who hold low wage jobs for most of their lives.

Currently, older black women are as likely as white women to draw on widow benefits. Blacks face several significant disadvantages with regard to widow benefits, however (Social Security Administration 2004). First, as with spousal benefits, theirs are smaller than white women's. Average widow benefits for white women were $911, and for black women $710 (Social Security Administration 2004). Second, black women are more likely than white women to have earned their benefits. In essence, black women are subsidizing white women's widow benefits. Third, black women's incomes make up a greater percentage of household income than white women's do (Herd 2006a). In 1997, for example, that figure was 44 percent, versus 36 percent for white women (Castro 1998). It is married couples with relatively equivalent incomes who see the smallest returns on their contributions to Social Security.

These disadvantages may be even more pronounced for younger cohorts of women. Young black and poor women will have difficulty qualifying for spouse and widow benefits because they are increasingly likely to remain unmarried. The percentage of women born between

Figure 4.4   Predicted Percentage of Women with Ten-Year Marriage, 1945 Birth Cohort

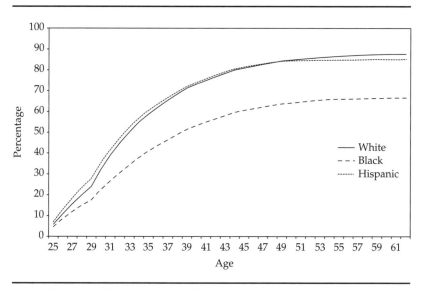

Source: Current population survey, see Harrington Meyer, Wolf, and Himes 2006.

1960 and 1964 who will never marry is 5.4 percent for college graduates and about 12 percent for nongraduates. The race differences are even more striking. Approximately 7 percent of white women will never marry, but 36 percent of their black counterparts will not (Goldstein and Kenney 2001). Just being married is not enough, however. Social Security requires those who divorce to have been married for at least ten years. Harrington Meyer, Wolf, and Himes (2006) demonstrate that smaller portions of younger cohorts are marrying long enough to be eligible for spouse and widow benefits. The patterns are much more pronounced for younger black women than for whites and Hispanics, as is clear from figures 4.4, 4.5, and 4.6. They predict that among women born in the 1960s, the proportion of white and Hispanic women who reach old age qualified for spouse or widow benefits will hover just above 80 percent, versus just 50 percent of black women. The growing race gap in marriage, coupled with the spouse and widow benefits, will likely lead to increasing inequality among older women for future cohorts.

The ways in which spouse and widow benefits reinforce race, class, and marital status inequality among women is a striking but generally overlooked aspect of Social Security. Retired worker benefits redistribute resources from those with greater resources to those with fewer, but spouse and widow benefits tend to have the opposite effect. Given the

Figure 4.5   Predicted Percentage of Women with Ten-Year Marriage, 1955 Birth Cohort

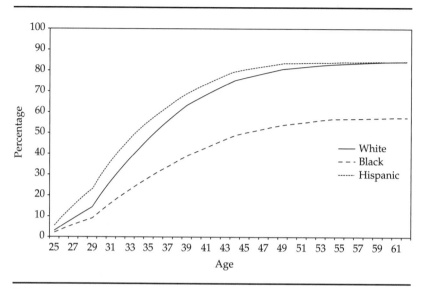

Source: Current population survey, see Harrington Meyer, Wolf, and Himes 2006.

Figure 4.6   Predicted Percentage of Women with Ten-Year Marriage, 1965 Birth Cohort

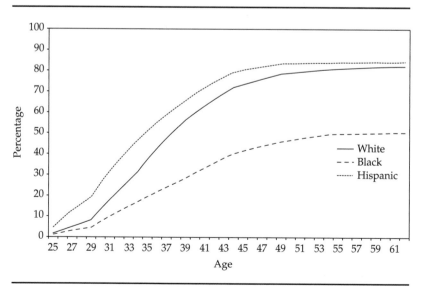

Source: Current population survey, see Harrington Meyer, Wolf, and Himes 2006.

recent welfare reform debates villainizing poor single mothers who do not work, it is surprising that we have not reformed these benefits to make them more responsive and redistributive (Seccombe 1999; Estes 2001). The reality is that in old age the state distributes very little Social Security income to poor, single women who have worked, but significant Social Security income to wealthier married women who have held few jobs in their lifetimes.

Supplemental Security Income

The old age welfare state, like much of the U.S. welfare state, is a two-tiered system of social provision. Some have access to generous social insurance through Social Security, and others have access to means-tested social welfare through Supplemental Security Income (SSI). Many older persons, because their Social Security benefits are meager, leaving them well below the poverty line, receive both. Numerous scholars have documented how earlier in the life course, our two-tier system is gendered, with women more likely to receive smaller and more stigmatized means-tested social welfare benefits than men (Abramovitz 1988; Acker 1990). Moreover, scholars emphasize that it is largely poor, black, and single women, rather than middle- and upper-class white women, who remain concentrated in the second benefit tier (Mink 1998). The latter is certainly the experience for those in late life. Married middle- and upper-class white women with little or no earnings history have access to the relatively generous Social Security system through spousal and widow ben-

Table 4.3   Older Individuals Receiving SSI Benefits, 2001

Sex	
Male	27
Female	73
Race-Ethnicity	
White	56
Black	28
American Indian	2
Asian-Pacific Islander	15
Hispanic	24
Marital Status	
Married	26
Widowed	44
Divorced	21
Never married	9

Source: Social Security Administration 2004.

efits, whereas as table 4.3 shows, poor, black, Hispanic, and unmarried women are more likely to access the inferior means-tested SSI program.

SSI is an important source of income for the very poor. This income and asset-tested program was created in 1972 for the poorest older and disabled people. About 6 percent of older Americans receive SSI payments; 73 percent of these recipients are women who are more likely to rely on the means-tested program because of their higher poverty rates and longer life expectancies (Social Security Administration 2004). Because of lifelong lower earnings and higher rates of chronic illness and disability, blacks are also more likely than whites to rely on SSI. Although they comprise only 8 percent of the aged population in 2000, blacks account for 28 percent of SSI recipients sixty-five and older (Himes 2001; Social Security Administration 2004). About 60 percent of the aged on SSI are also receiving Social Security, but because of low or sporadic earnings, their Social Security benefits are meager. For the remaining 40 percent of older SSI recipients, SSI is their only source of income (Social Security Administration 2004). Although these are important benefits for those who receive them, they do little to reduce poverty and they come with many strings attached.

SSI has not been particularly successful at improving income security for poor older Americans, for several reasons. First, it does not improve income enough to move many beneficiaries above the poverty line. Federal benefits are set at around 78 percent of the federal poverty line. Moreover, the benefits are reduced by one-third for those who do not live alone. Benefit reductions due to co-residence become increasingly problematic as people age and face declining income and health. Some states supplement SSI benefits, but as they have struggled with the cost of education and Medicaid, these supplements have declined over time. In 2003, the inflation-adjusted average was $161.67, down from $180.43 in 1975 (Social Security Administration 2005b). Only two states, California and Connecticut, offer supplements that, when added to the federal benefit, put single older beneficiaries above the poverty line (SSA 2005b; Harrington Meyer 2005).

Second, SSI eligibility guidelines include a strict earnings restriction. Under federal guidelines, the first $65 in earned income, along with an additional $20, is disregarded each month. Any additional earnings decrease benefits by $1 for every $2 earned. As a result, fewer than 2 percent of SSI recipients report earnings (Social Security Administration 2005). By contrast, Social Security has an earnings test only for early retirees. Those who retire after the designated age for full Social Security benefits face no earnings penalties. The employment rate for those age seventy and older—though most retire earlier—is about 13 percent for men and 20 percent for women (U.S. Census Bureau 2005a; He et al. 2005).

Figure 4.7   Percentage of SSI Recipients Sixty-Five and Older

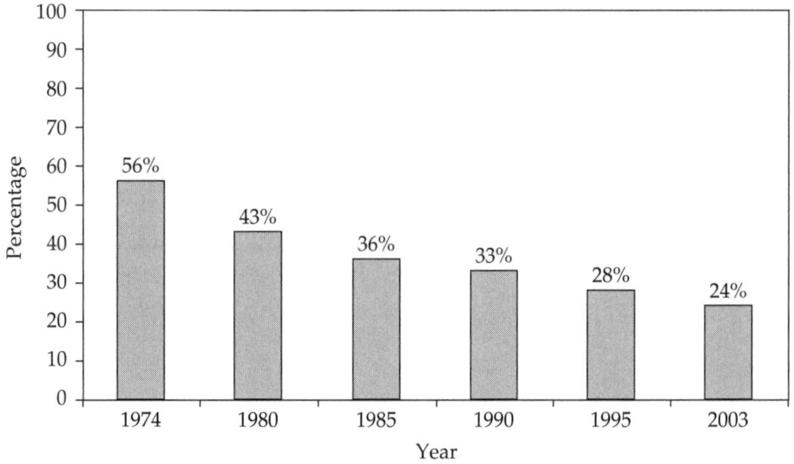

Source: Social Security Administration 2004.

Third, SSI eligibility guidelines include a strict asset test. In 1972, when SSI was created, asset limits were set at $1,500 for individuals and $2,250 for couples. In 1989, these limits were raised to $2,000 and $3,000. They have not been raised since (Social Security Administration 2004; Harrington Meyer 2005). We calculate that if these guidelines had kept pace with inflation, they would be three times the size of the current levels, at $6,607 for individuals and $9,912 for couples.

Fourth, because SSI is means-tested, accessing the program is both cumbersome and stigmatizing. Providing updated information about income, assets, and living arrangements is burdensome for many older persons. The Social Security Administration estimates that just 60 percent of poor older Americans receive SSI benefits (U.S. Congress 2004). Between 30 and 40 percent of those who are eligible do not apply. Poor older Americans who do not apply are either unaware of the benefits, overwhelmed by the lengthy eligibility forms, or too stigmatized to endure the scrutiny of a means-test (Quadagno 1999; Harrington Meyer and Bellas 1995).

The proportion of older SSI recipients has been falling over time because poverty among the aged has declined, the income and asset tests are highly restrictive, and the program remains cumbersome and stigmatizing. As figure 4.7 shows, between 1974 and 2003 the percentage of SSI recipients age 65 and over dropped from 58 percent to 18 percent (Social Security Administration 2005). Part of the decline in SSI use may also be linked to the Personal Responsibility and Work Opportunity Reconciliation Act (PRWORA). Passed in 1996, PRWORA deems most legal (and all illegal) immigrants ineligible for public assistance under SSI and Medicaid (Harrington Meyer 2005; Social Security Administration 2002). Katherine Newman (2003) reports that when the legislation was passed, about one in four SSI recipients were noncitizen legal immigrants. Reductions in SSI eligibility have hit inner cities, where many immigrant older people live with few other resources on which to rely, particularly hard.

Private Pensions

Private pensions are a vital source of income in old age. After Social Security, they provide the second largest stream of income for most older people and often are the difference between being below or above the poverty line (Smeeding, Estes, and Glasse 1999). Although we tend to think about private pensions as a market approach to retirement income, in fact, government subsidies make them a part of the welfare state. The government spends over $100 billion a year on tax subsidies for private pension plans (Weller and Singleton 2002). Only some older Americans have access to pensions. Among older people in the top income quartile, 63 percent have some pension income. Among those in the bottom two income quartiles, only 20 percent do (Employee Benefit Research Institute 2004). This has significant implications for women's retirement in that private pensions play a large role in determining retirement income and poverty rates. Ultimately, private pension distributions reflect employment inequalities. They tend to reinforce rather than reduce old age income inequality.

Currently, older women are significantly less likely to receive pensions than older men and when women do receive pensions their size is significantly smaller. In 2003, 28 percent of women versus 45 percent of men sixty-five and older received a pension. Among the women who did receive them, the average pension was just half that of men's (McDonnell 2005). That this cohort of women, born mainly in the 1920s and 1930s, was less likely to be employed and earned less than men largely drove these differences. Moreover, even for women who worked, occupational segregation and low rates of unionization left them less likely than men to receive a pension in retirement (Farkas and O'Rand 1998).

However, for younger women, the situation is changing. Women are increasingly likely to participate in pension plans that they will have access to in retirement. In 1972, 38 percent of full-time private sector female workers had pension coverage, versus 54 percent of their male counterparts (Johnson, Sambamoorthi, and Crystal 1999). By 2000, full-time private sector male and female workers were equally likely to have such coverage (Even and Macpherson 2004). Women, however, are twice as likely as men to be out of the labor force or to work part time. Thus, when you include all working and nonworking individuals, about 50 percent of men participate in pension plans, but only 38 percent of women do. Nonetheless, there have clearly been improvements in women's access to pensions.

Over time, the reasons for lower pension coverage among women have changed. For young women, one of the strongest determinants of whether they will receive a pension, and the size of the one they do receive, is whether they have children. In a study comparing women born from 1928 to 1937 and those born from 1944 to 1953, Janice Farkas and Angela O'Rand (1998) found that though children did not have a negative influence on participation in pensions for the older cohort of women, they did on the probability that the younger cohort of women would participate. Occupational segregation explained the lack of pension for most of the older cohorts and the presence of children explained the lack of pension for most of the younger cohort. In the past, older women were unlikely to obtain a job with good fringe benefits; today, younger women are more likely to be able to do so, unless they have children. Increasingly, it's not being a woman that interferes in the labor market, it's being a mother.

One thing that holds constant for today and tomorrow's older women, however, is that the average value of their pensions is, and will likely remain, much lower than men's (Even and Macpherson 2004). There has been very little improvement over time. In 1975, the average pension benefit was $800 for women and $3,600 for men. By 2000, the average was $1,900 for women and $6,400 for men. Thus, the gap did decline slightly in percentage terms, though in dollar terms it of course grew (Even and Macpherson 2004). These estimates, however, include those individuals with no pension income. In fact, almost all of the growth in women's average pension benefit is driven by more women acquiring pensions than by increases in the size of those benefits.

What does the future hold for younger cohorts? It's not entirely clear. Estimates range from modest to no improvement (Even and Macpherson 2004; Moore 2006). Researchers are not optimistic that the gender gap in pensions will diminish much for future cohorts, for several reasons. First, despite improvements, women's cumulative wages remain substantially lower than men's due to greater responsibility for unpaid care work and greater exposure to discrimination in the labor force. As noted earlier, these differences are not expected to change much for future cohorts. Second, the shift from defined pension benefits to defined contribution plans appears to be contributing to gender differences in private pensions for future cohorts. Richard Johnson, Usha Sambamoorthi, and Stephen Crystal (1999) found that among full-time workers with pension coverage who were approaching retirement age, men's average private pensions were 76 percent higher than women's. However, among those with a single defined benefit plan, men's average pensions were just 30 percent more than women's. Among those with defined contribution plans, men's average benefits were 170 percent higher than women's.

In contrast to the old fashioned defined benefit plans, which spread risk and responsibility for retirement income, defined contribution plans are consistent with the increasingly popular market-friendly approach. Defined contribution plans maximize individual choice, risk, and responsibility. Early studies suggest that the shift from defined benefit to defined contribution plans will be problematic for women because the degree to which employees, as opposed to employers, are now responsible for their pension savings is changing. In essence, the risks associated with retirement savings are being transferred from employers to employees, and from groups to individuals. Indeed, in the past, most people received defined benefit pensions. After working for an employer for a certain number of years, employees received a monthly pension benefit in retirement. The longer one worked, and the more one earned, the larger the benefit.

Within the past fifteen years, however, the majority of pensions have shifted to defined contribution rather than defined benefit (O'Rand and Henretta 1999; Shuey and O'Rand 2004). Roughly 25 percent of the labor force enjoys both. Between 1979 and 2004, the proportion covered only by defined benefit plans dropped from 62 percent to 10 percent and the proportion covered only by defined contribution plans rose from 16 percent to 63 percent (EBRI 2004). The difference is critical. Employees, as opposed to employers, are now responsible for pension savings (Shuey and O'Rand 2006). The employee contributes up to a certain percentage of their salary to a pension every year and the employer contributes based on that amount. What the employer puts in varies widely, ranging from nothing to a full match of the employee's contribution.

The shift to defined contribution plans has increased the individual financial risk older workers face in three ways. First, it is easier for employees to opt out of defined contribution plans. With a defined benefit plan, individuals were generally automatically enrolled and the amount invested was set by the employer. With defined contribution plans, employees have more opportunity to either opt out or to contribute relatively small amounts. Few contribute the maximum. On average, just 8.4 percent of workers in 2001 were making maximum contributions to their 401(k) plans (Munnell and Sundén 2004). Those with lower incomes were particularly unlikely to be investing. Whereas 53 percent of those earning more than $100,000 annually were making maximum contributions, just 0.1 percent of those making less than $10,000 annually were doing so. Women tend to earn less and contribute less.

Second, workers may withdraw money from these plans before retirement. For example, about half of all workers cash out their pensions rather than transfer the money to a new retirement account (Munnell and Sundén 2004). Of particular concern for women, in light of high divorce rates, is that marital dissolution substantially increases the risk that women will cash out their pensions. These risks do appear to be increasing for younger cohorts of women (Shuey and O'Rand 2006).

Third, in a defined benefit plan, losses due to poor investments are spread across all workers in the organization. In a defined contribution plan, individuals absorb the entire risk. For those with relatively low earnings, more limited contributions, or more intermittent employment, these risks are much harder to absorb. To the extent that women, and particularly less-educated women in lower-paying positions, contribute less, they have a more difficult time absorbing investment losses. Ultimately, under defined contribution, when the money is gone, the money is gone. Women's longer life expectancies leave them particularly likely to outlive their meager pension investments.

Finally, there is evidence that employers are decreasing their contributions toward 401(k) plans. In other words, defined contribution plans are becoming even more market friendly in that they are becoming less onerous for employers. In 1997, company contributions towards 401(k) plans as a portion of payroll were 3.2 percent. By 2001, this had fallen to 2.5 percent (Munnell and Sundén 2003). This means that the responsibility for private pension funding is being transferred even more fully from employers to employees. Reduced subsidization of retirement income is particularly problematic for low earners, including women, blacks and Hispanics, and single mothers.

Initially, some experts argued that the shift to defined contribution plans might prove advantageous for women, who tend to move in and out of employment more frequently than men. The argument was that they would accrue assets in a portable defined contribution plan rather than in a defined benefit plan that rewarded a lengthy tenure with a single employer. The reality, however, is quite different (Shuey and O'Rand 2004, 2006). In 1989, employers had contributed 7.75 percent of pay to women's pensions versus 6.13 percent to men's (Bajtelsmit and Jianakoplos 2000). By 1998, employer contributions had dropped to 5.52 percent for women's plans and 5.67 percent for men's. Everyone is getting less and a small gender gap has emerged. Further, the size of women's defined contribution plans lags well behind that of their defined benefit plans. Among those born between 1931 and 1941, women's average defined benefit savings were 77 percent of men's and those of their defined contribution plan just 37 percent (Johnson, Sambamoorthi, and Crystal 1999). In fact, a recent simulation estimates that women's pension wealth in defined contribution plans will be 25 percent lower than in traditional defined benefit plans, and 50 percent lower in 401(k) plans than in traditional defined benefit plans (Even and Macpherson 2004). That is, gender inequality in private pension income is expected to increase for future cohorts.

The shift to defined contribution embodies the market-friendly approach of individualized choice, risk, and responsibility. In practice, it reveals how benefits linked tightly to wages tend to replicate or even magnify inequalities generated in the labor force. Defined contribution plans concentrate risk and reduce subsidization or redistribution (Shuey and O'Rand 2006). Women, due to their lower labor force participation and earnings, fare better in systems that spread risk across larger groups and redistribute resources from higher to lower earners—systems that embrace family-friendly distributive principles, such as defined benefit private pensions and, even more so, public pension systems.

Private Pensions and Marital Status

Married women have two ways to receive pensions, his job or her job. Unmarried women have just one. Thus, gender, race, and class differences in access to pensions are confounded by differences in marital status. Although more and more women have access to pensions based on their own work history, many will remain dependent on their spouses' pensions due to slightly lower participation rates and substantially lower pension sizes. Being married provides women with much greater access to pension income. Among married women currently in their sixties, 84 percent have access to either his or her pension. The comparable rates are 55 percent for separated and divorced women, 46 percent for widowed women, and 65 percent for never-married women (Rogowski and Karoly 2002). After controlling for women's work histories, race, economic resources, and children, unmarried women are 70 to 80 percent less likely to have access to a pension than married women (Yabiku 2000). Moreover, access to one's pension through employment has been increasing over time for married and widowed women, where most of the increase in labor force participation has been concentrated, but has remained relatively stagnant for divorced and never-married women (Even and Macpherson 2004). Additionally, the size of those pensions has risen rapidly for married and widowed women over age sixty-five, but barely changed for divorced and never married women (Even and Macpherson 2004). With the general retreat from marriage, particularly among black women, these trends portend economic trouble for younger cohorts of women.

Widowed women actually experienced improved access to private pension income until the mid-1980s. Historically, adherence to family-friendly principles caused legislators to extend protections to widows, shoring up their fiscal situations. On retirement, individuals may choose to take their defined benefit contribution as either a single life annuity or a joint survivor annuity. The joint survivor annuity leads to smaller monthly payments, but guarantees that survivors, generally widows, will receive pension income after the death of their spouses. In the early 1970s, only about 48 percent of men chose the joint survivor annuity, but not all men had the option because employer-sponsored plans were not required to offer it (Holden and Nicholson 1998). After the passage of the Employment Retirement Income Security Act (ERISA) in 1974, which required employers to offer the joint survivor option as the default coverage, the rate rose to 64 percent. Further protection for widows was enacted in 1984 by the Retirement Equity Act, which required that pension recipients receive written consent from their spouses to take the individual annuity payout. Consequently, survivor benefit coverage rose from 70 percent in 1982 to 77 percent in 1990 (Aura 2001). The recent shift to market-friendly defined contribution plans has dismantled much of that protection, however. Defined contribution plans do not offer the same spousal protections currently in place for defined benefit plans. As soon as these pensions are rolled over into an individual retirement account, spouses lose control over them.

Divorced women, who comprise a rapidly growing segment of unmarried older women, often have more difficulty accessing their former spouses' pensions. Such matters are usually decided during the divorce because pensions are considered a total family asset. If negotiated, women can obtain a certain share of their former spouses' pensions. Most divorced women, though, rely on their own pensions. Divorced women are 7 percent more likely than married to have a benefit in their own name (Rogowski and Karoly 2002). However, because they rarely have access to men's private pension income, and because they are more likely to cash out of defined contribution plans, divorced older women's pension income is only 60 percent that of married women's (Shuey and O'Rand 2006).

Ultimately, the extent to which unmarried women have fewer and smaller pensions depends heavily on their socioeconomic status before their divorce or the spouse's death. Divorced women who are more highly educated and have consistent lifetime work histories are better able to offset pension losses linked to the end of their marriages. Widowed women's likelihood for a reasonable pension income also depends on their own earnings, but even more on whether their spouse took the joint survivor option. Most studies show that white and wealthier men are more likely than black and poorer men to take reduced pension payments in the short term so that their wives are guaranteed pension payments as widows (Johnson, Uccello, and Goldwyn 2003). Those with more limited economic resources are often unable to afford taking a reduced pension, no matter how much they may want to pass income on to their wives when they die.

Inequality Among Women

Women are catching up to men in their chances of having a pension, then, but the pensions they are acquiring are often less valuable. Moreover, there is growing variation among women, related to class and race. The forecast for less-educated and black women, in particular, is bleak. As figure 4.8 shows, in 1979, 35 percent of women without a high school degree had a pension compared to 60 percent of women with at least a college degree. By 2003, 19 percent of women without a high school degree had a pension compared to around 61 percent of women with at least a college degree (Even and Macpherson 2000, 2004; EBRI 2004). These educational disparities in pension receipt bode poorly for black women. Currently, 14 percent of black women, versus 7 percent of white women, do not have high school degrees. At the same time, whereas 30 percent of white women have at least a bachelor's degree, only 15 percent of black women do (Proctor 2003). In fact, the pension prospects for young minority women are little different than for older women today. Among those age sixty-five and older, 57 percent of white women and

Figure 4.8   Pension Coverage Rates Among Employed Women Twenty-Five to Fifty-Four

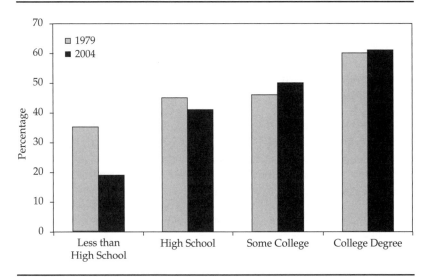

Sources: Even and Macpherson 2000; EBRI 2004.

44 percent of black women have some pension coverage. Among women age thirty-three to forty-two, 64 percent of white women but only 49 percent of black women have some retirement coverage (Verma 2003).

Class and race differences among women determine not only their probability of having a pension, but also the size of that pension. These differences are growing. Among women born between 1936 and 1940, those within the highest quintile of earnings had a defined contribution pension 25 percent larger than that of women in the bottom earnings quintile. Among women born between 1956 and 1960, those in the top earnings quartile will have a defined benefit pension 250 percent larger than that of women in the bottom quintile (Toder et al. 1999). Thus much of the growing inequality among women is linked to the shift from defined benefit to defined contribution plans. Even and Macpherson (2004) estimate that high earners, but not low earners, will have benefits that are 25 percent larger in defined contribution plans than under defined benefit plans. This growing inequality bodes poorly for black women and women without high school degrees. The wage gap between these groups of women and white women and women with college degrees has been growing, and differences in the sizes of their pensions are growing right along with it (Bowler 1999). The evidence is that low earners fare worse in defined contribution plans than they did in defined benefit plans. Thus, among the aged, the shift toward market-friendly principles of maximum individual choice, risk, and responsibility is leading not only to increasing gender inequality, but also to increasing race, class, and marital status inequality (Even and Macpherson 2004; Herd 2005c).

Asset Income

Having asset income in retirement is an area of growing importance for older Americans. As the welfare state and corporations turn more and more of the responsibility for retirement savings to individuals, the extent to which people can save is an extraordinarily important determinant of their well-being in old age. Women lag far behind men in accruing assets.

Gender disparities in household asset levels are mainly an issue for those who are not married. Because wealth is examined at the household level, asset differences between married women and men are, de facto, nonexistent. The main source of difference is between unmarried men and women. Among the current older population, unmarried men have assets that are almost 30 percent higher than unmarried women's (Levine, Mitchell, and Phillips 2000). Much of the explanation is due to the gender gap in wages, given that income is the primary determinant of asset levels (Levine, Mitchell, and Phillips 2000). Another part of the explanation is that marital dissolution has a more negative effect on assets for women than for men, though trend analyses show that the gender gap regarding the financial consequences of divorce is shrinking (Wilmoth and Koso 2002; McManus and DiPrete 2001).

Among younger cohorts, asset differences between married and unmarried women will be driven mainly by whether they were single mothers (Yamokoski and Keister 2006). Among those currently age sixty-five to seventy-five, the asset income of women who were single mothers for ten or more years was one-third that of continuously married mothers. Even after controlling for current marital status, educational attainment, and race, long-term single mothers had a median net worth $44,000 less than their continuously married counterparts. Even short-term single mothers had a median net worth $57,000 less than their counterparts (Johnson and Favreault 2004). The prospects for younger women are not much brighter. Among those who were fourteen to twenty-two in 1979, married parents had median assets worth $96,000 but single mothers only $6,000 by 2000 (Yamokoski and Keister 2006). Fewer assets means less to invest, less ability to absorb losses, less income in old age, and greater risk of poverty in old age.

Inequality Among Women

Gender disparities in asset levels are significant, but they pale in comparison to disparities by race and ethnicity. For women currently in their sixties, even after controlling for marital status and educational attainment, black and Hispanic women had a total net worth averaging $100,000 less than that of white women (Johnson and Favreault 2004). The prospects for younger minority women are also not much brighter. Using data from the 1990s, Amy Orr (2003) showed that average net worth for white mothers was $87,000 and for black mothers was $16,000. These asset differences are the primary driver of black and white differences in retirement income. They help explain why Hispanic and black older women were more than twice as likely as whites to be poor (Johnson and Favreault 2004).

Explanations for race differences in asset accumulation are plentiful. Black women are increasingly less likely to be married, and therefore less likely to have access to assets in a two-adult household. In 1970, the percent of black women married relative to white women age sixty-five and older was 87 percent. By the year 2000, this had fallen to 58 percent (Harrington Meyer, Wolf, and Himes 2006). About 20 percent of unmarried older women qualify as asset poor, but only 3 percent of married older women are (Wolff 2002). Black women are also increasingly likely to be single mothers, and single mothers' wealth is around 10 percent that of married parents (Wolff 2004; Yamokoski and Keister 2006). Even when comparing people with similar socioeconomic and demographic characteristics, however, whites have considerably more assets than blacks and Hispanics (Conley 1999; Krivo and Kaufman 2004). The mean wealth ratio in the 1990s was .24. Only 30 percent of this gap could be explained by income, education, and marital status differences (Gittleman and Wolff 2000). Moreover, racial and ethnic inequalities in assets have been growing since the 1960s (Conley 1999). The black-white net worth ratio dropped from .19 to .14 between 1983 and 2001 (Wolff 2004). As Edward Wolff (2004) points out, much of this gap can be explained by the fact that between 1998 and 2001 white household assets rose by 34 percent compared to just 5 percent for African Americans (Wolff 2004).

Housing wealth is a predominant source of these differences. It is also one of the key factors associated with income security in old age. A home is the largest single asset older people own (Wolff 2002). Whereas just 6 percent of homeowners qualify as asset poor, more than 70 percent of those who rent do (Wolff 2002). The accrued savings in home value is particularly useful in old age to offset large economic losses, such as the death of a spouse or catastrophic medical expenses (Venti and Wise 2001). However, African Americans and Latinos, have been, and continue to be, systematically less likely to own homes (Blau and Graham 1990). In 2000, almost 75 percent of white Americans owned their own home but fewer than 50 percent of black and Latino Americans did (Yinger 2001). In addition, the value of properties owned by blacks and Hispanics is much less than that of those owned by whites. Since the early 1970s, race and ethnic gaps in the value of people's homes have been rising (Krivo and Kaufman 2004; Wolff 2004). Between 1998 and 2001, Hispanics experienced a real decline in their housing wealth.

The explanations for this phenomenon range from white flight to real estate practices that affect racial and ethnic differences in mortgage rates (Krivo and Kaufman 2004). Discrimination plays an important role. The first level occurs outside the housing market and is a product of structural inequities built into the educational system and labor market, which leads to lower socioeconomic attainment, and accounts for almost one-third of housing wealth differences (Krivo and Kaufman 2004). The second level occurs within the housing market (Krivo and Kaufman 2004). The most recent study of discrimination, conducted in 2000 by the Urban Institute and the Department of Housing and Urban Development, continued to find bias in the housing market. In the sales market, blacks are around 17 percent more likely to be discriminated against than whites and Hispanics 20 percent more likely (Ross and Turner 2005; Turner et al. 2002). For example, real estate agents limit what properties they show people. Black and Hispanic home buyers learn about 13 percent fewer houses than their white counterparts (Ross and Turner 2005; Turner et al. 2002). There are some encouraging signs, however, that discrimination has weakened over time. Adverse treatment against both blacks and Hispanics in the sales market dropped by about one-third between 1989 and 2000 (Ross and Turner 2005; Turner et al. 2002). There was evidence, however, of increases in certain forms of adverse treatment. Blacks were more likely than in 1989 to be steered away from predominantly white neighborhoods and Hispanics were less likely to receive help with financing than whites were (Ross and Turner 2005; Turner et al. 2002). A third level of discrimination occurs among lending institutions (Munnell et al. 1996; Smith and Cloud 1996; Yinger 2001). Alice Munnell and colleagues (1996) found that black and Hispanic home buyers were 82 percent more likely than comparable white buyers to be turned down for a loan. Another study found that white applicants received more detailed loan information, and, most important, better loan rates, than comparable black and Hispanic applicants (Smith and DeLair 1999).

Racially and ethnically stratified wealth has not only disturbing implications for today's older Americans, but also significantly negative implications for their children. It influences people's ability to buy homes. Whereas almost 25 percent of whites receive help from a family member for a house down payment, just 6 percent of blacks do (Charles and Hurst 2002). Further, a lack of assets means a limited ability to transfer those assets to children as an inheritance; direct inheritance differences account for up to 20 percent of the racial gap in wealth (Menchik and Jianakoplos 1997). Overall, inheritances account for between 50 and 80 percent of Americans' net worth (Yamokoski and Keister 2006).

Asset accumulation is shaped predominantly by sociodemographic differences such as education and marital status, and market forces including wages, fringe benefits, and real estate and mortgage practices. The lack of government intervention to help women—especially single, poor, and less-educated women—save, invest, buy houses, and otherwise accumulate assets is problematic. The evidence suggests that reliance on market-friendly solutions leads to market-based forms of inequality. The paucity of relevant family-friendly welfare benefits means that the blunt forces of the market are unrestrained. The result is that inequality linked to gender, race, class, and marital status is growing and may well continue to grow among future cohorts of older people.

Discussion

Although the economic picture for older women has improved substantially, women receive substantially less than older men in every source of income, whether we look at Social Security, private pensions, or assets. Moreover, inequality is rising among women. Older blacks and Hispanic women's Social Security, pension, and assets are substantially less than white women's—and that gap is growing.

Policy solutions linked to the private market are problematic given that the private market solutions already in place are fueling growing inequality. Even though private pensions are federally subsidized and come with strings attached, employers are not required to distribute private pensions in ways that are equitable or would reduce inequality. Thus private pensions, subsidized by taxpayer dollars at $100 billion a year, are leading to more, not less, inequality by gender, race, class, and marital status. Because of the emphasis on individual choice, risk, and responsibility, the move toward defined contribution plans may be prompting even more inequality. Moreover, the move toward defined contribution makes federal intervention even less likely. Historic government efforts to regulate private pensions and protect people in defined benefit plans have now been almost entirely circumvented by the shift to defined contribution plans. At a certain level, such debates are becoming almost moot because private pension coverage is on the decline for all groups—even among higher-income people in large firms. This leg of the three-legged stool is already weak and growing weaker.

By contrast, Social Security, with its universal coverage, redistributive formula, and socialization rather than individualization of risk, currently provides a very strong leg. We actually could build an even more robust Social Security program in response to changing families and workplaces. We could also have a system that provides higher income replacement rates. The U.S. system has a replacement rate of 45 percent compared to about 65 percent in all OECD countries (OECD 2005). In chapter 7, we discuss several moves that would provide a more robust program that would be more family friendly and therefore lessen gender, race, class, and marital status inequality. We are well aware, however, that many policy makers are moving in the opposite direction: toward a market-friendly privatization of public pensions. Privatization of Social Security would lead to outcomes that look a lot like what we currently have with private corporate pensions; far from reducing inequality among the aged, such a program would replicate inequalities generated by the market.

= Chapter 5 =

The Business of Health

We are slowly discovering that we can't pay for the business of health care along with health care.

Dr. Linda Peeno, Louisville, Kentucky, physician and
former medical director at Humana and Blue Cross/
Blue Shield of Kentucky (Britt 2004)

GOOD HEALTH is not randomly distributed in old age. Older women, blacks, Hispanics, and people with less income and education are less healthy than their counterparts. They also have much lower average incomes and therefore fewer resources with which to deal with poor health. Access to health insurance is also not randomly distributed. Those under sixty-five rely on private market health solutions. The results have been problematic in that 44 million Americans are uninsured (Holtz-Eakin 2004). Those over sixty-five rely on a nearly universal health insurance plan, but the coverage is incomplete, thus requiring private market supplemental coverage, and for low-income Americans, public subsidies to fill in the gaps. Here we explore inequalities in health and health care over the life course and, in particular, in old age. It is clear that our patchwork health insurance system, with a mix of coverage through private insurance, Medicare, and Medicaid, is neither adequately insuring against the costs of ill health nor fiscally sustainable. Proponents of market-friendly policies argue that we must reduce government funding and regulation of the health industry to maximize individual consumer choice, risk, and responsibility (Herd 2005a). As the *Congressional Quarterly* put it, the goal was "to unleash 'free market forces' to attack the persistent problems of cost and accessibility of health care" (cited in Barlett and Steele 2006, 88). Attempts to deregulate and privatize, however, have proven particularly problematic for disadvantaged groups and served to increase rather than decrease inequality in old age. Indeed, advocates of family-friendly universal policies point out that efforts to contain costs and increase access by privatizing public health benefits have failed. What they have accomplished instead, much of it under the radar, is an erosion of the redistributive aspects of these programs. Proponents of family-friendly policies support a complete reversal, focusing on a universal health insurance program that emphasizes prevention for all ages, extending coverage to all, reducing inequality in old age, and, just maybe, reducing costs in the long run.

Gender, Race, Class, and Health Inequality

Poor health is often associated with old age. Sixty percent of those sixty-five and older have more than one chronic condition and nearly 40 percent of those eighty-five and older are at least partially disabled by chronic illness (Jette 1996; Quadagno 2001). The emerging story over the last few decades, though, is that most, but certainly not all, older people are living longer and healthier lives (Manton and Stallard 1996; Rieker and Bird 2000). If 60 percent of those sixty-five and older have at least one chronic condition, 40 percent have none. Older men, whites, and those with greater income and education have better health and mobility. By contrast, older women, blacks, Hispanics, and persons with less income and less education are more likely to have poor health and to experience accompanying functional limitations (Mirowsky and Ross 2003b; Halfon and Hochstein 2002; Himes 2001; Herd 2006b; Williams and Collins 1995). The question is, why is health inequality in old age so persistent?

Health Differences Between Women and Men

The great paradox with respect to gender differences in health is that generally men have higher mortality and women have higher morbidity. Throughout the twentieth century, life expectancy increased dramatically for all Americans, but the gender gap widened. In 1902, women lived an average of three years longer than men. By 2002, they lived an average of five years longer. Among those born in 2002, men will live an average of seventy-five years and women an average of eighty years (NCHS 2005b). At every age, men are more likely than women to die of fatal conditions such as heart disease, stroke, cancer, flu, cirrhosis, diabetes, HIV, unintended injuries, suicide, and homicide (NCHS 2005b). The top two leading causes of death are the same for men and women—heart disease, and stroke. Men and women, though, have somewhat different patterns of disease that lead to somewhat different patterns of health (Rieker and Bird 2000; Macintyre, Hunt, and Sweeting 1996).

Where men tend to report higher rates of life-threatening conditions, women tend to report higher rates of chronic conditions such as anemia, thyroid conditions, migraines, arthritis, hypertension, urinary incontinence, osteoporosis, gall bladder conditions, colitis, eczema, and depression (NCHS 2004; Halfon and Hochstein 2002; Rieker and Bird 2000; Himes 2001; Kaiser Family Foundation 2001; Haug and Folmar 1986;

Weitz 2007; Mirowsky and Ross 2003a). For example, women are 50 percent more likely than men to have arthritis, the most common chronic condition. Women are also 20 to 30 percent more likely than men to have acute illnesses and short-term infections such as the flu or serious colds. Although women live longer, they are sicker and report more functional limitations than men at all ages. In charting active and inactive life expectancy, Mark Hayward and Melonie Heron (1999) show that women spend longer portions of their lives with health problems that impede activity than do men. Still, it is important not to overstate gender differences in health. Women have considerably higher rates of mental health illness, but only slightly higher rates of physical morbidity (Macintyre, Hunt, and Sweeting 1996).

Health Differences Among Women

All women tend to live longer than their male counterparts, but white and Asian women tend to live significantly longer than black, Hispanic, and Native American women. For example, of those born in 2002, white women will live an average of almost eighty-one years and black women just under seventy-six (NCHS 2005b). Neither the Centers for Disease Control and Prevention nor the National Center for Health Statistics releases life expectancy statistics for Hispanic or Asian groups. Work by Mark Hayward and Melonie Heron (1999) shows dramatic differences in life expectancy for those born in 1970. Figure 5.1 shows that for those who had reached age twenty in 1990, Asian, white, and Native American women can expect to live to an average age of eighty-four, eighty-three, and eighty-one respectively, whereas Hispanic and black women will live on average to just age seventy-eight and seventy-six.

The leading causes of death for white, black, and Hispanic women are heart disease and cancers, but for Native American and Asian women these top two are reversed. Disease patterns differ substantially by race and ethnicity. Black and Hispanic women (and men) have higher rates of infant mortality, arthritis, hypertension, diabetes, cirrhosis, obesity, HIV, injury due to violence, and other illnesses (NCHS 2005b; Himes 2001; Kaiser Family Foundation 2001; Haug and Folmar 1986; Mirowsky and Ross 2003a). As a result, blacks and Hispanics have higher rates than whites of chronic conditions and functional limitations (Himes 2001; Quadagno 2001; Smith and Kington 1997). For example, only 58 percent of older black men report their health as good to excellent, versus 65 percent of Hispanics and 74 percent of whites (Himes 2001). Hayward and Heron (1999) show that black, Hispanic, and Native American women and men spend longer portions of their lives with health problems that impede activity than whites do. Native American women are hardest hit, with an average of nearly eighteen

Figure 5.1   Life Expectancy in 1990

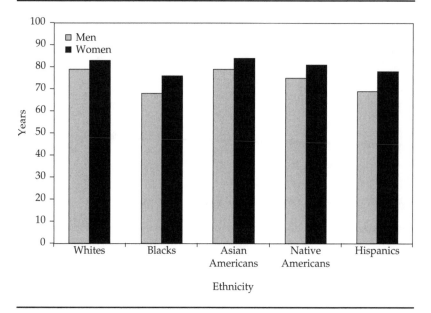

Source: Hayward and Heron 1999.

years of inactive life in old age, compared with about ten years for Asian and white women.

Explaining Health Differences

In explaining health inequality, proponents of market-friendly policies emphasize individual choice, risk, and responsibility. After all, it is estimated that about one-third of the difference in health by socioeconomic status is due to individual differences in lifestyle and behavior (Lantz et al. 1998). By contrast, proponents of family-friendly policies emphasize how structural constraints, which impact health through a range of mechanisms, including individual behaviors, lead to accumulated advantage or disadvantage.

Individual Risk and Responsibility   There is little question that individual lifestyle behaviors vary significantly by gender, race, and class. Indeed, gender differences in lifestyle explain some—but certainly not all—of the gender differences in health (Potter 1992; Rothman 1986; Rieker and Bird 2000; Mirowsky and Ross 2003a). Numerous studies have shown that men are more likely to engage in riskier health behaviors, including drug use, dangerous sports or hobbies, violence, and occupations such as mining or construction where injury or illness are more common (Rieker and Bird 2000; Ross and Bird 1994). By contrast, women are more likely than men to engage in health protective behaviors, such as healthy diet, regular exercise, regular health screenings, and more frequent visits with doctors (Ross and Bird 1994; Weitz 2007).

For both women and men, those with lower incomes and less education tend to have higher rates of risky behavior, such as drinking and smoking, and lower rates of healthy behavior such as regular exercise and physicals (Lantz et al. 1998). We can look at specific health behaviors and see significant differences by gender, race, and class. The question is, why. For example, although smoking is generally down, older black men are twice as likely to smoke as older white men or any older women (NCHS 2004). Similarly, body sizes are growing generally, but older women and older blacks and Hispanics are significantly more likely than men or older whites to be overweight or obese (Himes 2001). Supporters of individualistic explanations suggest that poor health behaviors contribute to lower incomes and standards of living (Smith 1999). Conversely, good health behaviors can help people overcome disadvantages in the job or marriage market. Critics of individualist theories caution that individual lifestyle behaviors are shaped by social, economic, and cultural factors (Himes 2000a, 2000b, 2001; Quadagno 1999; Link, Phelan, and Fremont 2000). For example, higher rates of smoking have been linked to strategic advertising practices by tobacco companies, and lower rates of physical exercise have been linked to more dangerous neighborhoods (Luke, Esmundo, and Bloom 2000; Link, Phelan, and Fremont 2000; Ross and Mirowsky 2001).

Collective Risk and Responsibility   By contrast, supporters of family-friendly policies point out that individual choice, risk, and responsibility are shaped by a wide array of collective forces. Even if differential rates of obesity, smoking, and drinking by socioeconomic status were not driven by structural factors, they still explain just one-third of the relationship between socioeconomic status and health (Lantz et al. 1998). Differential exposure to discrimination, stress, and resource strain shapes health and health behavior (House et al. 1990; Lantz et al. 2005; Hayward, Pienta, and McLaughlin 1997; Link, Phelan, and Fremont 2000). Disadvantaged groups have higher levels of stress and strain, which may translate into higher rates of morbidity. For example, discrimination and the fear of discrimination have been linked to cortisol and blood pressure levels, which may ultimately affect health outcomes (Harrell, Hall, and Taliaferro 2003; Williams 2000). Indeed, health inequality may be best explained by the accumulation of advantage—or disadvantage—over the life course as a result of gender, race, and class inequality (Link and Phelan 1995; Link, Phelan, and Fremont 2000; Harrell, Hall, and Taliaferro 2003; Williams

2000). Various structural advantages and disadvantages accumulate over the life course, setting people on different types of trajectories and exaggerating health inequalities by older ages (Elder 1985, 1998; O'Rand 1996).

Gender differences in health are linked to gender differences in discrimination, stress, resources, paid and unpaid work, and domestic violence. Women are more likely than men to experience stress related to paid work, poorly paid work, and conflicts between paid and unpaid work (Rieker and Bird 2000). Several studies show that women have less autonomy, authority, and control at work, and therefore experience higher rates of physical and mental distress (Ross and Mirowsky 2001, 2003a, 2003b; Padavic and Reskin 2002; Turner and Turner 1999). Eliza Pavalko and her colleagues (2003) found that perceived discrimination leads to higher levels of functional limitations, such as having difficulty standing, stooping, lifting objects, walking, and reaching. Women's wages are significantly lower than men's, and low incomes lead to higher rates of mortality, chronic illnesses, functional limitations, depression, and psychological disorders (House 2002). Poorer women can expect their health disadvantages to accumulate throughout their lives, leaving them not only poorer but also sicker in old age (House 2002). The link between low income and poor health is a double-edged sword. Because women live an average of five years longer than men, they are at greater risk of accumulating age-related illnesses and have fewer resources with which to respond (Himes 2001; NCHS 2005b; Rieker and Bird 2000; Padavic and Reskin 2002).

Gender differences in health are also linked to the conflict between paid and unpaid work. Women continue to have disproportionate responsibility for unpaid cleaning, feeding, and care work. The stress of these chores, often in combination with the stress of paid work, is linked to poorer physical and mental health (Mirowsky and Ross 2003a; Bird 1999; Ross and Bird 1994; Scharlach 1994; Stephens and Franks 1995). At younger ages, women still have the lion's share of the responsibility for unpaid domestic labor and child care (Bianchi et al. 2000; Ross and Bird 1994; Bird 1999). Women's disproportionate responsibility is linked to poorer health outcomes. Chloe Bird (1999) found that men's lower contribution to household work partially explains their lower rates of depression. Inequities in the distribution of this labor, as opposed to the overall amount, were what prompted women's depression (see also Mirowsky and Ross 2003a). One of the emotional consequences is that women get more distressed than men about parental and marital strain (Simon 1998). Moreover, women leaving employment to raise their children reduce their income and social support, which is problematic for their emotional and physical health (Mirowsky and Ross 2003a; Waldron, Weiss, and Hughes 1998). Indeed, mothers who stay at home with young children are more depressed than any other group of women (Mirowsky and Ross 2003a).

In older age, women provide roughly 75 percent of all care work for frail older persons (Stone 2000; Estes 2001; Quadagno 2001; Moody 2002; Herd and Harrington Meyer 2002; National Alliance for Caregiving and AARP 2004). Care work adversely affects the roughly 45 million care workers in terms of economic, physical, emotional, and social health (Stone 2000; Hooyman and Gonyea 1995; Kaiser Family Foundation 2002). Caregivers report higher rates of physical and psychological distress, loneliness, family tension, sleeplessness, exhaustion, inadequate exercise, anxiety, depression, chronic conditions, and drug misuse (Baumgarten et al. 1992; Pavalko and Woodbury 2000; National Alliance for Caregiving and AARP 1997, 2004; Collins, Schoen, and Joseph 1999; Adam 1999; Bird 1999; Hoyert and Seltzer 1992; Brody 1990; Stephens and Franks 1995; Pavalko and Woodbury 2000; Harrington Meyer and Herd 2001). Ultimately, caregivers face worse health due to the stresses of care work, yet they are less likely to have the time, energy, or resources to obtain care for themselves. Compared to noncaregivers, caregivers were twice as likely to forgo needed medical care and to miss filling a prescription due to cost (Collins, Schoen, and Joseph 1999). Being sick, tired, and depressed stifles people's energy and ability to focus on anything other than their most immediate responsibilities. The longer individuals provide care, the more of an impact it appears to have. Long-term caregiving weakens individuals' immune systems and leads to accelerated aging at the cellular level. Caregivers reporting very high stress levels, compared to those reporting low levels, aged an equivalent of an extra ten years (Epel et al. 2004; Kiecolt-Glaser et al. 1991; Pavalko and Woodbury 2000).

Finally, violence at the hands of men also takes a dramatic toll on women's physical and emotional health. More than 30 percent of female murder victims are killed by an intimate partner, versus 4 percent of men (Rennison 2003). As figure 5.2 shows, this rate is basically the same as it was in the mid-1970s. Intimate partner violence accounts for 20 percent of nonfatal violence against women versus 3 percent for men (Rennison 2003). Nonfatal assault includes rape, robbery, aggravated assault, and simple assault. Beatings often escalate when women are pregnant. Estimates are that 4 to 17 percent of women are abused during their pregnancies (Cokkinides and Coker 1998; Gazmararian et al. 2000; Stewart and Cecutti 1993). Ultimately, abused women face higher rates of sleep disorders, anxiety, depression, suicide, and alcohol and substance abuse, not to mention the toll it takes on their self-esteem (Umberson et al. 1998; Dutton and Painter 1993; Gleason 1993; Orava, McLeod, and Sharpe 1996; Straus and Gelles 1990). Thus women's poorer health is ultimately linked to less status, power, control, and resources at work and at home.

Figure 5.2   Murders by Intimate Partners

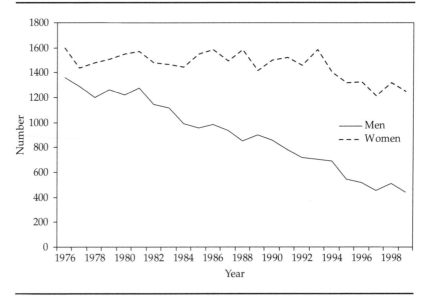

Sources: Rennison 2003; Rennison and Welchans 2000.

Race and ethnic differences in health are similarly linked. At work, blacks and Hispanics face barriers in hiring and promotions, receive less return on their investments in education, and often face overt and covert bigotry (Padavic and Reskin 2002; Hayward and Heron 1999; Williams 2000; Feagin 2000). Blacks and Hispanics tend to have more dangerous and physically demanding jobs and greater exposure to pollutants at work (Weitz 2007; House 2002; Smith 1999; Williams and Collins 1995; North et al. 1996). They are also more likely than whites or Asian Americans to be unemployed, homeless, migrant workers, and imprisoned, all of which are linked to significantly worse health (London and Myers 2006; Williams 2000; Weitz 2007).

At home, blacks and Hispanics face barriers in buying and renting homes, attending good schools, and receiving needed health and social services. Blacks, Hispanics, and the poor are much more likely to live near toxic waste dumps, polluting industries, and congested freeways and thus face greater exposure to contaminated air, water, and soil (Weitz 2007; House 2002; Smith 1999; Williams and Collins 1995; North et al. 1996). Because they are more likely to be poor and to live in inferior and overcrowded housing in more dangerous neighborhoods, many blacks and Hispanics report higher rates of lead poisoning, injury, infection, gas poisoning, asthma, and injury from fire (Reading 1997). Blacks and Hispanics are more likely than whites to live in neighborhoods that are dangerous or dirty, both of which interfere with good health. These and other forms of structural inequality constrain choices, elevate stress levels, tax immune systems, and increase the likelihood of illness throughout the life course (Freund, McGuire, and Podhurst 2003; Williams 2000). These structural factors help to explain higher rates of cancer, hypertension, and other forms of poor health (Bullard 1993, 1994; Fitzpatrick and La Gory 2000).

There is some question among health scholars about the extent to which race and ethnic differences in health are entirely explained by socioeconomic differences or whether racial discrimination continues to play a role (London and Myers 2006; Weitz 2007; Hayward, Crimmins, and Miles 2000; Mirowsky and Ross 2003a; Quadagno 2001; Williams and Collins 1995; Bullard 1993; Mutchler and Burr 1991; Smith and Kington 1997). Older African Americans have higher rates of many chronic illnesses. Mark Hayward and his colleagues (2000) suggest that this is almost entirely due to socioeconomic differences. Given the preponderance of evidence about the degree of race and ethnic inequality in education, income, housing, health and health care, and so on, however, it seems likely that both factors continue to be at work (Williams 1997). Moreover, attributing race differences solely to income and education fails to address how race patterns in income and education arose in the first place.

Finally, class differences in health are linked to less status, power, control, and resources at work and at home. Education and income are key components of class differences in health outcomes (House 2002; Herd 2006a; Herd, Goesling, and House forthcoming). Poor people have difficulty meeting basic needs such as good nutrition and safe and healthy home and work environments, which are imperative to good health (Herd, Schoeni, and House 2007). Both those with little education and those with low incomes have high levels of stress, which play a significant role in the onset of disease (Lantz et al. 2005). They are also more socially isolated, which is predictive of poor health (House, Landis, and Umberson 1988; Turner and Noh 1988; Turner and Marino 1994). Finally, they have a limited sense of control over their lives, and increased levels of hostility and hopelessness, which are also correlated with poor health (House 2002; Ross and Mirowsky 2001).

Those in low-wage jobs, who are driven by educational attainment, also face poorer health outcomes. Those with low-status jobs tend to face more routine or simple tasks that provide them with fewer subjective or objective rewards, greater risk of injury or illness, less social integration, and little control over their days. Such jobs are associated with higher morbidity and higher mortality rates (Link, Phelan, and Fremont 2000; Marmot et al. 1991, 1997; Turner and Marino 1994). Low-wage work can be stressful, but being unemployed is also linked to adverse health outcomes. Those who are unemployed have higher rates of numerous physical and mental health problems (Mirowsky, Ross, and Reynolds 2000). Several studies show that women who are not employed have significantly worse health than those who are employed (Ross and Bird 1994; Mirowsky, Ross, and Reynolds 2000).

To the extent that less educated and more poorly paid people return each evening to poorer neighborhoods, they tend to face higher stress at home as well. Shortages of resources, control, and hope contribute to an overall health disadvantage (Mirowsky, Ross, and Reynolds 2000; Weitz 2007). The high levels of noise, crime, graffiti, garbage, and violence associated with poor urban and generally highly racially segregated areas induce higher levels of mental illness, morbidity, and mortality (House 2002; Smith 1999; Ross and Mirowsky 2001; Williams and Collins 1995). Moreover, class differences widen as individuals age (Herd 2006a; House, Kessler, et al. 1990; House, Lepkowski, et al. 1994). Scholars debate whether low incomes, bad jobs, and limited educational attainment lead to poor health or vice versa, but studies increasingly suggest that the link runs both ways (Kaplan and Lynch 2001; House, Lepkowski, et al. 1994; Menchik 1993; Case, Lubotsky, and Paxson 2002). For our purposes, the important matter is this: the factors that shape health and the factors that shape income must both be addressed in the policy arena.

Those with poorer health also tend to be less likely to have health insurance. Lack of insurance, or insurance through poverty-based Medicaid, can impede access to health care, particularly if providers refuse to accept these patients (Weitz 2007; Harrington Meyer 2000; Rieker and Bird 2000; Harrington Meyer and Pavalko 1996). Even among those who are insured, there is evidence that providers may treat women, lower-income people, and blacks and Hispanics differently. Whether due to lack of insurance, type of insurance, or covert gender, race and class discrimination, disadvantaged groups often wait longer for needed care, undergo more undesirable treatments, and suffer higher mortality (Fessenden et al. 1998; Whittle et al. 1993; Gornick et al. 1996; Geiger 1996; Institute of Medicine 2002). *Newsday* used the Freedom of Information Act to sue for access to medical records at Long Island hospitals and found that blacks receive only one-fourth as many bypasses and one-third as many angioplasties as whites with similar diagnoses. They also found that blacks wait twice as long for kidney transplants (Fessenden et al. 1998). Jeff Whittle and his colleagues (1993) found that among Veterans' Hospital patients with heart disease and chest pain, blacks were less likely to receive catheterization, angioplasty, or bypass surgery than whites. Marian Gornick and colleagues (1996) found that among Medicare beneficiaries, blacks are at least 50 percent less likely than whites to have bypass surgery, angioplasty, or hip replacement. Blacks also go to the doctor less and receive fewer mammograms and flu shots. They are more likely than whites to go to the hospital and to die. Blacks are three times more likely than whites to have a lower limb amputation due to diabetes whereas whites are significantly more likely to have vein stripping procedures that save the limb. Jack Geiger (1996) reviewed ten years of studies on the effect of race and class on medical treatment in the United States and noted that the most startling fact was their consistency. Blacks are consistently less likely to receive angioplasty, catheterization, bypass surgery, vein stripping, mammograms, less invasive vaginal hysterectomies, renal transplants, hip and knee replacements, and flu shots.

Some scholars dismiss these studies, arguing that blacks go to the doctor later and therefore sicker, have more complications with their conditions, and are more likely to be medically noncompliant (Institute of Medicine 2002; Satel 2001). Others suggest that the long legacy of mistreatment of blacks by the medical profession, including the Tuskegee experiments, has caused blacks to shy away from doctors and procedures. The Institute of Medicine (2002) reviewed more than a hundred studies on racial differences in treatment. It found widespread and persistent race differences in treatment, even when controlling for insurance, income, co-morbidity, and severity of illness. Although some of these differences are due to confounding factors, others are linked to bias, prejudice, and stereotyping on the part of providers.

The Changing Business of Health Care

Health care for older persons must be understood in the context of the broader U.S. health care system. Access to health care in the United States is determined mainly by access to health insurance. The United States is the only developed nation that does not provide health insurance to all citizens. We spend more in total dollars, per capita, and as a share of the GDP than any other country, but our health outcomes are among the worst in the industrialized world (Davis et al. 2006; NCHS 2005b; Quadagno 2005). U.S. health care costs, in relation to the GDP, have risen from 5 percent in 1965 to over 16 percent in 2005 (MedPac 2005; Congressional Budget Office 2005). The Congressional Budget Office predicts that total health care expenditures will usurp 20 percent of the GDP by 2015. Unsurpassed spending has not, however, bought unsurpassed health. More than twenty countries have longer life expectancies and lower infant mortality rates than the United States (NCHS 2005b). Rather than a single insurance pool, we have a complicated system wherein workers and their families rely on insurance through their jobs or do without, the poor rely on Medicaid, and older people rely on Medicare and a web of supplemental policies. The result is that some have excellent insurance and others are underinsured or uninsured.

Does having health insurance matter? Yes. Although having health insurance does not eliminate socioeconomic disparities in health, it does have an impact (Barlett and Steele 2006). Health insurance and health

Figure 5.3   Full-Time Employees in Medium and Large Firms Receiving Employee-Based Health Insurance

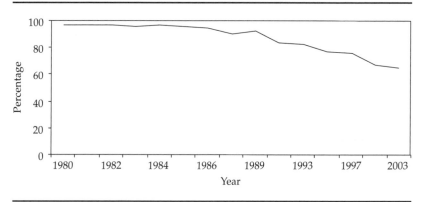

Source: EBRI 2005a, table 4.1a.

care probably account for about 10 to 20 percent of the relationship (McGinnis, Williams-Russo, and Knickman 2002). Those without health insurance tend to receive less preventative care and later diagnoses. As a result, they have poorer overall health and higher mortality (Navarro 1993; Hadley and Holahan 2003; Barlett and Steele 2006). One recent study found that 47 percent of the uninsured, compared to just 15 percent of the insured, had postponed seeking care because of cost (Kaiser Family Foundation 2003a).

Reliance on Employer-Based Health Insurance

Until age sixty-five, most in the United States rely on employment-based health insurance coverage. Such insurance, however, has declined substantially since the 1980s. Historically, those working in larger firms with good pay receive good benefits; those with lower pay often receive fewer benefits. Even in medium and larger firms, which have always been most likely to offer health insurance, coverage of employees has diminished. Figure 5.3 shows that the proportion of full-time employees in medium and larger firms receiving employee-based health insurance dropped from a fairly stable 97 percent in the earlier 1980s to just 65 percent by 2003 (EBRI 2005b, 2005c). Among workers who are part time, temporary, and self-employed, only 21 percent now have insurance through their jobs (Ditsler, Fisher, and Gordon 2005). Diminishing employment-based coverage has led to escalating uninsurance. In 2004, 17 percent—roughly 44 million Americans—were not insured (Holtz-Eakin 2004; Mills and Bhandari 2003; EBRI 2004; Seccombe and Amey 1995; Harrington Meyer and Pavalko 1996). Single

Figure 5.4   Non-elderly U.S. Population with Health Insurance 2004

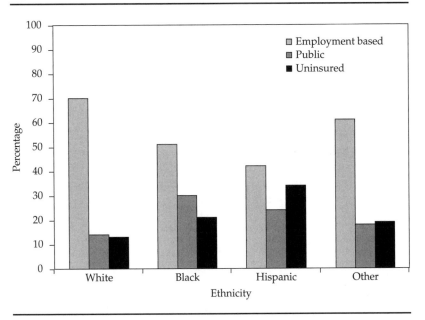

Source: EBRI 2005b.

people, part-time and low income workers, and those with less education are most likely to be uninsured (Holtz-Eakin 2004; EBRI 2004).

Women are less likely than men to have insurance through their own
jobs. In 2004, among those age eighteen to sixty-four, 51 percent of men,
and only 39 percent of women, had employment-based health insurance
(EBRI 2004). Women are twice as likely as men to be insured through a
spouse's job. In 2004, 26 percent of women and only 13 percent of men
had insurance through their spouse. Although dependent coverage helps
to offset the paucity of coverage women have through their own jobs,
they are at risk of losing that coverage should their partners lose their
jobs or the marriages end through death or divorce (Harrington Meyer
and Pavalko 1996).

Blacks and Hispanics are significantly less likely than whites to be
insured through their jobs and more likely than whites to be uninsured
altogether. Figure 5.4 shows how coverage varies by race. Whereas 70 percent of whites younger than sixty-five are covered by employment-based
health insurance, only 52 percent of blacks and 42 percent of Hispanics
are covered (EBRI 2004). One result is that blacks and Hispanics are more
likely to rely on public health insurance. Among those under sixty-five,
14 percent of whites, 30 percent of blacks, and 24 percent of Hispanics are

on public health insurance. Another result is that blacks and Hispanics are significantly more likely—1.6 and 2.6 times, respectively—to be uninsured that whites.

Lower-income people are also significantly less likely to be insured through their jobs. Among those age eighteen to sixty-four in 2004, with family incomes below $10,000, only 12 percent had employment-based health insurance (EBRI 2005a, 2005b). By comparison, among families with incomes of $50,000 or higher, 82 percent had employee-based coverage. The dearth of employment-based health insurance among lower-income families leads to higher rates of uninsurance. In 2004, among those with family incomes below $10,000, 35 percent were uninsured (EBRI 2005a, 2005b). Among those with family incomes of $50,000 or more, 9 percent were uninsured. Ironically, health care workers are among the most likely to be uninsured: 32 percent of all health care workers in the United States were uninsured in the mid-1990s (Navarro 1993).

Rather than provide health insurance to all its citizens, the U.S. government encourages employers, through tax incentives, to cover workers. These tax breaks amount to $190 billion in lost revenues a year (Hacker 2006). They fund a system defined by exclusivity. Employers can and do avoid hiring persons with certain medical conditions, exclude preexisting conditions, set limits on amount of coverage for some conditions, exclude others altogether, and shift costs for premiums and exclusions to employees. The United States is the only major country in which losing a job means losing health insurance; roughly one-third of Americans have stayed in a job they did not like merely to retain their health insurance coverage (Harrington Meyer and Pavalko 1996; Navarro 1993). Insurers have quite a bit of leeway concerning whom they cover and what sorts of profits they will realize. There is evidence of insurers skimming the healthiest patients, refusing to cover those with greater health care needs, restricting coverage of needed treatments, and micromanaging the physician-patient relationship (Quadagno 2005; Navarro 1993). Insurers are highly motivated to contain costs by restricting coverage.

All of the paperwork that accompanies this restriction requires a stable of employees. Blue Cross has more administrative employees in the state of Massachusetts than the entire national health program for all of Canada (Navarro 1993). In the last four years, health insurance premiums rose nearly 60 percent (Holtz-Eakin 2004; Britt 2004). The consequence, at least in part, is that the health insurance industry is reporting banner profits, yet covering a smaller percent of the population. Profits, and salaries for the top echelon, have doubled in the past four years (Britt 2004). In a period where the Standard and Poor's (S&P) 500 saw profits rise an average of 5 percent, profits of the top seventeen health insurers rose 114 percent, hitting $414 billion in 2004. Average salaries for the top five executives at sixteen health insurance companies nearly doubled, hitting

$3 million a year. Pacificare Health Systems, for example, reported a 51 percent increase in profits between 2000 and 2003. Its CEO received a 777 percent raise. His compensation in 2003 was $6.4 million. He is not alone. The average pay of the top five executives at Pacificare increased by 355 percent in that time frame, hitting $2.8 million in 2003 (Britt 2004). Our premiums cover these salaries. The cost of salaries and paper shuffling is enormous; between 15 and 25 percent of U.S. health care dollars go toward administration (Navarro 1993; Holtz-Eakin 2005; Barlett and Steele 2006). U.S. administrative costs in the health care industry are three times those in Canada (Barlett and Steele 2006). Shifting to a single national health insurance plan alone could drop health care costs by 15 to 25 percent. It would also sidestep, perhaps even eliminate, the need for this powerful and profitable insurance industry.

As taxpayers, we are already paying for health insurance as a social benefit, but because we are distributing it through employment-based rather than welfare state mechanisms, we have little control over how the benefits are distributed (Quadagno 2005; Harrington Meyer and Pavalko 1996; Estes 2001). In the United States, the distribution of health insurance benefits is gender, race, and class biased. Whites, men, full-time workers, and highly paid workers are most likely to have health insurance. Minorities, women, part-time, and low-wage workers are more likely to be uninsured or rely on poverty-based programs. As a social experiment in providing a basic necessity through employment, rather than through the welfare state, the U.S. health care system is revealing. The same sorts of inequalities that emerge from the market are replicated and amplified by the market-based distribution of benefits. For those 44 million Americans who do not have regular access to health care, this social experiment has been a failure.

Medicare

Historically, retirees faced high health care needs with little access to health insurance. Since 1965, however, Medicare has provided nearly universal health care benefits to the aged, blind, and disabled. It is a pay-as-you go, defined-benefit program. Those who are eligible for Social Security are generally eligible for Medicare. Medicare Part A, which is fully funded by the FICA payroll tax, is the mandatory component that covers hospital stays and short-term nursing home stays. Medicare Part B, which is financed by premiums and general tax revenues, provides optional coverage of up to 80 percent of the cost of physician visits and services. Medicare has done a remarkable job of increasing access to certain kinds of health care for the aged. Before the program began, 56 percent of the aged had hospital insurance. In 2006, nearly 97 percent did (Harrington Meyer 2005; Social Security Administration 2006). Other kinds of health

Figure 5.5   Increases in Medicare and Medicaid Spending

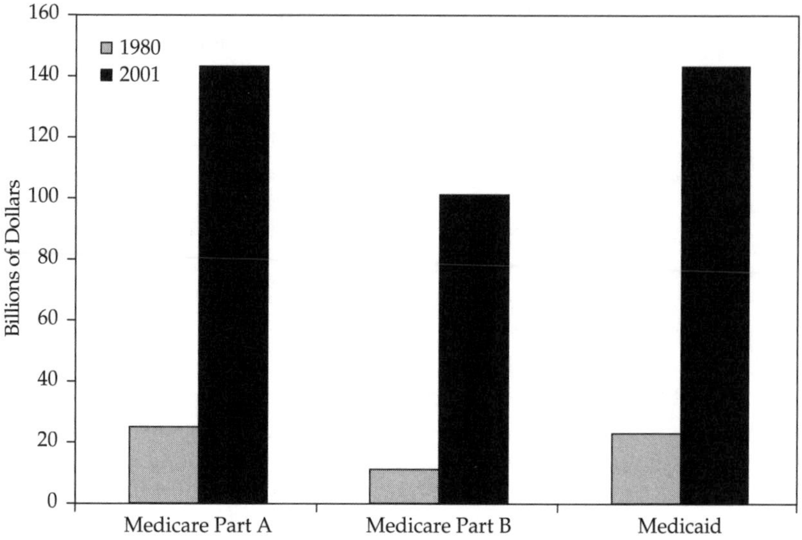

Source: Social Security Administration 2002.

care, most notably long-term care, remain out of reach for many. The entire system also operates at very high costs, the highest in the developed world.

Medicare costs rose dramatically from the moment the program was implemented; cost containment has been on the front burner for decades (Marmor 2000; Moon with Herd 2002). Total Medicare expenditures in 2004 were $301 billion, or $7,400 per beneficiary (Holtz-Eakin 2005). Figure 5.5 shows that in 1980, Medicare Part A costs totaled $25 billion. By 2001, those costs had risen 470 percent, to $143 billion. Even more dramatically, Part B costs rose by 800 percent between 1980 and 2001, from $11 billion to $101 billion (Social Security Administration 2002). Much of the money goes toward health care for the very old, the very poor, and the very sick (MedPac 2005). Even for the relatively young and able, per capita expenditures are up dramatically.

Cost Cutting   Constraining costs has historically been accomplished by either restricting services, restricting fees, or raising beneficiary costs (Herd 2006c). In an effort to curb runaway costs in 1984, HCFA implemented a prospective payment system (PPS) aimed at reducing unnecessary medical treatment and cutting costs. This legislation changed the way Medicare paid for services, moving from a retrospective cost plus profit system to a prepaid system that allocated a pre-set amount per person per primary diagnosis. By certain measures, the effort succeeded: hospital stays were shortened dramatically and the rate at which total costs were rising slowed measurably (Harrington Meyer 2005; Estes 1989, 2001). Studies also revealed, however, that hospitals and clinics increased the extent to which they exported unprofitable care, discharged clinically unstable patients, and made multiple readmissions (Glazer 1990; Estes 2001). Both the quantity and quality of care work changed as hospitals discharged patients quicker and sicker and Medicare and Medicaid coverage of home care dried up (Glazer 1990; Hooyman and Gonyea 1995). With little training, families are often expected to take on highly technical work including chemotherapy, apnea monitoring, phototherapy, oxygen tents, tubal feedings, dressing changes, and more. Carol Estes (1989) calculated that in the first five years of Diagnostic Related Groupings (DRGs), more than 21 million days of care work had been transferred to families from hospitals. Nona Glazer (1990) estimated that the medical industry saves at least $10 billion in wages annually because of the unpaid care work provided by family members. More recently, a CBO report estimated that the annual cost to replace all donated long-term care with professional services would be between $50 and $103 billion (Holtz-Eakin 2005).

In the wake of PPS, the demand for postacute care rose dramatically. Initially, though demand rose, postacute services did not expand because Medicare officials refused to allow the expansion. In the late 1980s, however, a series of court cases by families desperate for Medicare home health services challenged the restricted interpretation of the Medicare policies (Harrington Meyer 2005; Moon with Herd 2002). Consequently, throughout the 1990s home care and skilled nursing care grew exponentially. Though it had been less than $1 billion in 1980, figure 5.6 shows that between 1992 and 1997, Medicare home health care payments rose from $7 billion to $18 billion.

The relief that families received in the 1990s was short lived. Concerned by rapid Medicare cost increases, legislators pushed through the Balanced Budget Act of 1997. It included a series of cost cutting measures, including reducing payments to hospitals and shifting home health care from Medicare Part A to Part B. The net effect of this and other measures in the act was an increase in the Part B premium, restricted access to home health and other services, and even higher out-of-pocket expenses for the aged (Moon with Herd 2002). Total Medicare expenditures on home health care for older persons dropped from $18 billion in 1997 to just under $13 billion in 1998, and $8.4 billion in 1999 (see figure 5.6). This reflects a 28 percent decrease in a single year and a 53 percent decrease in just two years (MedPac 2005). Total expenditures have crept back up slowly, but the overall share of the total Medicare budget devoted to

Figure 5.6   Medicare Home Health Care Expenditures

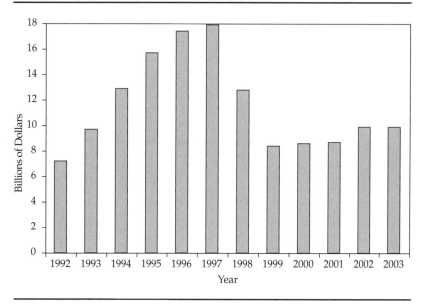

Source: MedPac 2005.

home health care has dropped by half in just a decade, from 8 percent in 1994 to just 4 percent in 2004 (MedPac 2005).

After the 1997 act, the commitment to home care plummeted in several other ways as well. As figure 5.7 shows, the number of Medicare licensed, participating home health agencies peaked at 9,808 across the United States in 1996. By 2000, the number had dropped to 7,317 (MedPac 2005). In other words, the number of home health agencies covered by Medicare dropped 25 percent in just four years. Some of that reduction reflects a much-needed crackdown on fraud and abuse, but much is due to funds drying up. Figure 5.8 shows that the number of persons receiving home health care benefits dropped from a high of 3.6 million in 1996 to 2.4 million by 2000, reflecting a 33 percent decrease in four years. Many of these decreases in coverage have rebounded slightly, bringing us back to roughly 1992 levels. But the help each individual person is getting has shrunk. Figure 5.9 shows that per person home visits peaked at seventy-four visits in 1996. By 2000, that had dropped to thirty-seven visits, reflecting a 50 percent drop in just four years. By 2003, per person home visits were down to thirty-one (MedPac 2005). Per person home health care visits have not rebounded to the 1992 level of fifty-three visits per year mainly because the 1997 Balanced Budget Act instituted changes in payment policies such that providers are now reimbursed in a lump sum based on the patient's condition.

Figure 5.7   Medicare Home Health Care Agencies

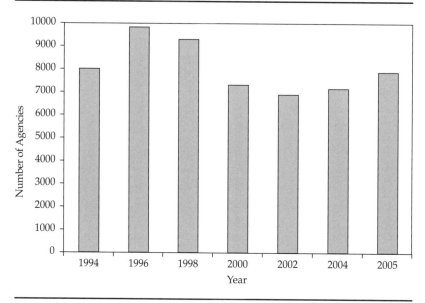

Source: MedPac 2005.

Figure 5.8   Recipients of Medicare Home Health Care

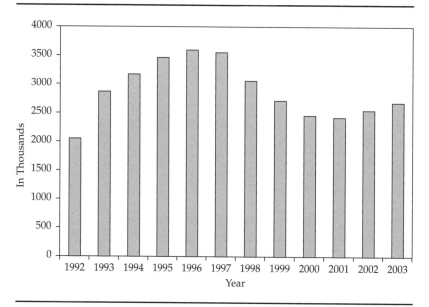

Source: MedPac 2005.

Figure 5.9   Medicare Home Health Care Visits per Person Served

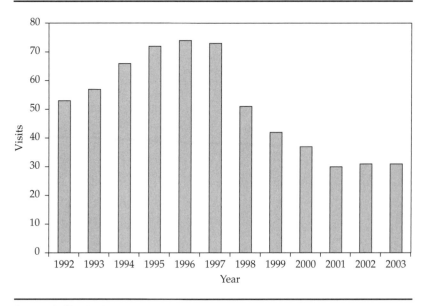

Source: MedPac 2005.

They had been reimbursed on the basis of services provided. Like 1984 PPS policies applied to hospitals, this move encourages home health care providers to provide fewer services. Moreover, the crackdown has spawned a shift in type of care, toward therapies and away from home health aid services (MedPac 2005).

Care Shifting   With these policy changes, much of the responsibility for providing care has shifted to families, and much of the responsibility for paying for it has shifted back to the aged, increasing their dependence on informal caregivers and causing many to do without needed care (Estes 2001, Harrington Meyer and Kesterke-Storbakken 2000; Moon with Herd 2002). The amount of unpaid care families assume has increased dramatically and is now estimated at between $50 and $103 billion annually (Holtz-Eakin 2005).

Cost Shifting   Cost shifting to those age sixty-five and older has also been significant. Although Medicare is nearly universal in terms of eligibility, it has never been comprehensive. Recent estimates suggest that it covers less than 45 percent of old age health care costs (Moody 2002; Quadagno 1999). In addition to premiums and co-payments, Medicare recipients pay deductibles, co-insurance of 20 percent, any costs above the allowable rate, and uncovered goods and services such as long-term care, preventive care, dental care, vision, and eyeglasses (Harrington Meyer 2005; Social Security Administration 2006; EBRI 2004, 2005b, 2005c). With respect to nursing home care, for example, Medicare covers portions of the first hundred days of nursing home care as long as certain conditions are met. In fact, after day twenty, the co-pay is more than $100 a day, making the monthly co-pay more than $3,000. Premiums have risen dramatically. The Medicare Part B premium increased 244 percent between 1980 and 1990. In 1993, the Part B premium was set at 25 percent of the cost of Part B services, and the Balanced Budget Act of 1997 made this a permanent condition. Between 2003 and 2004, the Part B premium rose again, this time by 13.5 percent, hitting an all-time high of $66 a month. The Part B premium is expected to continue rising at rates much higher than the cost of living. The Medicare trustees predict that by 2030, the monthly Part B premium will increase to $150 in 2004 dollars (Johnson and Penner 2004). Because the Part B premium is deducted from Social Security benefits before the checks are mailed, the net effect may be smaller Social Security benefits across the board. Medicare deductibles and co-payments have also risen sharply. For example, between 1980 and 1990, the Part A deductible for hospital stays increased by 250 percent, from $180 to $628 (Waxman 1992). By 2003, it had risen to $840 (EBRI 2004, 2005b). Additionally, Medicare reimbursement rates have been curtailed since the 1997 BBA, and providers are transferring costs above the assigned rate to patients (Moon with Herd 2002). By 2003, out-of-pocket health care expenses were consuming more than 20 percent of the average Medicare recipients' income (Kaiser Family Foundation 2003).

Generally, the legacy for Medicare has been one of generous coverage of acute care and much more limited coverage of long-term care. Medicare's benefits are so spotty, and exclude so many of the very benefits that older people are likely to need, that Richard Margolis (1990) quips that Medicare must have been created for some other group than the aged. Certainly the coverage is less than most Americans count on from their employer-based plans; one study found that fully 82 percent of employer-based plans had more generous coverage than Medicare (Moon with Herd 2002). Aware that out-of-pocket expenses are particularly burdensome for lower-income old people, Medicare officials implemented several different Medicare Savings programs. Everyone else, however, is simply spending more on their health care. The story grows more complex because some benefits are retrenched and others are expanded as Medicare increasingly relies on the private market.

Privatization of Medicare   Changes to Medicare policy have been plentiful, but many have gone unnoticed by older people and their families. In part, the legislation is so complex that many are unable to understand the parameters of the debate. In part, the focus is almost always on

Social Security rather than Medicare. Perhaps most insidiously, however, many of the changes initially appear to be gains—thus they go unchallenged. Pro-market privatization proposals are wrapped in the popular universal framework of Medicare; the fact that privatized plans undermine the redistributive features of universal programs goes undetected (Herd 2005a). Proponents of market-friendly approaches argue that we cannot continue to contain Medicare costs by merely raising taxes or cutting benefits (Herd 2006c). Rather, as the Cato Institute's Peter Ferrara (1980) argues, we should take advantage of the efficiencies, incentives, competition, and productivity of the private sector. The trouble is that the evidence suggests that efforts to privatize Medicare have actually increased costs and that further privatization would reduce the program's progressiveness (Herd 2005a). Privatization is well under way with Medicare; here we focus on the impact of Medicare's HMO and drug benefit programs.

Medicare HMO and PPO Options   Privatization has been part of Medicare for decades. In 1982, the Tax Equity and Fiscal Responsibility Act (TEFRA) developed HMO or PPO options under Medicare. Many providers attracted the healthiest clients and then used the difference between costs and reimbursement rates to make benefits—and profits— more generous. Enrollments rose from just 6 percent of all Medicare beneficiaries to 11 percent between 1994 and 1996 (Biles, Nicholas, and Guterman 2006). Amidst concerns that Medicare was reimbursing HMO and PPOs at too high a rate, Congress then readjusted Medicare reimbursements to providers. When the Balanced Budget Act of 1997 created Medicare plus Choice (M+C), enrollment in Medicare PPOs and HMOs was at its zenith, 16 percent. By 1998, however, reduced federal payments began to undermine their popularity (Kaiser Family Foundation 2003; Moon with Herd 2002; Herd 2006c). With time, this exercise in privatization no longer proved lucrative for the PPOs or HMOs and they responded accordingly. By 2000, M+C plans had pulled out of many service areas, cut benefits, and raised premiums. Enrollment dropped. In 2003, just 12 percent of Medicare enrollees remained in the program. Part of the attraction with privatized options was that they initially reduced out-of-pocket costs and covered prescription drugs (Harrington Meyer 2005; Kaiser Family Foundation 2003). As federal reimbursements tightened, and profits dipped, benefits diminished. For example, the share of M+C plans that included drug coverage dropped from 84 percent in 1999 to 69 percent in 2003, and among those who offered drug benefits, 60 percent covered only generic drugs. Similarly, though M+C plans did not initially charge enrollees a premium surcharge, by 2002, 62 percent charged premiums averaging $60.50 a month (Kaiser Family Foundation 2003).

To reverse declining enrollments, the 2003 Medicare Modernization Act replaced M+C with Medicare Advantage (MA) and increased reimbursements. A broad selection of HMO, PPO, and other plans became available, and enrollments slid up. Critics of these privatized options continued to warn that private firms skim the healthiest older people for these programs to keep costs down (Biles, Nicholas and Cooper 2004; Herd 2005a). Moreover, critics worried that the care might be inferior to that of traditional fee-for-service plans. Evidence on the quality of care is mixed, and suggests that in particular those with many health problems do not tend to fare well in either M+C or MA plans (Kaiser Family Foundation 2003; Moon with Herd 2002; Quadagno 1999). Moreover the sickest tend to pay more. A recent study by the Commonwealth Fund (Biles, Nicholas, and Guterman 2006) shows that though costs under Medicare Advantage are lower for those in good health, they are often higher than they would be under traditional Medicare for the sickest beneficiaries. Further, because the sickest Medicare beneficiaries are concentrated within traditional Medicare, not HMOs, the wealthiest and healthiest beneficiaries are receiving greater subsidies than are some of the poorest and sickest beneficiaries (Biles, Nicholas, and Cooper 2004; Herd 2005a). These results demonstrate quite explicitly the extent to which privatization undermines the redistributive aspects of welfare programs (Harrington Meyer 2005; Herd 2005a).

Hopes that privatization might reduce Medicare expenditures have not been realized (Herd 2005a, 2006c). A 2001 U.S. GAO report shows that Medicare paid an average of 13 percent more per person in private plans than it would have had those persons received care under the traditional Medicare program. In 2005, the government was paying an extra $546 per enrollee in private plans. Brian Biles, Lauren Nicholas, and Barbara Cooper (2004, pg. 3) report that in 2005, every MA plan "in every county in the nation, for every Medicare plan enrollee, will be paid more than the average of fee-for-service costs." What is the total cost for the Medicare Advantage experiment—an experiment that was justified by the premise that it would reduce Medicare costs? The cost is roughly $2.75 billion per year, assuming that the rate of participation in MA programs remains at 12 percent. As that rate increases, so will the cost. By 2007, 18 percent of Medicare enrollees were in MA (MedPac 2007). These higher costs are particularly problematic given that the private plans do not even include the poorest and sickest beneficiaries (Herd 2005a; Biles, Nicholas, and Cooper 2004). The CBO estimates that Medicare Advantage will add $14 billion in new Medicare costs over its first ten years (Biles, Nicholas and Cooper 2004; Congressional Budget Office 2005).

Congressional leaders appear to be wedded to market-friendly policies championed by the Cato Institute and other conservative think tanks. The impact of these reforms, though, has been problematic. Thus far, taking advantage of market efficiencies and incentives has increased government expenditures and regulatory involvement and decreased services to the sick and poor. Privatizing has chipped away at the effectiveness of the old age welfare state by undermining the more family-friendly redistributive features that reduce old age inequality. Incredibly, despite evidence that privatizing Medicare is raising costs and reducing redistribution, many legislative proposals currently under consideration attempt to privatize Medicare costs through similar sorts of capitated plans.

Medicare Prescription Drug Plan   The 2003 Medicare Modernization Act, which added a prescription drug plan, provides another perspective on the efforts to privatize Medicare. Historically, the absence of prescription drug coverage was particularly problematic because on average older people take 3.8 medications per day and prescription drug costs have risen sharply (Palmer and Dobson 1994). Older women have more chronic illnesses and as a result take more prescription drugs. Older women's average prescription drug costs are 14 percent higher than men's (Moon with Herd 2002). Older people had a variety of mechanisms for obtaining at least partial coverage of drug costs; many received prescription coverage through their retiree health insurance, Medicare HMOs, Medigap policies, or Medicaid. Overall, though, 25 percent had no prescription coverage at all, and others had high out-of-pocket costs (Hoadley 2006). At the end of 2003, Congress finally responded to demands from the aged for Medicare coverage of prescription drugs, creating an optional Medicare Part D. The degree of privatization in the plan is unprecedented (Hoadley 2006). Instead of offering a single, universal benefit through Medicare, Congress required older people to select (and pay a premium for) one private drug plan from a sea of complex and ever-changing private options.

The benefit itself is complex. Beneficiaries will pay approximately $35 in monthly premiums, a $250 annual deductible, and then a 25 percent co-pay for all drug costs from $251 to $2,250. Most seniors would then pay all of the next $2,850 in drug costs, a portion of the plan dubbed the doughnut hole. Then, an emergency benefit kicks in that pays annual drug costs in excess of $5,100 (Kaiser Family Foundation 2004). The complexity of the program has proved problematic. Finding accurate information has proven to be difficult. In an audit, Congress's Government Accountability Office placed 900 calls to the ten largest companies offering Part D coverage. As Robert Pear reported in the *New York Times*, they received accurate and complete information in only 30 percent of the calls ("Investigators Find Medicare Drug Plans Often Give Incomplete and Incorrect Data," July 11, 2006, p.1). Real costs to beneficiaries were often underestimated by up to thousands of dollars. Lack of reliable information undermines the pro-market initiative. Part D was constructed on the premise that older people would act as informed consumers, making choices among dozens of competing plans (Herd 2006c). As Maine Senator Olympia J. Snowe commented, "any program that relies on choice must ensure that those choices are well informed." Indeed, acting as informed consumers has proven difficult for older persons both because reliable information is hard to obtain and because they do not know what their futures hold. Decisions about prescription drug plans are based on current health but the cost-effectiveness of those choices will be decided by future health.

The impact of the drug benefit for poor older people is difficult to evaluate. Initially, state legislators were pleased that Medicaid expenditures might diminish as primary responsibility for drug coverage for poor older people shifted from Medicaid to Medicare. As the legislation proceeded, however, it became clear that states would have to shoulder much of the cost. Because the Medicare drug benefit would provide prescription drugs to Medicaid recipients, states expected a reduction in Medicaid expenditures. Federal legislators quickly deflated their expectations by inserting a "clawback" clause. States are required to make a monthly payment to Medicare equal to 90 percent of the projected reduction in 2006, with that proportion declining slightly over time to 75 percent (Centers for Medicare and Medicaid Services 2005a, 2005b; Families USA 2005a, 2005b). Many states are now worse off than before and desperate to find ways to reduce Medicaid costs at the state level (Robert Pear, "Officials' Pitch for Drug Plan Meets Skeptics," *New York Times*, Sunday, July 17, 2005, p. 1).

Poor older people who did not previously have prescription drug coverage stand to gain the most from the new policy. After paying premiums and co-pays they are expected to save about 23 percent on out-of-pocket drug costs per year (Hoadley 2006). However, poor older Medicaid recipients may have fared better under the old regime. In the past, low-income Medicare recipients who also qualified for Medicaid generally received prescriptions at no cost. The new Medicare prescription drug benefit requires co-payments of $2 to $5 per prescription per month. The Congressional Budget Office estimates that these fees are expected to rise roughly 10 percent per year, though Social Security checks are only expected to rise 2 to 3 percent per year (Park et al. 2003). Moreover, many states are responding to the clawback clause with talk of cuts. Several states, including Florida, Mississippi and Missouri, are already planning to cut thousands from their Medicaid rolls. If they do, these people will lose a variety of medical services including personal care, vision, dental, podiatry, hearing, and case management (Families USA 2005a, 2005b).

There are other shortcomings of the new drug benefit legislation. First, out-of-pocket expenses may be as high as $3,600 a year. Second, only prescriptions on an approved list are be covered and counted in the benefit coverage. Third, because lawmakers wanted to be sure that beneficiaries would bear some of the costs, seniors are prohibited from purchasing any Medigap policies that would cover uncovered drug costs (Park et al. 2003; Kaiser Family Foundation 2003b, 2005). They may, however, be able to enroll in Medicare Advantage HMO or PPO plans that provide comprehensive prescription coverage at no extra cost. Fourth, the cost of the program is expected to hit at least $400 billion in its first ten years, though many estimates show the cost coming in much higher (Hoadley 2006). Finally, the program is so complex that even the experts have been baffled. As the long-awaited January 1, 2006, implementation date neared, many groups that represent the aged were advising their constituents to wait before selecting their form of coverage because the legislation was so complex that experts were unsure how best to proceed.

While the act is proving problematic for older persons, it has been quite positive for drug companies' bottom lines. The legislation prohibits Medicare from negotiating costs with the drug companies (Kaiser Family Foundation 2003b). Because Medicare has so many enrollees, officials have historically controlled costs by negotiating prices with medical providers and suppliers (Herd 2005a). High numbers of beneficiaries have given the program leverage to negotiate lower prices. That legacy of price negotiation was severed with the new drug policy, which makes it more difficult for Medicare to contain prescription drug prices. In the six months following the implementation of Medicare drug plan, profits of the ten largest pharmaceuticals rose by over $8 billion (Waxman 2006). Advocates for this approach argue that strict price controls would reduce innovation. Price controls, however, could be implemented in such a way to maintain high enough profit levels to generate innovation. We may be paying much more than we need to be.

Medicare managed plans also received some benefits from the prescription drug plan (Herd 2005a). They are being encouraged to take Medicare patients. Although they served only 4.6 million seniors, they received an additional $1.3 billion for 2004 and 2005 via the 2003 Medicare Modernization Act. Urban Institute analyst Robert Berenson suggests that the administration was so keen to maintain or even increase HMO coverage of Medicare recipients that by 2006 Medicare would pay HMOs 25 percent more than the traditional Medicare costs for the same beneficiaries (Kaiser Family Foundation 2003b). The other advantage Medicare HMO plans gained in the Medicare Modernization Act is that they can provide prescription drug coverage, but Medigap plans cannot (Herd 2005a). For those in Medigap plans, it would be far easier to enroll in a Medicare Advantage plan than to purchase both a Medigap plan and a prescription drug plan on top of it.

There are few who question that something must be done. The financial outlook for Medicare is bleak. Costs are rising sharply because overall health care costs are rising sharply, the use of new medical technologies drives up fees, and baby boomers are entering old age and making claims (Palmer 2006; Herd 2006c). In 2004, federal Medicare expenditures topped $312 billion. Those costs are expected to continue escalating. Total costs for Part A and Part B and Part D are projected to grow from 2.6 percent of gross domestic product in 2005 to 13 percent by 2079 (Centers for Medicare and Medicaid Services 2005a). The number of enrollees is expected to double between 2000 and 2030, rising from 40 to 80 million beneficiaries (MedPac 2005). The level of Medicare expenditures is expected to exceed that for Social Security in 2024 and, by 2079, to represent almost twice the cost of Social Security. The policy focus, though, has been almost entirely on reforming Social Security; the much larger problem of what to do about Medicare has not been a central part of the debates. Few Medicare reform proposals are even being seriously considered.

What, then, should be done? Cost-shifting trends have been particularly burdensome for older women, blacks, and Hispanics. Privatization, however, does not appear to be the answer. Evidence that privatization does not work is growing. The private long-term care insurance market has required a lot of regulation and still remains too expensive, too complex, and too selective to be of use to most older people. HMO and PPO programs for the aged have been heavily subsidized, yet have increased rather than decreased costs. Medicare Part D extends coverage to prescription drugs, but Medicare expenditures have risen dramatically. In the end, the private market plans from which the recipients must select are prohibitively complex, Medigap coverage of prescription drugs is now outlawed, and out-of-pocket expenses have risen. We review market-friendly solutions in chapter 6 and family-friendly solutions to this quandary in chapter 7.

Medigap Supplemental Insurance

It's ironic that Medicare costs are so high given that the program covers only 44 percent of old age health care costs (Quadagno 2005). Medicare premiums, co-pays, deductibles, amounts above the allowable rate, and exceptions mean that most older people must turn to market-based supplemental Medigap insurance. The ones who end up with the lowest out-of-pocket costs rely on employment-based health insurance. Retiree health insurance, though, has dropped significantly in recent years. Even among large employers, who are most likely to offer retiree insurance, the proportion who offer coverage has dropped from 66 percent in 1988 to just 36 percent in 2004 (MedPac 2005). In 2002, 55 percent of retirees fifty-five to sixty-four, and 34 percent of those sixty-five and older, had employer-sponsored health coverage (EBRI 2004, 2005a, 2005b). White, male, full-time and highly paid workers are more likely to accrue these benefits, but even for those groups, coverage is on the decline and the GAO (2001) expects the declines to continue. Moreover, the diminishing pool of employers who still offer retiree coverage are pushing more of the costs onto retirees and tightening restrictions on benefits. The EBRI (2004) reports that most employers have tightened eligibility requirements, capped benefits, and increased cost-sharing for those covered by retiree benefits.

Although reliance on retiree health insurance is waning, reliance on private Medigap policies is growing. These supplemental insurance packages are purchased out-of-pocket by the elderly through premiums. In fact, 66 percent of Medicare beneficiaries pay premiums on supplemental policies that cover Medicare premiums, co-pays, deductibles, and exclusions such as eye exams and hearing aids (Centers for Medicare and Medicaid Services 2005a). Whites are more likely to have supplemental coverage, particularly when poor. Some 48 percent of poor whites but only 17 percent of poor blacks and Hispanics have Medigap coverage (Centers for Medicare and Medicaid Services 2005a, 2005b, Harrington Meyer and Herd 2001). Recent studies show that access will become increasingly difficult because supplemental insurance premiums have risen significantly and are expected to continue to do so (Alecxih et al. 1997). Between 1992 and 1996, rates rose between 20 to 40 percent in certain states, leaving even more women and older minorities without supplemental insurance (Moon with Herd 2002).

Privately purchased Medigap policies are the quintessential market-friendly old age policy. As a private market product, however, these supplemental insurance policies for the aged got off to a rough start. Almost immediately, there was evidence of price gouging, duplicate coverage, and severance of coverage. Eager to find a way to regulate the market, Congress intervened and created categories of plans labeled A through J (Moon with Herd 2002). The aim was to ensure that older people received fair coverage for their dollars. Although this regulation significantly reduces fraud and confusion among beneficiaries, problems with these plans continue. First, prices vary significantly by geographic location. For example, in 1999, the average Medigap plan price in California was $1,600, compared to a national average of $1,185 (GAO 2001). In Utah, the average plan price was $706 (GAO 2001). Second, once older people have passed the six-month period of open enrollment at age sixty-five, only those who have lost coverage because an HMO plan is eliminated or an employer drops coverage are protected by the open enrollment rules. Others, if they have preexisting conditions, including Alzheimer's, diabetes, hypertension, migraines, and rheumatoid arthritis, can be denied coverage (GAO 2001). The GAO (2001) found that insured older persons are often told that they will not receive insurance coverage of asthma, glaucoma, impotence, Parkinson's disease, or ulcers. Finally, policies that initially appear affordable often become unaffordable over time if older Americans buy attained age-rated instead of community-rated plans. The attained age-rated plans cost less to start with, but increase in price as beneficiaries age (GAO 2001).

Reductions in employment-based health insurance and retiree insurance, as well as gaps in Medicare coverage, leave older Americans to fill the gaps with private supplemental policies. Despite government oversight, older people are often unprotected from rising premiums, dropped coverage, increased deductibles, decreased coverage, caps, exclusions, fraud, and mismanagement (GAO 2001). The reliance on private supplemental policies shifts responsibility for the aged out of the welfare state and the corporate sector and into the private market. That means all expense and risk falls squarely on the shoulders of older individuals and their families. Those with the fewest resources, who often have the poorest health, are least likely to be able to obtain and retain private insurance. They are increasingly likely to do without insurance and, at times, needed care (Moon with Herd 2002; Harrington Meyer 2000).

Medicaid

Since 1965, Medicaid has provided comprehensive coverage of health care for the poor aged, blind, and disabled. Those on SSI and TANF are generally eligible; others may become eligible, particularly if their health care needs are high. All together, 20 percent of the U.S. population receives Medicaid. Most are poor adults, children, or disabled persons. The elderly account for just 10 percent of enrollees, but for 23 percent of total Medicaid expenditures (Congressional Budget Office 2005). Over the years, Medicaid has grown to be the largest payer of nursing home care, covering two-thirds of all nursing home stays by the time of discharge (Congressional Budget Office 2005). Older people rely on Medicaid to cover institutional care when their assets and savings are either depleted or have been transferred (Grogan and Patashnik 2003). The program itself may well be the most comprehensive health care plan available in the United States. Generally, beneficiaries receive free acute care, hospitalization, diagnostic testing, treatments, doctor visits, prescription drugs, and nursing home care, as well as some coverage of vision, dental, and medical appliances. Such coverage is costly. Total federal Medicaid expenditures topped $190 billion in 2006. When state expenditures are added, the annual budget exceeds $300 billion. The Congressional Budget Office (2005) predicts that by 2015, the federal costs alone will exceed $363 billion, comprising 2 percent of the GDP.

Unlike younger recipients, for whom Medicaid is the sole source of insurance, most older recipients are dually enrolled with Medicare as the principal insurer. Medicaid covers only expenses Medicare does not.

The numbers of older people on Medicaid have been remarkably stable since the early years of the program, with 4 to 6 million older persons receiving benefits every year for the past three decades (Social Security Administration 2002; Congressional Budget Office 2005). Given that the numbers of older people have risen dramatically in that time, a smaller share of the aged receive Medicaid benefits. In 1970, more than 16 percent of those sixty-five and older received Medicaid; in 2000, fewer than 13 percent received Medicaid benefits (Quadagno 1999; Social Security Administration 2002).

Even though the proportion of older people receiving Medicaid is going down, spending is going up. Total Medicaid expenditures for just those sixty-five and older rose from $21 billion in 1990 to $39 billion in 2006 (Social Security Administration 2006; Congressional Budget Office 2005). Per person expenditures for the aged have risen from $3000 in 1975 to more than $13,000 in 2004. Medicaid is a federal-state program and the costs borne by states have become burdensome; Medicaid spending for all ages is now one of the largest items on every state budget. On average, states spend about 17 percent of their budgets on Medicaid, second only to education, which consumes an average of 47 percent of state budgets (Kaiser Family Foundation 2004). At the federal level, Medicaid is a relatively small program, but because all of the cost is borne through general tax revenues, and the program lacks a broad-based constituency, cost containment is a priority (Estes 2001).

The cost for Medicaid would be a lot higher if all of the poor aged, or even all of the eligible aged, claimed benefits. Eligibility for Medicaid, however, is restricted by both income and asset tests. Federal guidelines for full benefits set the income test well below the federal poverty line, at just 73 percent; thus many poor older people are ineligible (Kaiser Family Foundation 2003). However, many states have established more generous provisions, and some states have established limits that approach the federal poverty line (Social Security Administration 2002). Moreover, the asset tests for full benefits, set at $2,000 for an individual and $3,000 for a couple, have been in effect since 1989.

Some 6 million, or 16 percent, of older Medicare enrollees are also Medicaid recipients. Full Medicaid benefits cover costs Medicare does not, including the Medicare Part B premium, nursing home care, and all Medicare co-pays and deductibles (Kaiser Family Foundation 2003a; Social Security Administration 2002; Harrington Meyer 2000; Quadagno 1999). Because full coverage is so comprehensive, and because health care providers are prohibited from charging costs above the allowable rates to Medicaid recipients, full Medicaid coverage reduces out-of-pocket expenses from 20 percent to just 5 percent of annual income for dual enrollees (Kaiser Family Foundation 2003a).

A smaller subset of dual Medicare and Medicaid enrollees receive limited coverage under new rules that relax eligibility guidelines. Since 1998, Medicare recipients with incomes below 100 percent of the federal poverty line, and assets up to $4,000 for an individual and $6,000 for a couple, may be eligible for the Qualified Medicare Beneficiary Program (QMB). QMB covers the Medicare Part B premium and most deductibles and co-pays. Those with incomes between 100 and 120 percent of the poverty line, and assets up to $4,000 for an individual and $6,000 for a couple, may be eligible for the Specified Low Income Medicare Beneficiary (SLMB) program which covers the Part B premiums (Kaiser Family Foundation 2003a). For those who are enrolled, QMB and SLMB benefits help by reducing out-of-pocket costs to 13 percent of total annual incomes (Kaiser Family Foundation 2003a).

Because the process of applying is complicated and stigmatizing, and the rules of eligibility are so restrictive, fewer than one-third of poor older people actually receive Medicaid (Congressional Budget Office 2005). In fact, only half of those who are eligible for Medicaid receive the benefit (U.S. Congress 2000; Moon with Herd 2002; Kaiser Family Foundation 2003a). QMB and SLMB also involve complex application procedures. Only 55 percent of those who qualify for QMB actually participate, and only 16 percent of those who qualify for SLMB actually participate (Moon with Herd 2002; Quadagno 1999).

For those older Americans who rely solely on Medicaid for their health insurance, or dual eligible beneficiaries who need treatments or care that Medicare does not cover, access to that care can be problematic. As a poverty-based program, Medicaid generally prohibits health care providers from charging patients any amount over Medicaid assignment. One consequence is that many doctors, clinics, labs, hospitals, and nursing homes refuse to treat Medicaid patients. Others use a variety of mechanisms to cap the proportion of Medicaid patients they see (Harrington Meyer 2000; MedPac 2005; Congressional Budget Office 2005). For example, among primary care physicians in the United States in 2002, 85 percent were accepting new private payers and 83 percent were accepting new Medicare recipients, but only 66 percent were accepting new Medicaid patients (MedPac 2005). The lower reimbursement rates cause doctors to distinguish, and often discriminate, on the basis of payer source. Between 1980 and 1997, nursing homes and other health care providers could sue the state on the grounds that Medicaid reimbursement rates were too low, using provisions in the Boren Amendment to the federal Medicaid Statute in the Social Security Act. That amendment was repealed, however, with the Balanced Budget Act of 1997. As Medicaid rates stalled out, private pay rates continued to rise. One result is that hospitals, clinics, nursing homes, and other providers became even more likely to eliminate or limit Medicaid admissions.

Another result is that private payers in all types of health care facilities are subsidizing the costs of care to Medicaid patients in the same facility. They do so because providers set two price lists; one price for Medicaid patients and another, generally substantially higher, for those with private insurance. Because older women, blacks and Hispanics, and unmarried persons are more likely to be on Medicaid, they are more likely to face denial of or delays in treatment or admission (Wallace et al. 1998; Harrington Meyer and Kesterke-Storbakken 2000).

The transfer of long-term care back to the jurisdiction of family caregivers is just as pronounced under Medicaid as it is under Medicare. In the wake of the 1997 budget act, the number of Medicaid recipients receiving home health care dropped from 1.8 million to 1.2 million, a 34 percent decrease in a single year (Social Security Administration 2002). The total Medicaid dollars devoted to home health care dropped 78 percent the same year, from $12.2 billion in 1997 to $2.7 billion in 1998. As a result, the average annual Medicaid dollars per home care recipient dropped 66 percent, from $6,600 in 1997 to $2,200 in 1998 (Social Security Administration 2002).

Moreover, for those admitted to nursing homes, Medicaid policy shapes life in unparalleled ways. Unlike Medicaid recipients in the community, who keep their income and receive free health care through Medicaid, Medicaid recipients in nursing homes become wards of the state. In other words, all of their Social Security and any private monies go to pay the nursing home costs; Medicaid is merely payer of last resort. Medicaid recipients in nursing homes are permitted to keep only a small monthly personal needs allowance, which ranges from $30 to $70 depending on the state, to cover basic necessities not covered by Medicaid, including clothing, haircuts, transportation, phone calls, cable, stamps, dentures, glasses, orthopedic shoes and devices, and dental work (Harrington Meyer and Kesterke-Storbakken 2000). A few states have indexed the personal needs allowance to cost of living increases, but the federal monthly rate of $35 has remained steady for nearly two decades.

In an effort to curb Medicaid expenditures, states have taken several tacks. Many states have raised co-payments for prescription drug coverage and some services. Others have reduced the scope of coverage, eliminating dental and vision care, or limiting the number of prescriptions, physician visits, or pieces of medical equipment per year (Ku and Broaddus 2005). The impact is higher out-of-pocket expenditures. Between 1997 and 2002, the average annual growth rate for out-of-pocket expenditures for poor Medicaid recipients was 9.4 percent, though their incomes rose just 4.6 percent per year in that time. Thus, out-of-pocket expenses rose at twice the rate of incomes; poor adults on Medicaid now spend 2.4 percent of annual income on out-of-pocket medical expenses (Ku and Broaddus 2005).

Another cost containment mechanism is Medicaid estate recovery. Because they are prompted to do so by the 1993 Omnibus Budget Reconciliation Act, nearly all states are pursuing estate recovery, though they do so with varying vigor. When applying for Medicaid coverage of nursing home care, applicants are permitted to except their home and car if they can demonstrate that they may be able to return to them or that they are needed by a dependent. The estate recovery provision requires states to recover Medicaid expenses for nursing home, community-based, and hospital care for all aged recipients (Centers for Medicare and Medicaid Services 2005a, 2005b). The recovery is made from Medicaid patient estates after they die, before the remainder is distributed to those cited in the will (Wood and Sabatino 1996). Actual recovery efforts are somewhat unevenly applied; understandably, states are more likely to pursue estate recovery when it appears that costs regained would outweigh the legal and administrative costs of the recovery itself. Supporters argue that estate recovery helps replenish the coffers for this financially strapped program. Opponents maintain that estate recovery discourages the aged from seeking needed medical care and undermines the very meaning of the term health insurance (Schwartz and Sabatino 1994). Laura Katz Olson (2003) argues that estate recovery converts a public benefit into a loan that must be paid back by family members who forgo items they would have received through the will. Family members who lived with the older person, many of whom may have provided intensive care work, may be impoverished and forced from their homes (Katz Olson 2003). In any case, estate recovery does not generate large sums of money. The amount of money collected by the top ten estate recovery programs averaged only about 1 percent of Medicaid nursing home expenditures in 1993. Total estate recovery in all states was $124.8 million in 1995, less than one-half of 1 percent of Medicaid nursing home expenditures for the aged (Wood and Sabatino 1996; Wiener and Stevenson 1998).

The strength of Medicaid is that it provides comprehensive health care services to poor older persons, reducing out-of-pocket expenses and inequality in old age. The weakness is that the eligibility guidelines are strict and outdated, and reimbursement rates are low and getting proportionately lower. Medicaid retrenchment has primarily taken the form of gatekeeping. Income and asset requirements, as well as provider reimbursement rates, have not kept pace with cost of living increases. The overall effect is to minimize the proportion of older people who are eligible and minimize access to benefits among beneficiaries. With long-term care needs left unmet by both the welfare state and private market insurance options, the pressure is even greater on families to provide care to the frail elderly.

Private Long-Term Care Insurance

After older people themselves, Medicaid is the biggest payer of nursing home care. Those who wish to bypass paying for nursing home care out-of-pocket or through Medicaid can purchase private long-term care insurance. Private long-term care insurance policies may cover home care, community-based care, or institutional care. Selecting a plan is complicated because cost and benefits vary dramatically by the type of coverage, age and health of the insured, and state or region of the country. Despite government regulation, the plans have proven fairly unstable. Put off by high premiums, fraud, overcharges, and general mismanagement, many people will not purchase the coverage (Angel and Angel 1997; Estes 2001). Moreover, those with serious health care problems often find that no plan will accept them (Quadagno 1999; Angel and Angel 1997). Indeed, many who can afford and who seek out private long-term care insurance coverage are denied because of preexisting conditions, smoking, drinking, or specific health problems (Quadagno 2005; GAO 2001). Estimates are that as many as 40 percent of older people could probably afford private long-term care insurance premiums if the market were more reliable and better managed (Congressional Budget Office 2005; GAO 2001). Women, blacks, Hispanics, and unmarried older persons are particularly likely to have old age incomes so low that such premiums would be formidable (Angel and Angel 1997; Hooyman and Gonyea 1995). In another example of the limitations of the provision of health insurance coverage through the market, most estimates are that only about 7 percent of the aged have private long-term insurance (Moon with Herd 2002; Holtz-Eakin 2005).

Shifting the Burden

Efforts to control health care costs have led to shifts in costs and care work from the government to older people and their families. Cost shifting has been profound. Indeed, we are four decades into the Medicare and Medicaid programs and the costs of health care for the aged are a greater burden than before the program began. Figure 5.10 shows that out-of-pocket expenses for the elderly rose from 15 percent of annual income in 1965 to 19 percent in 1990. By 1998, the average older person spent 22 percent of income on health care expenses. By 2025, out-of-pocket health care expenses are expected to reach nearly 30 percent (Moon with Herd 2002). Each year, one-third of the near poor are reduced below the poverty line by out-of-pocket health care expenses. Because they have poorer health and lower incomes, older women, blacks, Hispanics, and the unmarried are particularly likely to be made poor by their out-of-pocket health care expenses (Moon with Herd 2002; Angel and Angel 1997). Medicare provides universal health care to nearly all older Americans, but the program is not well tailored to the health needs of older people. Medicaid provides coverage to the poor and to disabled older people, but gaps in that coverage are growing as efforts to contain

Figure 5.10   Out-of-Pocket Health-Care Expenses, Sixty-Five and Older

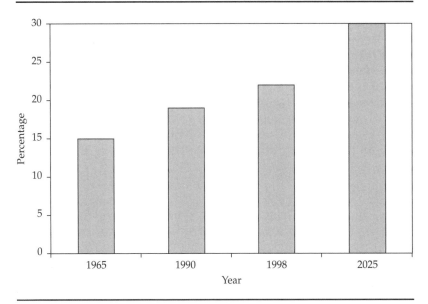

Source: Moon with Herd 2002.

costs eclipse efforts to provide coverage. The costs of old age health care are increasingly shifted back to older persons and their families. The poor, and those with considerable illnesses, have great difficulty making do, even with supplemental Medigap and Medicaid policies in place.

Shifting of care work may have been even more pronounced. It is hard to overstate just how much informal care work is performed each year in the United States. Robyn Stone (2000) points out that there are forty unpaid informal care workers for every paid formal care worker. One in four U.S. households are engaged in care work for frail older relatives at some time in a given year. The effects of the transfer of responsibility for care work are most strongly felt by women. Women have higher rates of chronic illness, longer life expectancies, and fewer resources than older men, thus the greatest demand for long-term care. Moreover, as unpaid care workers, they perform as much as 75 percent of all long-term care (Estes 2001; National Alliance for Caregiving and AARP 1997, 2004; Moody 2002). Peter Arno, Carol Levine, and Margaret Memmott (1999) estimate that in 1997 alone, if we replaced free care for paid services, the value of family caregiving was $196 billion.

The shifting of care work to families, and particularly women, may adversely affect caregivers in terms of economic, physical, emotional, and social health of those providing the care (Stone 2000; Hooyman and

Gonyea 1995; Kaiser Family Foundation 2002; Scharlach 1994; National Alliance for Caregiving and AARP 2004; MetLife Mature Market Institute 1999). Proponents of family-friendly policies agree that welfare states have both the potential and the moral imperative to reduce hardship among the hard-pressed and spread the burdens of unpaid care work (Harrington Meyer 2000; Hobson 2000; Sainsbury 1994; Lister 1997; Zimmerman 1993). In contrast to the market-friendly approach that maximizes individual choice, risk, and responsibility, we argue that the state must support unpaid care by providing economic and social supports for those who do care work and providing alternative sources of care for those who do not.

Discussion

The existing Medicare and Medicaid programs provide desperately needed access to health care for the aged—rich and poor. These programs are imperfect. We have itemized numerous shortcomings. Even more, we have stressed how efforts to contain costs for these two programs by relying on the market—whether employer benefits, HMOs, or private insurance policies—have increased rather than decreased inequality among the aged. The market-friendly policies already implemented—under the justification of cutting costs—disproportionately negatively affect lower-income groups by shifting costs and care work back to older people and their families. Recent efforts to provide health care benefits to older people by letting the market replace the welfare state are simultaneously failing to cut costs and to reduce old age inequality.

Why don't we follow the lead of other nations and adopt national health insurance? Jill Quadagno (2005) argues that early on, doctors feared the regulations they assumed would accompany national health insurance. They were backed by unions and employers who preferred to provide health insurance directly to employees as a way to build loyalty. Over time, all these opponents became overwhelmed by the inefficiencies of multiple insurance pools, the weight of the uninsured, and of course skyrocketing costs. They stopped opposing, if never directly favoring, national health insurance. Other opponents were on the horizon, however, namely insurers who stand to profit under the current multifaceted arrangement and might, in fact, disappear under a single-payer plan. It's a story of those with tremendous power wielding that power for financial gain (Estes 2001; Navarro 1993; Katz Olson 2003). Caught in the crosshairs are the millions who are uninsured and countless more who are underinsured.

There are myriads of ways to adopt national health insurance. A radical approach would be to implement a universal single-payer plan that was modeled on Canada's health care system. One incremental approach is to expand Medicare coverage to those under age sixty-five. Private insurers could still maintain a role by providing supplemental coverage and thus retain some level of private market interaction (Hacker 2006). At the same time, everyone would have coverage and the government would have more leverage than it does now to control costs. Regardless of how we do it, the most important goal is that we maintain universal eligibility for the elderly and expand that coverage for younger Americans (Hacker 2002, 2006).

There is little question that the current system is not working. Businesses are slashing coverage for current and retired employees. The Medicare surplus is nearly gone and as enrollments rise, deficits will skyrocket. States are stressed by the burden of Medicaid expenditures and dramatic cuts to these programs loom. Given our experience to date with senior HMOs and private long-term care insurance, the private market does not appear to be the answer for health insurance. Managed care for the aged has lead to increased, rather than decreased costs. Private long-term care insurance has stalled out leaving only a handful with meaningful coverage. Indeed, given the evidence of these failures, ongoing efforts to privatize Medicare make little sense.

These trends suggest it is time for a change and the overwhelming majority of people in the United States agree. Most are dissatisfied with the U.S. health care system and want a major overhaul. In every major poll since 1952—the first year Gallup asked the question—the majority of Americans have favored a federally financed national health insurance plan (Navarro 1993; Quadagno 2005). Is change in the direction of family-friendly, rather than market-friendly, welfare policy possible? In chapter 7, we return to this question.

Chapter 6

Market-Friendly Proposals: Entrenching Inequality

Is there as strong a political economy case for eliminating government management of the retirement industry as there is for eliminating its management of most other industries? My answer is yes.
      Nobel Laureate economist Gary Becker, "A Political Case for Social Security Reform." op-ed, *Wall Street Journal*, February 15, 2005

W E ARE in the midst of a major transformation of welfare states from publicly provided benefits aimed at protecting workers from the market to privately provided benefits aimed at encouraging workers to fend for themselves through the market (Gilbert 2002; Hacker 2002; Myles and Quadagno 2000). Market-friendly conservative groups want to minimize government involvement in the free market by minimizing social welfare and maximizing individual choice, risk, and responsibility. Their family-friendly opponents worry about the stratifying effects of such efforts, arguing for welfare expansions that will minimize inequality linked to gender, race, class, and marital status.

Despite the shortcomings we have articulated thus far, Social Security and Medicare, the two key programs in the U.S. old age welfare state, do far more to offset gender, race, and class inequality than they do to reinforce it. Both programs redistribute resources from wealthier to poorer Americans. Studies show that redistribution is palatable to most Americans as long as everyone benefits from the program (Korpi and Palme 1998). Universalism provides political cover for progressive benefit distribution, what Theda Skocpol labels targeting within universalism (1991). The most spectacular legacy of the old age welfare state is that poverty amongst the elderly has plummeted over the past thirty years, yet among children and working age adults, who have no universal programs, it has barely budged. Thus, minimizing income and health inequality in old age requires us to maximize the strength of these universal old age programs. This could be easy given how popular both programs are; most middle-class Americans remain firm in their support. Over the past few decades, public opinion polling has showed that 70 to 90 percent of the public supports current or increased spending on Social Security and Medicare (AARP 2005; Pew Research Center 2005; Public Agenda 2005; Quadagno 2005; Street and Sittig Cossman 2006). Fewer than 2 percent of Americans would support less spending on Medicare (Public Agenda 2005). Medicare has even expanded to cover prescription drugs, in the midst of a war, an exploding budget deficit, and general welfare retraction.

Instead of strengthening the programs, however, many proposals currently on the reform agenda aim to devolve, dismantle, or privatize the entire system. We examined the current old age welfare state in chapters 4 and 5, showing how it structures stratification in health and retirement. Here we look at the current reform agenda, showing how it does nothing to correct the problems we have articulated thus far. We explore the extent to which many policy proposals currently under consideration emphasize fostering a healthy market rather than offsetting the vagaries of a healthy market.

Fixing or Sinking Social Security?

Since their inception, Social Security and Medicare have been popular targets for retrenchment. Historically conservative politicians paid a high price for proposals to slash them. For example, Republican nominee Barry Goldwater's suggestion that participation in Social Security be made "voluntary" became a source of ridicule, a symbol of his "radical conservativism" (Derthick 1979,187) and contributed to his landslide loss to Lyndon Johnson in the 1964 election (Herd and Kingson 2005). Throughout the 1970s and 1980s, conservative opponents of Social Security and Medicare attempted to reduce or means-test these programs by arguing that we could no longer afford them, they shifted resources away from children, or they were inefficient and ineffective. When those efforts failed, conservatives developed market-friendly proposals wrapped in the popular universal framework of Social Security and Medicare (Herd 2005a). What they discovered is that any proposal that significantly threatens the benefits of middle-class Americans is doomed to failure. The new policy approaches maintained a universal framework, keeping middle-class Americans happy and sustaining the program's popularity, while dismantling the programs' redistributive facets. Essentially, conservatives have borrowed the progressives' tool of universalism. Now, though, universalism provides a cover for redistributing resources toward the market instead of providing a cover for the redistribution of resources toward the poor.

Recent proposals to privatize Social Security provide striking evidence of this trend. Dozens of reform proposals dot the political landscape, but

Figure 6.1   Workers Fully Insured Under Social Security

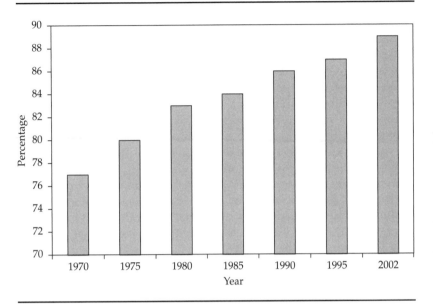

Source: Social Security Administration 2004.

virtually none of them address the sweeping sociodemographic changes or the sources of inequality we have concerned ourselves with in this book. The clash between demographic trends and Social Security's bread-winner benefit structure will have profound implications for women's well-being in old age, yet there has been little public discussion about addressing this outdated benefit structure (Herd 2005b). Why? For the past fifteen to twenty years, the reform agenda has been driven by pro-ponents of market-friendly welfare programs. Their aim is to reduce the redistributive elements of Social Security, which is likely to increase gender, race, class, and marital status inequality in old age.

Between the 1930s and 1980s, liberals governed the Social Security pol-icy agenda of programmatic expansion. In 1962, 69 percent of those sixty-five and older were receiving Social Security benefits. By 2000, more than 90 percent of those were (GAO 2003). Further, as figure 6.1 shows, between 1970 and 2002, the percentage of workers fully covered rose from 77 percent to 89 percent (Social Security Administration 2002). Much of the absolute decline in poverty among women, and among the elderly overall, can be traced to the automatic cost of living increases to benefits implemented in the early 1970s, as well as changes that expanded the pop-ulation eligible for Social Security benefits (Engelhardt and Gruber 2004).

Attacks on Entitlement

By the mid-1980s, however, conservatives had developed a two-prong strategy to weaken support for Social Security (Herd 2005a). First, they made a generational equity argument: needed resources were being diverted from younger Americans to older (Quadagno 1996; Minkler 1986; Binney and Estes 1988). The media quickly picked up the debate. *Newsweek* even had a front page story titled "Greedy Geezers," which itemized the many public resources that went to the elderly rather than children (Minkler 1986; Quadagno 1996). In the end, demonizing the elderly was not a successful strategy. The generational equity argument has by and large faded into the background.

A second strategy has proven far more effective. The argument was that Social Security was facing a financial crisis (see Baker and Weisbrot 1999; Gilbert 2002). Conservative policy analysts argued that as the baby boomers aged, and the ratio of workers to retirees fell, it would become increasingly difficult for workers to continue supporting Social Security beneficiaries (Ferrara 1980). Because Social Security is a pay-as-you-go system wherein current worker taxes pay for the benefits of current retirees, a funding shortfall was inevitable. These rumblings started within conservative think tanks such as the Cato Institute and the Heritage Foundation in the late 1970s and early 1980s. In particular, Cato published Peter Ferrara's book *Social Security: The Inherent Contradiction* in 1980, which argued that given current demographic trends, the system was unsustainable. Gradually, conservative groups picked up the cost issue, pushing the idea of an overall entitlement crisis in which Social Security and Medicare spending would gradually overtake the budget (Quadagno 1996).

Having framed Social Security as financially unsustainable, conservatives saw their opportunity to control the debate over Social Security reform. It took some time, however, for them to shape reforms that Americans would accept. In 1982, President Reagan proposed massive cuts to Social Security benefits (Herd and Kingson 2005). Americans were furious and the proposed cuts evaporated. Instead, the 1983 Greenspan Commission President Reagan appointed led to an increase in the payroll tax and a tax on Social Security benefits for wealthier beneficiaries. The most significant retrenchment to come from this commission was that the age of eligibility increased from sixty-five to sixty-seven starting for individuals retiring in the early twenty-first century (Svahn and Ross 1983). Additionally, the penalty for taking early benefits was raised from a 20 to a 30 percent reduction in benefits (Social Security Administration 2006). These were relatively small changes, but they were the first moves toward retrenchment since Social Security was established in 1935 and have affected some groups disproportionately.

Although most women fared well under these incremental changes, the same cannot be said for blacks and the poor. The financial consequences of increasing the age of eligibility fall hardest on those with the shortest life expectancies and the worst health. Most hard hit were black and Hispanic men. Black men's average life expectancy is just sixty-six years; thus, on average, they do not live long enough to draw full Social Security benefits, though they are more likely to draw on its disability benefits. Among women, poor and black women have shorter life expectancies than wealthier white women (Crimmins and Saito 2001) and thus receive less back in Social Security benefits relative to the taxes they paid earlier in their lives. Moreover, those with poorer health and higher levels of functional disability, more often women, blacks and Hispanics, and less-educated and lower-income people, now pay a higher price for taking benefits between the ages of sixty-two and sixty-seven (Himes 2000a, 2000b; Social Security Administration 2006). Policy makers who aim to maximize individual choice, risk, and responsibility argue that older people who choose to retire early must pay the price. Critics, however, suggest that by age sixty-two many vulnerable groups are experiencing the health consequences of a lifetime of disadvantage and are simply not well enough to "choose" to continue to work in what are often low paying and physically demanding jobs until full retirement age (Estes 2001; Quadagno 2005; Hacker 2002).

The 1983 reforms, though problematic for black and poor men and women, did nothing to fundamentally change the shape of the program. In particular, calls to make Social Security a means-tested program roundly failed, likely because millions of middle-class Americans stood to lose by that change in particular. Nonetheless, for the first time since the program was enacted, retrenchment, rather than expansion, became the model for reform (Herd and Kingson 2005).

Proponents of current market-friendly policies appear to have learned from past policy failures and changed tactics (Herd 2005a). The newest reform initiative, privatizing Social Security, neither explicitly cuts benefits nor restricts eligibility by means-testing. Aware that Social Security has been popular precisely because all Americans benefit from it, conservatives look at privatization as a way to downsize the program without contradicting the beloved universal feature. How it does so, however, is little understood. Privatization of Social Security weakens progressive redistribution. Instead of talking about benefit cuts and means-testing, supporters have argued that workers' payroll taxes should be diverted to individual accounts and invested in the stock market to fund individual retirements. Individual accounts, de facto, restrict the program's ability to redistribute. Though the idea had been floating around since the early 1980s in conservative think tanks, the same think tanks and individuals who argued Social Security was facing a crisis, it was not

Figure 6.2   Elderly Dependency Ratios

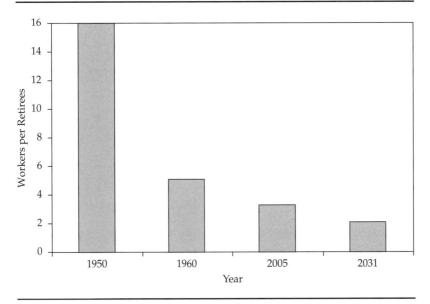

Source: Social Security Administration 2004.

until Republican leaders took it up in the wake of a booming stock market that it became a real political possibility.

When reelected in 2004, President Bush made the privatization of Social Security his domestic priority. Republican leaders backed a proposal in which people under age fifty-five would be permitted to divert up to 4 percent of their 6.2 percent FICA tax into personal investment accounts (President's Commission to Strengthen Social Security 2001). The creation of individual accounts was defended on several grounds. First, generations come in different sizes. The ratio of workers to retirees has dropped substantially. In 1950, as figure 6.2 shows, the dependency ratio was sixteen workers to every retired beneficiary. By 2005, that ratio had dropped to 3:1. By 2031, it is expected to be 2:1 (Quadagno 1999). Second, conservatives wanted to encourage an ownership society with individual ownership and responsibility for old age income. Ownership would allow more individual choice, risk, and responsibility, and perhaps even the possibility of willing unused monies to dependents. The aim was to get government out of the retirement business. Finally, as Nobel prize-winning economist Gary Becker argued in a 2005 *Wall Street Journal* editorial, the reason to privatize Social Security is that it would force us to stop hiding the real size of the annual budget deficit behind the Social Security surplus. Once we realize how large our budget deficit really is, he surmised, we might become more fiscally responsible.

Preserving Entitlement

Opponents to privatization responded quickly. Generations do come in different sizes and the dependency ratio really will drop to 2:1. Does this amount to a fiscal crisis? No. Although many liberals and most New Democrats bought into these arguments, the crisis was severely overstated (Quadagno 1996; Estes 2001). Indeed, the program's fiscal shortfall could have been fixed by a 1 to 2 percent increase in the payroll tax, which has not been raised since 1983 (Social Security Administration 2005b; Congressional Budget Office 2004a). Supporters of privatization specifically argued that Social Security is financially unsustainable in its current form, but the money spent in President Bush's recent tax cut would have largely offset the seventy-year shortfall. However, as we will discuss later, these solutions would not address the monies the government has borrowed from the Trust Fund.

Those who are hesitant to raise the FICA tax by a full percent might instead embrace any one of the other more modest solutions for shoring up the fiscal soundness of Social Security. Broadening the eligibility base is a solution that would expand the revenue base and commitment to the program simultaneously. Initially, only select workers were covered by Social Security, but over time most were incorporated. State and local government employees were excluded because of questions about whether the federal government could tax state governments. In the 1950s, Congress allowed states to elect voluntary coverage for their employees (Munnell 2005). In the 1980s, it extended mandatory coverage to new federal employees. Finally, in the 1990s, it extended mandatory coverage to state and local employees who had no other pension plan. Currently, about 95 percent of employees are covered, but among state and local employees, nearly 30 percent remain outside the system (Munnell 2005). Pulling those 30 percent into Social Security would increase contributions.

Raising the cap on taxable earnings would increase revenues and strengthen the redistributive features of the Social Security program. As we explained in chapter 4, workers now pay the Social Security component of the FICA tax only up to $90,000 of earnings per year; thus the tax covers only 85 percent of all earnings. We would need to raise the cap to $140,000 to cover 90 percent of earnings (AARP 2005). Indeed, the tax cap could readily be restored to 90 percent and then indexed to rise automatically with earnings.

Another solution, to reduce expenditures by raising the age of early retirement from sixty-two to perhaps sixty-four, could reduce the fiscal shortfall slightly but would contribute to greater inequality in old age. Alicia Munnell and Annika Sundén (2004) found that such a move might reduce poverty among the elderly both because many people would continue to work during those years and then would, on average, receive a higher benefit. Increasing the early retirement age does little to improve Social Security financing, however, because benefits are actuarially reduced to keep average lifetime payments constant, regardless of when benefits are claimed. Most important, they found that about 10 percent of those who take early benefits are in poor health and without an alternative source of income. They would be unable to continue working or to draw Social Security benefits. Thus, hardest hit by both the increase in the full and the proposed increase in the early age for eligibility are those who are unable to continue working due to poor health or unemployment. Lower-income women and blacks and Hispanics are more likely to be affected by both (Moon with Herd 2002; Himes 2001; Harrington Meyer 1996, 2005; Angel and Angel 1997).

One resolution that will not fix Social Security's fiscal problems, however, is privatizing it (Harrington Meyer 2005; Herd and Kingson 2005; Herd 2005a). Privatization will make the fiscal shortfall, and old age inequality, worse. Currently, the program is expected to experience a shortfall in 2042. If we divert funds to private accounts, this will happen as early as 2018. Additionally, because we would have to simultaneously fund the new individual accounts and the old collective account, and cover the administrative costs of creating billions of individual accounts, estimates are that it would run $1.5 to $2 trillion in extra monies to make this policy change (Diamond and Orszag 2002).

Privatizing Social Security?

Although the aim of social insurance is to spread risk, making it collective, privatization concentrates risk, making it individual. Individual ownership means individual risk. Those whose investments fared poorly would themselves fare poorly in old age. Moreover, despite all the discussion of maximizing consumer choice, there would be little choice of investments, particularly for low earners who would be forced to set their assets into annuities yielding guaranteed benefit payments but little control over their assets (President's Commission to Strengthen Social Security 2001; Hacker 2006; Herd and Kingson 2005).

Promoters of market-friendly policies argue that they want to get government out of the retirement business. One of the great ironies in the push towards private accounts and individual responsibility, however, is that the federal government's role would in fact increase (Harrington Meyer 2005; Herd and Kingson 2005; Herd 2005a). Currently, administrative costs for Social Security run at around 1 percent. The basic role for the Social Security Administration is to cut checks. By contrast, according to the Congressional Budget Office (2004b), government regulation of millions of tiny personalized accounts would increase administrative fees from less than 1 percent to somewhere between 5 and 30 percent.

Increasing administrative fees means more government involvement, but of a very different type.

For example, to protect beneficiaries as the current structure does, the Presidential Commission on Social Security's 2001 recommendation was that the government be primarily responsible for deciding where individuals may invest their money and educating them on how to do it (Herd and Kingson 2005). The heavy government involvement and limitations on choice reflect lessons learned from other nations' experiences with privatization. Britain's numerous problems with its almost fully privatized system made it clear that most people did not fare well with a lot of choice and little government intervention (Orszag 1999). The government would have to choose which accounts Americans' trillions of dollars would flow into. Imagine the lobbying effort, and the potential conflicts associated with it, of mutual funds companies vying to be on the list of approved investments. The government would face a growing conflict between protecting beneficiaries and supporting business. Indeed, they already have. Writers at the President's Commission explained, for example, that it would take more than a year for workers' money to actually be deposited into their accounts. Businesses would have to do additional paperwork, leading to new costs, for contributions to be immediately credited. The interest of business won out in this conflict. There will be many other choices for the government to make if these accounts are created, both at their inception and in gradual reforms that occur during implementation.

Supporters of privatization generally argue that the buildup of the Social Security surplus has encouraged irresponsible spending. The trust fund has been lent to the U.S. government and will need to be repaid (Herd and Kingson 2005; Quadagno 1996). Payroll taxes were increased to create a surplus that would see us through the aging of the baby boomers. The extra revenue could have been used to buy stocks, private bonds, or pay down the debt, but was instead spent on general revenue items like roadways and education. In essence, the government borrowed money from Social Security to pay for nonentitlement budget items, including defense spending. Current U.S. government debt totals put out by the Department of the Treasury already account for money owed to Social Security beneficiaries through the Trust Fund. In 2018, when incoming payroll taxes will no longer be enough to pay for current benefits, the government will have to redeem those Treasury bonds in the Social Security Trust Fund. This can be accomplished by taking the monies from general revenues, which would require either cutting spending or raising taxes, or by borrowing that money from other countries. The size of the national debt will not change, however, though its composition in regard to where the money has been borrowed from probably will. Regardless of how it is done, it must be done, because failure to repay these loans from the Social Security Trust Fund would constitute a fiscal crisis—the government is obligated to pay those monies.

Does the presence of the surplus actually encourage irresponsible fiscal behavior by the government? Some argue that because of the additional revenues coming in, we spent more than we would have otherwise (Becker 2005). The additional payroll taxes flowing into the government made the annual deficit look smaller than it actually was, encouraging politicians to spend more than they otherwise would have. For example, in 2004, the reported budget deficit was $475 billion. If the Social Security surplus had not been counted as real revenue, however, the deficit would have been $639 billion (Office of Management and Budget 2005). Becker argues that creating individual accounts, where individuals are responsible for funding their own retirement, eliminates the need for a trust fund and reduces the deficit threat. Others argue the Trust Fund was never the problem; we simply borrowed money from ourselves rather than from other sources, including foreign governments, or reducing spending, as Paul Krugman concludes in a 2001 *New York Times* op-ed column ("Reckonings: Sins of Commission," July 25, p. 17). Must we privatize Social Security simply because we lack the discipline to report the true size of the federal deficit?

Thus far, attempts by conservative policy makers to privatize Social Security have been unsuccessful. The determination to privatize was matched by the determination of the AARP and older Americans in general to keep the program intact. The AARP ran an ad campaign in which they admonished, "If you had a problem with the kitchen sink, you wouldn't tear down the entire house!" The cures were worse than the disease (Herd and Kingson 2005). Thus far, the politically untouchable universal social insurance program has remained untouchable (Quadagno 1994; Skocpol 1991; Korpi and Palme 1998).

Conservatives reframed welfare debates from family friendly to market friendly as they sustained the steady drum beat against universal welfare programs. They placed privatization, which was once considered a reasonable reform only by the radical right, at the top of the national agenda. The impact appears to have been somewhat modest. The privatization plan enjoyed little public support and the percentage of Americans supporting the concept of individual accounts has not really changed. In 2001, about 50 percent of Americans backed private accounts. In 2005, about 46 percent did so ("Polls on Social Security, in chronological order, of Americans aged 18 and older," http://www.pollingreport.com/social.htm, September 21, 2005). Support varies by age, however. The majority of the decline in support was concentrated among those older than fifty. Support was about 66 percent for those between eighteen and thirty and remained above 50 percent for those younger than sixty-five (Pew Research Center 2005). Thus, given the greater support for privatization by younger Americans, it may come back on the agenda in future years. National confidence in the Social Security program has also declined generally. A June 10, 2005, CBS *New York Times* poll showed that just 30 percent of American adults believe that Social Security will have enough money to pay their benefits when they get older (PollingReport.com, September 21, 2005). Nonetheless, an AARP poll (2005) showed that the public debate over privatization left many more informed and confident, leaving support for the program as strong as ever.

Social Security and Older Women

In the reams of papers on privatization, little discussion focuses on the implications of privatizing Social Security for women (for an exception, see Williamson and Rix 1999). How, then, would this kind of a reform affect women? The first problem involves longevity (Williamson and Rix 1999). Women outlive men by an average of about five years (NCHS 2004). In the private pension market, longevity has often been taken into account when determining benefit levels, causing women to receive smaller monthly benefits because they are expected to receive them for more years. In the private savings market, beneficiaries may take benefits in whatever size they please, but risk running out of funds before their death. With Social Security, however, gender differences in life expectancy have never entered the calculus. There is no risk that women will receive smaller pensions because of longer life expectancies or exhausting their benefits because they live longer than projected by their financial planner. If we shift to individual accounts, the program will operate as private savings and investments currently do. With advancing age, women, and particularly poor women, will end up with fewer benefits in a private annuity than their male counterparts. Given that women seventy-five and older are more likely to be poor than the younger old, reductions in their benefits would lead to real hardship. As figure 6.3 demonstrates, the poverty rate for women sixty-five to seventy-four is 10.8 percent, versus 14.1 percent for those seventy-five and older (U.S Census Bureau 2004).

The other problems with partial privatization have to do with women's relatively low earnings in comparison with men's (Williamson and Rix 1999). Working women still earn around three-quarters of what men earn (Castro 1998). Social Security's worker benefit is advantageous for low earners because income is redistributed from higher earners through the worker benefit. Under the current program, individuals with low earnings receive a benefit that is a higher percentage of their average lifetime earnings than high earning individuals do. Although currently

Figure 6.3   Poverty Rates Among Elderly Women, 2004

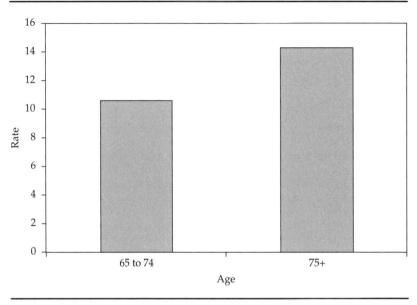

Source: He et al. 2005.

all tax dollars spent on Social Security are subject to the progressive benefit formula, under partial privatization plans a portion of those dollars
would now be diverted to individual accounts where they would not be
subject to the progressive benefit formula.

Those with lower earnings would have more difficulty than high earners increasing the size of their accounts for several reasons. First, lower
earners have less expendable income and therefore are less likely to put
a high proportion away for investments. Second, 10 percent of a low salary
amounts to much less than 10 percent of a high salary. Third, lower earners will spend a higher proportion of their investments on the administrative fees. Finally, those with more resources can afford to make riskier
investments and over the long term may end up with higher returns. The
level of financial risk individuals can take is proportional to the size of
their financial resources (Herd and Kingson 2005).

Currently, the one stable source of income that elderly people with
low incomes have is their Social Security benefit. Individual accounts
would leave older individuals with greater insecurity because large fluctuations in the stock market could be problematic for their income security in old age. One of the few concrete studies of privatization was done
in Galveston, Texas. On January 1, 1982, Galveston county opted out of
Social Security and developed a privatized system (Wilson 1999). The

Table 6.1   Galveston's Monthly Retirement Benefit as Percentage of Social Security's Benefit

Marital Status	Initial Benefit	After 15 Years	After 20 Years
Single			
Low	96	63	54
Middle	139	91	78
High	142	93	80
Very high	177	115	99
Married			
Low	59	38	33
Middle	82	54	46
High	87	57	49
Very high	108	71	61

Source: Wilson 1999.

study found that those with higher earnings had much higher benefits under this plan than they would have under the Social Security system. By contrast, low earners had lower benefits (Wilson 1999). Their initial benefit was about 4 percent lower. As table 6.1 shows, however, because Social Security includes automatic cost of living increases to offset inflation, the difference grew over time. For single low earners, then, after fifteen years, the benefit would be 63 percent of what it would have been under Social Security. More moderate single earners would have a higher initial benefit, but after fifteen years only 91 percent of that and after twenty years only 78 percent. By contrast, the initial benefit of the highest earners would be 177 percent of their Social Security benefit. After twenty years, it would be equivalent to what their Social Security would have been (Wilson 1999). Overall, they would have obtained a substantial gain through a private contribution system. Note that married people do not fare as well under the Galveston plan as they would have under Social Security because there are no spouse or widow benefits. In the one clear demonstration available to us, privatization led to increased inequality in old age.

Who Benefits from Privatization?

Certain interests in the private sector might benefit significantly from privatization and the reaction of the business community largely reflects this. They have been generally quite supportive of partial privatization, recognizing that billions of new dollars could flow into their coffers, despite some initial concern that caps on fees and the small size of many accounts might lead to lower than desired profits (Herd and Kingson 2005). New lobbying groups have popped up over the past few years.

Two of the more significant were the Coalition for the Modernization and Protection of America's Social Security (COMPASS)—which was formed by the Business Roundtable, the National Association of Manufacturers, and the Financial Services Forum (a group of CEOs of major banks, insurance companies, and securities firms)—and the Alliance for Worker Security. Others have been formed by the larger business community, which would generally benefit by having billions funneled into many publicly traded companies. The links between these lobbying groups and the Bush government are tight. COMPASS's director, Charles Blahous, actually left that organization to be staff director for the Presidential Commission on Social Security Reform, which eventually recommended that Social Security be privatized (Stevenson 2001). Aside from these new groups, think tanks such as the American Enterprise Institute, the Cato Institute, and the Heritage Foundation have been actively researching and lobbying for privatization for more than twenty years. Ultimately, it is nearly impossible to track down how much lobbying groups have spent—or are planning on spending—for Social Security reform. In the Medicare prescription drug reform campaign, lobbyist spending topped $100 million (*The Economist* 2005).

Over the past few decades, the Social Security reform agenda has shifted from talk of means-testing, increasing the age of eligibility, raising taxes, and lowering benefits to talk of privatization. For the most part, these market-friendly proposals fail to address the fiscal shortcomings of the program. They also fail to adequately address the changing sociodemographic changes, or the old age inequality, addressed throughout this book. In chapter 7, we analyze how family-friendly proposals aim to do both.

Privatizing Health Care

The old age health system is complex and expensive. It is comprised of thousands of different insurance pools: acute care, chronic care, informal care, Medicaid, long-term care insurance, Medicare, supplemental health insurance, and private insurance. Most acknowledge problems with complexities, gaps, and costs in the current system, but disagreement about how to solve them is significant. Over the past fifteen years, the family-friendly agenda to unify the system under a single national plan has been overtaken by a market-friendly agenda to further privatize, which will further complicate, rather than simplify the system. Moreover, ongoing privatization is likely to introduce greater inequality. Despite claims made by supporters, evidence that privatization will reduce costs or improve benefits is limited.

Just like Social Security, supporters of market-friendly welfare policy have always disliked Medicare. They fought off its creation for more than fifty years by arguing that it was the equivalent to socialized medicine, would interfere with the practice of medicine by doctors, and would be entirely too costly (Quadagno 2005). Much like Social Security, however, Medicare has engendered enormous public support. Even in the face of massive budget deficits, a recession, and a war, Americans recently received the largest expansion of Medicare since its inception with the addition of a prescription drug benefit. The universal principle, wherein everyone contributes and everyone benefits from a policy, has remained as firm with Medicare as it has with Social Security. Almost every older American, roughly 98 percent, relies on Medicare for health insurance (Centers for Medicare and Medicaid Services 2005a, 2005b).

Aware that they cannot successfully dismantle a universal program that is so popular, supporters of market-friendly policies have not attempted to eliminate Medicare or restrict the number of beneficiaries. Instead, they have focused on privatization—such as broadening the use of HMOs in Medicare, shifting more Medicare costs back to the elderly with premium and co-pay increases, and using tax incentives and cutbacks in Medicaid to encourage individuals to buy long-term care insurance (Herd 2005a). People want the government to guarantee their access to health care in old age (AARP 2005). Middle-class voters do not want their benefits threatened. Proponents of privatization are arguing, not unlike their strategy with Social Security, that a financial crisis in the program will necessitate privatizing Medicare. As with Social Security, there is no evidence that privatization will improve Medicare's fiscal problems. Already, proponents promised that HMOs would improve services and cost less. They did neither. Moreover, the push toward long-term care insurance has been stymied by expensive premiums and strict underwriting policies that prevent this from being a viable alternative for most Americans.

Medicare Cost Containment

Medicare's costs are skyrocketing, but are they too high? Over the past thirty years, Medicare has been far more successful than the private sector market at controlling health care costs (Boccuti and Moon 2003). Because so many people are insured in a single pool, Medicare is, in effect, able to buy cheaper in bulk. It has more leverage with providers to negotiate or demand lower prices from hospitals, physicians, and medical suppliers. Moreover, having a single, rather than multiple, administrative structure reduces costs. Average administrative costs in the private sector are 12.8 percent versus 3 percent in Medicare (Boccuti and Moon 2003). Though the average annual cost increases were 9.6 percent in Medicare between 1972 and 2002, they were 11.1 percent in the private sector.

Figure 6.4   Medicare and Overall Health-Care Spending to GDP

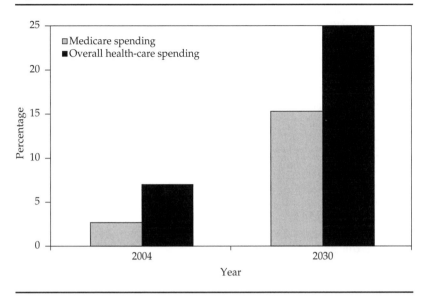

Source: MedPac 2005.

Nonetheless, the fiscal problems facing Medicare eclipse those facing Social Security. It is the elephant in the room that few are discussing seriously. Figure 6.4 shows the extent of rising Medicare and health care costs. Currently, Medicare comprises 2.7 percent of GDP. By 2030, it will comprise 7 percent (MedPac 2005). Increasing costs, in part, are linked to increasing numbers of older people living longer lives. But what is often ignored is that Medicare's fiscal problems are rooted in the larger problems of the U.S. health care system. For decades, increases in health spending have outpaced increases in any other expenses (Harrington Meyer 2005; Herd 2006c). Overall, health care spending is expected to rise from 15.3 percent of GDP to 25 percent from 2004 to 2030 (MedPac 2005). FICA contributions to Medicare's health insurance fund will fall below expenditures as early as 2011 (Social Security Administration 2005a). Preoccupation with Social Security has preempted serious efforts to address much more serious fiscal problems with Medicare.

Generally, potential solutions to Medicare's fiscal problems fall into five main categories (Herd 2006c). First, the government could reduce payments to health care providers and suppliers, but this might discourage providers from seeing Medicare patients. Second, service use on the part of beneficiaries could be limited, but this might cause some older people to do without needed care. Third, beneficiary cost-sharing could be increased, but this solution would be problematic for lower-income older people who already have difficulty covering rising out-of-pocket expenses. Fourth, the number of beneficiaries could be reduced, primarily by raising the eligibility age. Fifth, taxes could be raised. These first two ways of dealing with Medicare's financial problems have been tried in the past. Medicare, as the primary health insurer for older Americans, can act unilaterally to reduce payments and use. This is also how private health insurance companies cut costs. They pay hospitals, doctors, and health care suppliers lower fees and encourage their customers to use fewer health care services. There is one large difference, however, between the government and the private sector with regard to this approach. The sheer number of people that Medicare covers gives it more leverage to negotiate lower prices with health care providers and suppliers. Providers and suppliers can refuse to cover Medicare beneficiaries if they do not agree with the pricing, but the large number of beneficiaries makes this an option of last resort (Boccuti and Moon 2003). Individual health insurance companies, which cover much smaller numbers of beneficiaries, do not have this kind of leverage.

Reducing Payments to Providers and Suppliers   Reducing Medicare costs by reducing Medicare payments to health care providers and suppliers has been successful throughout Medicare's history. For example, in the early 1980s, when per capita Medicare costs had doubled in a single decade, Medicare cut costs by shifting from a fee-for-service to a prospective payment system for hospitals (Harrington Meyer 2005; Boccuti and Moon 2003). Instead of paying for an x-ray, blood testing, an EKG, and surgery for a beneficiary who went into cardiac arrest, Medicare began paying a single lump sum for the average amount it costs in total to treat such a patient. If the actual care costs more, the hospital absorbs the cost. If it costs less, the hospital keeps the extra. From 1967 to 1984, the average rate of increase in Medicare spending was 16.5 percent. After the implementation of these new payment procedures, annual spending increases dropped to 9.2 percent between 1984 and 1991 (Davis and Burner 1995).

Reducing costs is advantageous for older persons who pay 20 percent of their medical care out-of-pocket. It is particularly advantageous for the sickest and poorest beneficiaries who may be expected to cover 70 percent of their medical costs out-of-pocket by 2030 (Maxwell, Moon, and Segal 2001). Given that one-quarter of the elderly live below 150 percent of the poverty level (for a single person this is $12,741 a year), high medical care costs impose great challenges. Cost reduction comes with concerns about quality, however. Remember that many scholars claim that prospective payment systems led hospitals to discharge patients "quicker and sicker" to improve their profit margin (Harrington Meyer 2005; Estes and Red 1993). Indeed, hospital stays shortened after the implementation of the new payment system. Between 1981 and 1987, the average length of stay dropped from 10.2 to 8.5 days, about a 15 percent drop (Kominski and Witsberger 1993). The length of hospital stays has been continuing to shrink. Throughout the 1990s, it dropped by more than 10 percent (MedPac 2005).

The 1997 Balanced Budget Act included a variety of cuts in payments to providers, though some have been softened. Cuts in payments to hospitals were substantial, but the lobbying from hospitals caused legislators to make payments more generous in subsequent legislation. The portion of the 1997 act that extended PPS from hospitals to home care and nursing home providers remains (Moon with Herd 2002).

Ultimately, as Medicare continues to tighten its payment policies, beneficiaries may find that it is more and more difficult to access care, and that their care has shifted from hospitals to skilled nursing facilities and home care. Where will it be shifted to next? If Medicare reduces payments enough, health care providers and physicians may simply refuse to treat beneficiaries. This is already the case for Medicaid. Medicaid, the public health insurance program for poor Americans, has tremendous difficulty, many states, getting health care providers to participate because the reimbursement rates are so low (Harrington Meyer 2005). In some cases, they are only 20 to 30 percent of what Medicare pays. The result is that Medicaid beneficiaries have difficulty receiving care, particularly from primary care physicians (Sloan, Mitchell, and Cromwell 1978; Mitchell 1991; Fossett et al. 1992; Newacheck at al. 1998).

In a parallel move, the government can negotiate lower prices for the medical care products it covers. Medicare pays for medically necessary equipment, including artificial limbs, braces, wheelchairs, canes, patient lifts, hospital beds, commode chairs, and diabetes supplies. This will be particularly important over the coming decades as new medical care products are created for a rapidly expanding elderly population. Most economists believe that rising health care costs are almost solely due to new technologies (Cutler and McClellan 2001). If the government can better control the cost of these, considerable savings are possible.

The government, however, cannot currently negotiate lower prices for one of the most expensive medical products, prescription drugs. That this is the only product or service for which Medicare cannot negotiate says something about the power of the drug lobby. Even if Congress passed legislation permitting price negotiations, how would it work in practice is uncertain, given the hundreds of private insurance providers currently involved. Because Medicare will pay the going rate on prescriptions, initial evidence indicates that the new Part D coverage will rather dramatically expand Medicare's costs. The most recent estimate is that cost of the new plan will be $534 billion over the next ten years. This is troublesome, given that prescription drugs are the fastest increasing medical expense. Prescription spending grew by 450 percent between 1990 and 2004, from $40.3 billion to $188.5 billion (Kaiser Family Foundation 2006). Prescription drug costs are quite high in the United States relative to other countries. Conservative estimates are as much as 30 percent more (Danzon and Furukawa 2003). These high relative costs have led many older Americans to seek out lower prices in Canada or Mexico. Critics of the Medicare prescription drug policy call for reforms that would allow the government to negotiate lower prices. Opponents suggest that government price controls may reduce the incentive for companies to develop new and better treatments, services, and supplies (Aaron and Reischauer 1998a; Cockburn 2004). Ultimately, this could reduce the overall quality of medical care. The real question is not about price caps, however, but about how high profits need to be to keep innovation going. Given the massive profits in pharmaceuticals, and that they devote more money to advertising than they do to research, it seems there may be room for lower profits without undermining innovation. The United States currently spends twice as much as the rest of the developed world on health care, yet we have relatively poor health outcomes. Innovation, perhaps, but at what price?

Reducing Service Use   An alternative approach to reducing Medicare costs is to reduce the amount of health care services beneficiaries use. It is tricky, however, to differentiate between what constitutes unnecessary and necessary use of medical services. One of the most often proposed approaches is to control the use of untested and experimental treatments and services. If medical technology is a primary source of rapidly rising health care costs, Medicare could reduce access to experimental and unproven new treatments. If there is not solid evidence that they work, Medicare will not cover them. Thus far, reducing services has not been a priority. In fact, in the 1990s, the president added Alzheimer's coverage. In 2003, Congress added prescription coverage (Centers for Medicare and Medicaid Services 2005a, 2005b).

Some policy makers suggest that we could save money by streamlining care provided to Medicare's sickest beneficiaries. In fact, about 10 percent of beneficiaries account for 70 percent of payments (Davis and Burner 1995). Many are seeing multiple physicians, receiving overlapping services, or taking prescription drugs that interact poorly. Ultimately, Medicare could better coordinate care for such beneficiaries. Moreover, keeping tabs on the sickest beneficiaries could reduce costs by managing their illnesses more efficiently so they do not end up with high cost hospital visits. For example, carefully monitoring diabetes patients can prevent more long-term and costly outcomes such as blindness and loss of limbs.

Ideally, Medicare would reduce service use by improving health. Indeed, one of the most commonly proposed approaches to reducing health care costs is to cover and encourage preventative care. When Medicare was created in the mid-1960s, it was mainly intended to cover acute care in hospitals. In many respects, this was a reflection of an entire medical care system largely centered on acute care. Today, though, it is quite clear that it is less expensive to stop poor health before it occurs, rather than after. To some extent, Medicare has already shifted to a preventative approach. For example, it has expanded its coverage of preventative care services to include things such as mammograms and annual physicians' visits. A comprehensive emphasis on preventative medicine could improve the fiscal health of the program.

Increase Beneficiary Cost Sharing   Many proposed reforms include shifting more costs to the beneficiaries through higher premiums, co-payments, and deductibles. This strategy is exemplified by the Balanced Budget Act, which increased costs to beneficiaries and reduced the rate of growth in Medicare spending by almost 25 percent (Herd 2006c; Moon, Gage, and Evans 1997). Proponents argue that this approach provides direct cost savings through increased revenue, and indirect cost savings because higher out-of-pocket costs discourage use or prompt beneficiaries to seek less costly alternatives. Opponents, however, argue that Medicare beneficiaries are already heavily burdened with health care costs (Harrington Meyer 2005; Moon with Herd 2002). Beneficiaries currently devote 20 percent of their income to out-of-pocket health care costs. Further, out-of-pocket health care costs are particularly high among groups with the fewest resources. Those without high school degrees have out-of-pocket costs that are almost twice those of their counterparts with college degrees (Crystal et al. 2000). Moreover, those in the bottom income quartile have out-of-pocket costs that consume 30 percent of their income versus the 8 percent for the wealthiest individuals in the top income quartile (Crystal et al. 2000).

Projections for the future, without any changes to the current program, show that the situation will only deteriorate further. By 2025, beneficiaries' average out-of-pocket costs could rise to 30 percent (Maxwell, Moon, and Segal 2001). Vulnerable groups will face the harshest repercussions. Those in poor health and with no additional supplemental insurance outside of Medicare could devote 63 percent of their income to health care. Even more striking is the estimate that a low-income single woman age eighty-five or older and in poor health could spend 72 percent of her income on health care.

Raise the Eligibility Age   Another way to cut costs is to reduce the number of beneficiaries by delaying the age of eligibility. Many policy makers propose that we raise Medicare's eligibility age from sixty-five to sixty-six, or sixty-seven, or even higher. Recent estimates indicate this would reduce overall program costs by 8.7 percent (Herd 2006c; Waidmann 1998). Moreover, the incentives this change creates would likely increase employment rates among the near elderly, thus increasing tax revenues for both Social Security and Medicare. The primary justification for this change is that elderly health has improved significantly over the last half century. Older Americans are far more capable of staying in the labor force longer than ever before. Moreover, as mentioned, the eligibility age for Social Security will be age sixty-seven by 2010.

Delaying eligibility, however, could be problematic for Americans approaching retirement. Current estimates show that increasing the age of eligibility to sixty-seven would leave one in ten people between the ages of sixty-five and sixty-seven without any health insurance coverage and another 25 percent underinsured (Waidmann 1998). The lack of health insurance coverage could have severe ramifications for health. There is evidence that those uninsured just previous to retirement are more likely to die than those consistently insured (McWilliams et al. 2004). Moreover, delaying the eligibility age undermines the universal feature of the program. Because life expectancy varies so dramatically by gender and race, certain groups, particularly black men, may not, on average, live long enough to obtain benefits. In any case, studies show that this option would do little to improve Medicare's solvency; those between sixty-five and sixty-seven are the healthiest and the least costly.

Raise Taxes   One final measure that would shore up Medicare's fiscal outlook would be to increase payments into the system. This proposal, however, shores up the program in a way that spreads the costs across all working-age Americans. Currently, the FICA tax that goes to Medicare Part A health insurance is 1.45 percent for employers and employees. There is no cap on this tax, so, in contrast to Social Security's regressive tax structure, it is truly a flat tax (Harrington Meyer 2005; Herd 2006c). Payroll taxes for Medicare have not been increased since 1983, though overall health spending over the same period has increased dramatically. Some argue payroll taxes in the United States are already too high, but they are actually quite a bit below the rates of 25 to 30 percent in countries such as Sweden, France, Belgium, and Italy. To offset the shortfall for Medicare part A health insurance, the FICA tax would have to be raised by more than 3 percent, to a new total of 4.5 percent (Social Security Administration 2005a).

Ultimately, there is no easy solution to controlling Medicare's costs. The best strategy would likely be a mix of the options discussed. One thing is clear: privatizing the system is not an answer to Medicare's financial problems.

Privatization and Redistribution

These five approaches above have not received much attention in policy arenas in recent years, aside from shifting costs to beneficiaries, because supporters of market-friendly policies have focused the reform agenda on one thing: privatization. Similar to privatization proposals for Social Security, it is the redistributive part of Medicare that is being challenged (Herd 2005a). The link between privatization and redistribution is murkier when it comes to health care, so here we explore this link carefully. At the moment, the government is the primary health insurer for elderly Americans. The government decides how much beneficiaries pay and what services they receive. Everyone generally has access to the same services and pays the same basic premiums, co-payments, and deductibles. The costs of health care are distributed across all elderly Americans. Certainly, those who are sicker end up paying more because a co-payment of 20 percent, for example, leads to a higher dollar value the more services one uses. Ultimately, though, the costs of health care for the sickest and poorest beneficiaries are heavily subsidized by their healthier and generally wealthier counterparts.

Supporters of market-friendly policies argue that the government's role in health care should be limited, and the role of HMOs and private health insurance companies expanded (Herd 2005a; Herd 2006c; Lemieux 2003). Proponents of privatization argue that older Americans should be able to "decide what kind of health plans they want, the kinds of benefit packages they want, the medical treatments and procedures they want, and the premiums, co-payments, deductibles, and coinsurance they are willing to pay" (Moffit 2004, pg. 1). The most common proposal for privatizing Medicare is called premium support. Each older American would receive a voucher with which he or she would have to purchase a health care plan. Central to their proposals is that there would be many, perhaps hundreds, of insurance pools. The premiums, co-payments, and deductibles that beneficiaries paid would vary depending upon the HMO or health insurance company that covered them. The government would continue to act as an insurer, but if it failed to effectively compete with private sector companies it could be eliminated.

How do these privatized systems reduce redistribution? The privatized system would provide fewer services at higher costs for poor and sick Americans, who are disproportionately black, Hispanic, and women (Harrington Meyer 2005). Multiple pools make it much harder to spread and redistribute the costs of health care from the sickest and poorest beneficiaries to the healthiest and wealthiest. Even though there will be open enrollment, experts suggest that this much choice often leads to confusion. It is hard to navigate such a complex array of options. Moreover, it is likely the plans would be designed in ways to attract the healthiest beneficiaries. For example, plans that want to attract healthier older

Americans might include free gym memberships, but have very limited coverage for diabetes care (Moon with Herd 2002). Ultimately, the sickest would likely end up paying much more for their health care than they do in the current system, where sick and healthy beneficiaries are in the same pool (Herd 2005a, 2006c).

The problem is that HMOs and health insurance companies are very skilled at attracting the healthiest individuals who will leave them with the highest profits. Generally, they do this by designing insurance plans most attractive to people who are not sick. Sicker individuals end up concentrated in certain plans when people have multiple options (Rice and Desmond 2002). Under the premium support plan, the sickest and most costly beneficiaries would likely end up concentrated in traditional Medicare, leaving them with extraordinarily high premiums, deductibles, and co-payments (Rice and Desmond 2002).

Who then benefits with privatized plans such as premium support? Ultimately, the market broadly, and private health insurance companies and HMOs specifically, would gain (Herd 2005a). In a market-friendly welfare state, the primary goal is to foster a healthy market. For Medicare, that means diverting taxpayer dollars toward private health insurance companies and providers. In shifting from a single insurance pool under Medicare to hundreds of insurance pools under privatization, we ensure that administrative costs will increase. Health care providers would have many opportunities to insert fees and profits that will be difficult for the government to identify and regulate.

Unlike Social Security, which though threatened with privatization has yet to be altered, the underlying ideology of privatization has already become a part of Medicare (Herd 2005a, 2006c). Remember that Medicare Advantage currently covers about 18 percent of beneficiaries. Further, the prescription drug benefit expanded market involvement in Medicare in numerous ways (Kaiser Family Foundation 2004). First, it increased payments to Medicare Advantage to encourage more beneficiaries to opt out of traditional Medicare. Second, under the prescription drug benefit, the government is not the primary insurer. The government does not provide the insurance, therefore beneficiaries have to buy it on their own, with a subsidy, from private insurance companies. Beneficiaries in HMOs receive the coverage through them. Beneficiaries who want to remain in Medicare fee-for-service, generally those who are sicker and poorer, have to buy an additional policy from an insurer. Clearly, the overall incentive is to push more individuals into HMOs, even though such efforts have thus far increased Medicare costs. Finally, the prescription drug bill does not allow the government to use its leverage with prescription drug companies to negotiate lower costs for these prescription drugs. This lack of leverage will lead to higher priced prescription drugs, increasing the overall costs of Medicare.

The passage of the Medicare prescription drug bill makes the market-friendly strategy very clear. Supporters are using large universal policies to redistribute to the market rather than to the poor. Many conservatives were quite willing to expand a government social policy, but only if the expansion helped the private sector. Privatization would expand rather than restrict the government's role in old age health care, but redefines that role from one of provision to one of regulation. Privatization also magnifies inequality linked to gender, race, and class. Moreover, it does little to shore up the Medicare fiscal crisis. Indeed, privatization has thus far increased costs substantially. At last count, the government was paying an extra $522 per Medicare Advantage beneficiary (Biles, Nicholas, and Cooper 2004).

Discussion

Of the many market-friendly reform proposals currently under consideration, almost none adequately address inequality in old age. Moreover, proposals that focus on cost containment and privatization fail to respond to the sweeping sociodemographic changes that are redefining old age. Proposals that focus on privatization also fail to address the fiscal shortfalls, indeed, they make the shortfalls even larger. Market-friendly proposals are not designed to strengthen our two universal old age programs by improving benefits and reducing costs, they are designed to benefit markets. Supporters of privatization argue that they want to reduce government involvement. These proposals, however, do not get the government out of the retirement business. Instead they aim to put private enterprises, particularly investment firms and health insurance providers, more fully into it.

Given the ever-increasing focus and attention on market solutions to public problems, it is almost as if the primary concern of politicians is how to foster a healthy market. Who then will foster a healthy nation? Does the well-being of the market matter more than the well-being of citizens? Policy makers now argue that if government intervention offsets some of the negative ramifications of a market economy, such as poverty, it should be done in a very limited and focused way to avoid any interference in the market. Universal social policies most certainly do not fit this framework. Despite overwhelming evidence that universal policies are the most effective way to reduce inequality and poverty, then, we remain entrenched in a system where policy solutions are targeted and market focused (Korpi and Palme 1998). The result of these trends will likely be further entrenchment of gender, race, and class inequality.

═ Chapter 7 ═

Family-Friendly Proposals: Entrenching Equality

I N THE MIDST of an era marked by market-friendly proposals that would retrench and privatize old age welfare programs, we analyze a slate of family-friendly reform proposals intended to be universal, redistributive, affordable, and responsive to sociodemographic changes. The aim from a family-friendly perspective is to use the welfare state to mitigate rather than magnify old age inequality. Despite the clout wielded by market-friendly supporters such as corporate lobbyists, investment firms, insurance companies, pharmaceuticals, health care providers, and conservative think tanks, most polls show that the vast majority in the United States want the government to do more, not less, for older people (AARP 2005; Street and Sittig Cossman 2006). Although reforms to old age programs are needed, for many, old age benefits may still be too little too late. Reforms that will significantly improve the livelihood of the poorest and sickest older people need to be in place at every stage of the life course. Here we analyze reforms for both older and younger individuals.

In contrast to those who want to minimize government intervention and distribute public benefits through private markets, supporters of family-friendly policies reject the argument that a healthy market will naturally lead to a healthy and wealthy populace. Given that markets have long been a major cause of inequality, it makes little sense to draw heavily on them for cures. If structural elements drive poverty, inequality, and stratification, then structural rather than individual solutions are needed. Whether they are favored by conservatives or liberals, the evidence suggests that policies that primarily emphasize fostering healthy markets will lead to greater gender, race, class, and marital status inequality. By contrast, family-friendly policies are designed to rectify rather than replicate the inequalities resulting from social institutions such as labor markets, families, and education. Here we explore the family-friendly case for expanding the welfare state.

We also evaluate the premise that expanding the old age welfare state will cost more money. Many might argue that the family-friendly solutions addressed here are much too costly, and consequently Pollyannaish, in

156

an era of ballooning deficits, massive tax cuts, and war. As we assess this debate, it becomes clear that cost is not the real reason for our failure to redress current shortcomings in the welfare state. In fact, almost all of the family-friendly proposals analyzed here can be accomplished without increased revenues, and some, particularly in the case of health care, may lead to long-term costs savings. By contrast, most of the pro-market reforms currently on the table, in particular privatizing Social Security and Medicare, would entail substantial cost increases.

A New Social Security Reform Agenda

What does a family-friendly reform agenda look like for Social Security? To begin with, it involves maintaining and strengthening the program. This universal old age program is the most effective one we have for lifting people out of poverty (Quadagno 1999; Estes 2002). Supporters want to sustain its universal and redistributive features, something that can not be accomplished through privatization. The first step is to respond to the budget shortfall in a reasonable way. If we take no action now, in 2041 the contributions will cover only 80 percent of the payouts. If we take small steps now, we can easily offset that shortfall. As we argued earlier, the most efficient solutions include either raising the tax cap to $140,000 and pulling in all uncovered government workers, or raising the FICA tax by 1 percent. Either would be a reasonable and effective response to Social Security's impending fiscal shortfall.

Given that the fiscal crisis can be addressed, we turn our attention to fairly modest policy proposals that would cause the program to be even more effective at reducing gender, race, class, and marital status inequality in old age. These reforms focus on modifications that would help offset the costs born primarily by women whose waged labor is shaped by the demands of their unpaid care work. Preoccupation with the program's fiscal problems, and with privatization, has caused reformers to set aside the possibility of making benefits more gender accommodative and more responsive to changing family structures. Here we consider somewhat neglected proposals that have been put forth to make Social Security benefits more responsive to families.

Perhaps the most popular proposals involve changing the way we figure current spouse and widow benefits. One way to do this would be to implement earnings sharing, which is a proposal to credit each person in a marriage with having earned half of the annual household income, regardless of who actually did so. Later, if there is a divorce, each already has credit with Social Security for half of all of the household earnings. A second way would be to increase the widow benefit, which usually involves giving less money to a couple while the husband is alive and then more to the widow after he has died (Burkhauser and

Holden 1982; Burkhauser and Smeeding 1994; Favreault, Sammartino, and Steuerle 2002). We are not going to analyze the impact of these proposals because both continue to link benefits to marital status. Such proposals are worth considering, but are problematic precisely because they are aimed at increasing benefits to women with a qualifying marriage. They fail to take into account the economic well-being of those without qualifying marriages. They do nothing to help offset growing race differences in marital rates. They do nothing to attend to the growing legions of cohabiters, gay or straight, who often raise children outside of marriage. Indeed, such proposals further entrench marital status as an eligibility requirement and would only contribute to greater inequality in old age along race, class, and marital status lines (Harrington Meyer, Wolf, and Himes 2006; Herd 2005b, 2005c, 2006a).

The key to making Social Security benefits more responsive to changing families is to eliminate marital status as the primary criterion for eligibility. Linking benefits to marital status has proved problematic as fewer Americans enter marriage and more Americans leave it. Moreover, given the disproportionate representation of black women and women with low educational attainment among those who will never attain a ten-year marriage, removing the connection between benefits and marriage would likely reduce race and class inequality among women. Simply eliminating marital status benefits would still leave women with less income, given women's lower labor force participation and lower earnings. If women had access only to the worker benefit, they would face drastic benefit cuts and dramatic increases in poverty rates. Remember that currently, two-thirds of women are receiving marital-based benefits because their incomes are not high enough to produce a more generous worker benefit (Harrington Meyer, Wolf, and Himes 2006). Thus, the issue becomes how money spent on noncontributory marital status benefit might be distributed differently. That is, what if we took the money spent on marital status benefits and used it differently? Here we analyze the two most commonly suggested family-friendly reform proposals for Social Security family benefits: care credits and minimum benefits. Both proposals have roots in larger theoretical debates about whether the state should redistribute resources in ways that are market or family friendly (for more methodological and policy detail, see Herd 2005b, 2005c, 2006a).

Care Credits

Implementing care credits would reward parents for raising children. In essence, family benefits would be linked not to marital status, but to parenthood. As early as the Progressive era, upper-class women activists argued that women should be financially compensated for their care through mothers' pensions (Gordon 1994). Mothers were fulfilling their citizenship duties, not in employment but in raising future citizens and workers. Arguments for compensating care cropped up again in the 1970s during the wages for housework campaigns when, among other things, feminists argued that domestic labor should be included in the GNP. Such proposals have been on the table since the late 1970s (Herd 2006a; Holden 1979; Social Security Administration 1979; Burkhauser and Holden 1982). Feminist supporters of family-friendly policies argue that women should be financially compensated for raising children and for care work more generally. The root of gender inequality, by this logic, is the lack of recognition, both cultural and financial, for the work that predominantly women perform (Cancian and Oliker 2000; Folbre 1994; Seccombe 1974). The result of uncompensated care work is diminished access to economic resources and increased dependence on men. Over the past ten years, there has been a resurgence of calls for women's care work to be compensated (Harrington Meyer 2000; Cancian and Oliker 2000; Crittenden 2001; Folbre 1994; Herd 2006a; Hobson 2000; Knijn and Kremer 1997).

Proposals to reward unpaid care work through Social Security have come from feminist scholars, mainstream policy analysts, and politicians. The proposal we analyze, slightly modified from the proposal suggested by Al Gore in the 2000 election, would eliminate the spouse benefit, but not the widow benefit, and shift every beneficiary to a worker benefit. The proposal then introduces care credits to subsidize the worker benefit. Instead of compensating women for their lost earnings, a strategy that increases inequality among women by giving a lawyer more credit than a secretary for doing the same labor of raising a child, these care credits would be equivalent for all (Herd 2006a). Thus, out of the thirty-five earnings years used to calculate the worker benefit, parents could substitute up to five years for one child, up to nine years for more than one child, with an amount equal to half of the median wage (*News Hour with Jim Lehrer* 2000). Half of the median wage for adults working full-time, which was about $15,000 in 2000, was selected to make the program cost neutral. In other words, this proposal would not increase payouts through Social Security, but redistribute them slightly toward those who have low earnings due to children. This proposal differs from many care credits in that one need not be a stay-at-home parent or married to be eligible. Working parents may benefit from the credit as long as their wages are below half of the median wage.

Minimum Benefits

Implementing a broad minimum benefit would set an income floor that no beneficiary could fall beneath. Most western welfare states have some form of a universal minimum benefit. This family-friendly proposal has its theoretical origins in T. H. Marshall's (1950) conception of the social rights associated with citizenship. Americans are more familiar with political rights, such as equal access to the vote, and civil rights, such as equal access to the workplace and other civil institutions. Social rights deal with equal access to basic necessities, such as shelter and food. Marshall argues that without social rights citizens cannot act on their political or civil rights. For example, a homeless man cannot vote because he does not have an address. Critical to the definition of universal benefits is that eligibility cannot be tied to anything but citizenship, and increasingly to an even broader residency criterion due to rising immigration rates in most industrialized countries.

In the United States, the 1939 amendments, which also fashioned spousal and survivor benefits, added a minimum benefit for eligible workers. Although the minimum benefit was never particularly generous, it was eliminated in the 1981 Social Security amendments for budgetary reasons and its vulnerability to claims that it was largely benefiting housewives, those with limited employment histories, and military or government retirees who were double-dipping in the pension pools (GAO 1979; Harrington Meyer 1996; Herd 2005b, 2005c). Amendments to the program in 1972 instituted two measures intended to protect low-income older persons, but both have serious shortcomings. The first, a special minimum benefit, required a lengthy low-earnings work history to receive any meaningful benefit increase (Congressional Research Service 2000). Eligibility was defined so tightly and benefits were so restricted that few people receive the benefit. The second measure, SSI, provided an income safety net for the low-income aged and disabled. As we detailed earlier, however, the combination of stigma and strict eligibility guidelines causes SSI to cover only half of those eligible. Moreover, beneficiaries receive a guaranteed income that is just 76 percent of the poverty level (Social Security Administration 2006; Harrington Meyer 1996).

A broadly defined minimum benefit would be fairly effective at reducing poverty and inequality among low-income beneficiaries (Harrington Meyer 2005; Herd 2005c; Favreault, Mermin, and Steuerle 2006). It is a cost-efficient strategy in that it would substantially reduce reliance on SSI. How high should it be? Bernard Wasow (2004) proposes limiting it to households that currently receive 75 percent or more of their income from Social Security and have a total income below the poverty line. Such a poverty-based benefit, though, might be too restrictive. If the minimum were set equal to the federal old age poverty line, it would be nearly equivalent to the maximum spouse benefit and thereby eliminate the need for such a benefit. Thus the family-friendly proposal we analyze would eliminate the spouse benefit, shift every beneficiary to a worker benefit, and introduce a flat poverty-level minimum benefit. Any older U.S. resident whose Social Security benefit falls below the poverty level would have his or her benefit buffered up to the poverty level. A minimum benefit approach would create an income floor independent of marital or employment history.

A Combination

Finally, we will analyze the combined effect of implementing both the care credit and minimum benefit. Will these proposals simply substitute for each other or do they each uniquely affect the distribution of women's benefits? Although gender, race, and class inequalities are intertwined and mutually dependent (Collins 1991), will a policy designed to reduce gender inequality also weaken race and class inequities? Can a policy designed to reduce class inequality weaken gender inequality?

How Do Women Fare?

We evaluate these proposals in two ways. First, we examine how the reforms shape inequality among women. How do the reforms affect the distribution of noncontributory benefits, that is, benefits not linked to earnings, among women? What percentage of the benefits goes to wealthier versus poorer women? What percentage goes to black women versus white women? Second, we examine how the reforms shape inequality between men and women. How do the proposals affect the average size of women's benefits compared to the average size of men's benefits? Currently, women's benefits are about 68 percent those of men's. For those retiring between 2020 and 2030 the gap will shrink, but will remain at about 77 percent (for detailed discussion of data and methods, see Herd 2005b, 2005c). All of the following results are for women retiring between 2020 and 2030.

Figure 7.1 shows what portion of noncontributory benefits women with different household asset levels would receive under each reform compared to the current marriage based system. Under the current system, women in the bottom quartile receive 14 percent of noncontributory benefits, and those in the top quartile receive almost 40 percent—emphasizing the extent to which the current system reinforces class inequalities among women. Both the care credit and minimum benefit would shift more of these resources towards poor women. The care credit proposal raises the proportion of family benefits distributed to poor women to 23 percent. The minimum benefit is even more effective, raising the proportion of family benefits distributed to poor women to 28 percent. The care credit proposal shifts more benefits from women in the top asset quartile toward those in the third quartile. Both proposals leave about 28 percent of these benefits in the hands of women in the top quartile. Combining the care

Figure 7.1   Distribution of Noncontributory Benefits

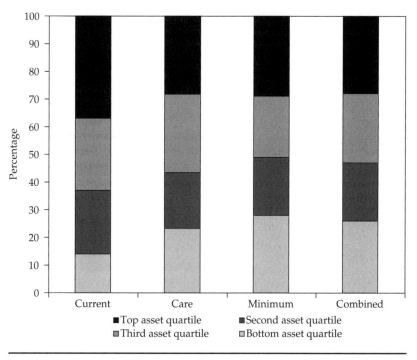

Source: Herd 2005b.

credit and minimum benefit proposals also pushes more benefits into the hands of poor women, but is slightly less effective than just simply using the minimum benefit to reduce inequality among women. Women in the bottom quartile receive 26 percent of these benefits under this proposal.

As figure 7.2 shows, all three of these proposals dramatically improve the race distribution of family benefits. Although black women represent about one-fifth of the population, they receive only 11 percent of family noncontributory benefits under the current marriage-based system. Care credits would raise black women's portion of family benefits to 19 percent, the minimum benefit would raise it to 21 percent, and the combination of a care credit and minimum benefit would raise it to 20 percent. Once again, the minimum benefit is most effective at redistributing to reduce inequality among women.

Finally, how would each of these approaches affect the gender gap in Social Security benefits? Figure 7.3 shows that the care credit and minimum benefit proposals have little impact. It is only by combining both proposals that the gap between women and men narrows. By introduc-

Figure 7.2   Distribution of Noncontributory Social Security Benefits

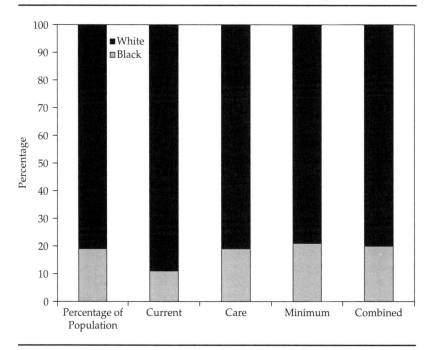

Source: Herd 2005b.

ing both measures, women's Social Security benefits would rise from the current level of just 76 percent to 81 percent of men's.

The Best Solution for Improving Inequality

Given the goal of minimizing inequality in old age, the best family-friendly approach is to maintain and strengthen the compulsory universal and redistributive features of Social Security. The fiscal outlook of Social Security can best be buttressed by raising the tax cap on earnings, bringing in all uncovered government workers, and, if need be, raising the FICA tax slightly. Moreover, the family-friendly proposals assessed here, the universal minimum benefit and the care credit proposal, make the program more responsive to sociodemographic changes and further reduce gender, race, class, and marital status inequality in old age. Whereas the child care credit is developed to be budget neutral, the minimum benefit would entail some cost increases. These increases, though, are substantially offset by the elimination of spouse benefits and by reductions in reliance on SSI. Indeed, a universal minimum benefit would make SSI

Figure 7.3   Women's Social Security Benefit as a Percentage of Men's

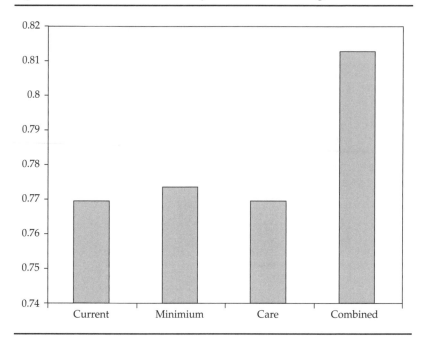

Source: Herd 2005b.
Note: Current = 0.769, Minimum = 0.774, Care = 0.769, Combined = 0.813.

for the aged unnecessary. Moreover, costs would be offset by reduced administrative costs. Administrative costs for SSI are much higher than those for Social Security because of SSI's complex eligibility guidelines.

Finally, the most controversial solution would be to eliminate widow benefits, thus completely dismantling the association between Social Security benefits and marital status. The extra revenues from this would easily offset the cost increases associated with the universal minimum benefit and the care credits, moving our proposals from essentially cost-neutral to cost-savings. Although many might argue with this strategy, our analyses show that widow benefits mainly accrue to middle- and upper-class white women (Harrington Meyer 1996). Given the goal of using old age policy to reduce inequality among the aged, we find that this policy would be effective. Even if we keep widow benefits, we find that the guaranteed minimum benefit would nearly eliminate poverty among older people, the care credit would reward parents for child rearing, and the entire Social Security system would be at least partially disentangled from the long-standing—and increasingly race- and class-biased—practice of rewarding marriage.

A New Health Insurance Agenda

Although we find that the best family-friendly proposal for Social Security involves strengthening the existing program, making it more responsive to changing families and reducing old age inequality, our findings for health insurance reform are very different. The existing old age health care programs are very expensive, provide spotty coverage, and are increasingly being privatized. These aspects only exacerbate gender, race, and class inequality. Unlike Social Security, Medicare does face an immediate and enormous fiscal shortfall. As we have argued, however, privatizing is not a solution that minimizes old age inequality or reduces costs. Market-friendly conservative proposals would redistribute taxpayer dollars to the market, particularly to investment firms, corporations, and private health insurance companies. Wealthier and healthier older Americans might fare better, but women, the poor, African Americans and Hispanics would almost certainly fare worse. Overall, these strategies would reinforce, rather than reduce, growing inequality in the United States.

So what should be done? Under the current system, access to health care is shaped by access to health insurance. Access to insurance is shaped by work status, marital status, type of illness, and so on. Family-friendly policies move away from this system and aim is to ensure universal access to health care for all, regardless. The central family-friendly proposal, then, is to implement a national health insurance plan for all ages, paid for through a progressive payroll tax. This can be accomplished either by a careful expansion and correction of the Medicare program, or by starting with a clean slate. In either case, this would eliminate the need for Medicaid, provide coverage to the 44 million Americans who are uninsured, permit more effective price leveraging, and prompt more emphasis on prevention (Barlett and Steele 2006; Hacker 2006; Quadagno 2005).

Can We Afford a Universal Single-Payer System?

A single-payer universal health insurance system could improve health given that the lack of insurance is a key explanation for individuals not receiving needed care. Indeed, when those who have been uninsured previous to retirement begin receiving Medicare at age sixty-five, their use of health services increases, their health improves, and their mortality rates decline (McWilliams et al. 2004). Moreover, universal health insurance would offset large financial losses some people experience with the onset of poor health (Cutler 2004; Hacker 2006). The best-kept secret, though, is that a single-payer plan may also cut costs.

Indeed, the United States spends more than any other industrialized nation, but our health outcomes are relatively low among these nations. Among industrialized nations, we come in near the bottom in terms of

**Figure 7.4   Health-Care Costs as a Percentage of GDP Among
Industrialized Nations**

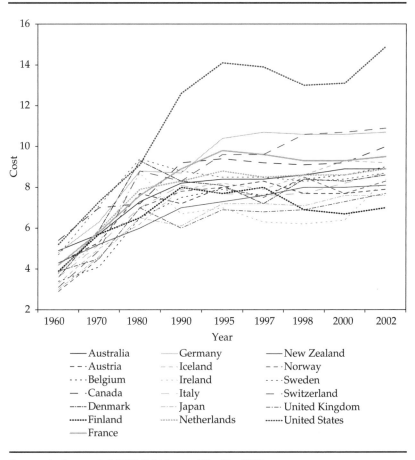

Sources: Anderson et al. 2000; Schieber and Poullier 1989.

overall population health, life expectancy, number of years spent without any disabilities, and infant mortality rates (Mathers et al. 2001;
Starfield 2000). The United States spends from 150 percent to 300 percent more on per capita health expenditures than every other industrialized nation. Moreover, health care costs consume 13.9 percent of GDP,
the highest of any industrialized nation. Germany, at 10.7 percent of GDP,
is our closest competitor. Health care costs in the United States are also
rising faster, as figure 7.4 shows, than in almost every other industrialized
country. From 1980 to 1995, the United States completely outpaced other
countries in its health expenditure growth. Despite optimism during the
mid- to late 1990s, when the United States substantially stemmed this

rate, putting it on average with other industrialized countries, by the early twenty-first century, it once again outpaces most other industrialized countries: average annual spending increased an average of 5.2 percent in OECD countries and 5.9 percent in the United States (OECD 2005). Given the United States' relative inability to constrain health care costs in a nonuniversal health care system, the question may actually be, can we afford not to turn to a universal single-payer system?

Opponents to a national health insurance plan present two main concerns—cost and quality. Despite popular myths that we could not afford it, current data suggest we could. Ultimately, countries with single-payer universal health insurance systems have been able to constrain costs for several reasons. First, they have lower administrative costs because there are fewer organizations involved in the administration of health insurance. This is the same reason that Medicare has lower administrative costs than the private sector in the United States. Scholars estimate that we could reduce overall health care costs by 15 to 25 percent if we were to shift to the more efficient administrative efforts of a single-payer plan (Hacker 2006; Barlett and Steele 2006; Holtz-Eakin 2005; Navarro 1993). Second, a single payer system places everyone in a single insurance pool and provides the single payer with sufficient leverage to better control the use and cost of health care services and products. Again, this is the same reason why Medicare costs have risen more slowly than private sector costs. It is easier for Medicare, with such a large pool of insurees, to negotiate lower prices from health care providers and suppliers, and this capacity would only grow with national health insurance (Boccuti and Moon 2003; Quadagno 2005; Hacker 2006; Barlett and Steele 2006). Third, because everyone is insured and therefore has access to health care, health inequality decreases and the emphasis on prevention increases.

This is not to say that a single-payer system is the perfect solution. Quality may indeed be affected in a variety of ways. Critics suggest that tightly controlled costs could diminish quality. For example, tightly regulating the costs of pharmaceuticals increases the risk that reduced profits will lead these companies to invest less in innovations in drugs and technologies (Cutler 2004). Similarly, tightly controlled costs may divert our best and brightest from entering medicine, increase the time we wait for medical services, and lead to various sorts of rationing. Tightly controlled costs would almost certainly interfere with profits and salaries for those in the insurance and pharmaceutical industries, but studies show that only a small proportion of profits are directed toward innovation (Barlett and Steele 2006; Hacker 2006; Quadagno 2005).

It is important, however, to consider carefully the merits of a single insurance pool for all ages. There would be little economic incentive for patient skimming or patient dumping. No one would be left uninsured.

We would eliminate the need for employer based health insurance, which would shift tremendous savings to employers. We would substantially reduce out-of-pocket costs to individuals and families. Moreover, we would be able to implement a progressive funding system to replace the existing regressive premium system. Further, because of the efficiencies of a national health insurance plan, we might finally bring ourselves in line with our peer nations by reducing total spending, per capita spending, and spending as a percent of the GDP. Many of the increased costs due to expanded coverage would be offset by disappearing costs—we would no longer need Medicare, Medicaid, or fledgling programs like SCHIP (the State Children's Health Insurance Program).

Perhaps most important, universal coverage might finally shift the focus from profit to prevention (Estes 2001; Navarro 1993). Starting early in the life course, we might ensure each new child preventative care that could help break the cycle of poorer families producing sicker children who then become poorer and sicker adults (Case, Lubotsky, and Paxson 2002; Barlett and Steele 2006). Because of its universal feature, national health insurance has tremendous potential as an intervention that reduces inequality by ensuring broad coverage regardless of employment, marital status, age, income, or assets (Korpi and Palme 1998). Although universal health insurance does not eliminate gender, race, and class disparities in health, it can help soften the blows associated with them.

Even supporters of a national health insurance policy recognize that there are limits to this reform. It is not a panacea. The evidence suggests that because the majority of the sources of poor health lie outside the health care arena, many of the solutions may as well. Given evidence that social and economic factors are often fundamental cause of poor health, national health insurance will only reduce, not eliminate, health inequalities (House et al. 1990; Link and Phelan 1995; Black et al. 1982). For example, if unequal education leads to unequal health, then one way to improve the health of the nation would be to improve the educational system (Ross and Wu 1996; Mirowsky and Ross 2003a, 2003b). Further, if low income and high inequality lead to poor health, then an important way to improve the health of the nation would be to reduce poverty and economic disparities (Case, Lubotsky, and Paxson 2002).

Solutions for Medicare

If we are unable or unwilling to move toward a national health insurance plan, supporters of family-friendly policies propose more minor adjustments to Medicare aimed at shoring up the program, maintaining its universal and redistributive features, and reducing inequality in old age. The most serious problems with the existing program are that costs are skyrocketing both for the government and, because of growing out-of-pocket costs, the aged. With respect to the first, the solution would be to wrap all older people under a single Medicare umbrella. This would control costs both by reducing administrative costs and further allowing the government more leverage to negotiate down the costs of health care services and supplies. The current tendency to create more choice, and to divide the aged into more and more risk pools, is exacerbating the problem of rising costs. Consolidating the risk pools, reducing administrative paperwork, and bargaining for reduced prices are critical to achieving lower costs. In particular, Medicare Advantage and the new Part D prescription drug program could be restructured to exclude the participation of private health insurance providers. At the very least, we could reduce payments to HMOs and increase control over the prices for Medicare prescription drugs in Part D. Reducing payments to HMOs alone would result in billions of dollars in savings.

With respect to growing costs for the aged, the problem is that Medicare coverage is so spotty. Out-of-pocket expenses for older people already consume 20 percent of their annual incomes and are expected to reach 30 percent by 2025 (Moon with Herd 2002). One solution is to fill out the current Medicare package. One of the biggest gaps in Medicare coverage is long-term care. Currently, most nursing home care is paid for by Medicaid or out of pocket. Overwhelmed by the costs of long-term care, many states are constraining Medicaid expenditures. The private market has offered a variety of long-term care insurance plans but, as we explained in chapter 5, there has been little take up. Only 5 to 7 percent of the public actually have long-term care coverage. Some older Americans simply cannot afford it, given that the average annual premium for a fifty-five-year-old American is $2,500 for three years of nursing home coverage (Connecticut Partnership for Long-Term Care 2006). Others have difficulty qualifying for the coverage because many plans refuse people with preexisting health conditions. Currently, Medicare covers the first 100 days of nursing home care, but the co-payment for days twenty-one through 100 averages more than $100 a day (Social Security Administration 2006; Harrington Meyer 2005). Eliminating co-insurance on the first 100 days would be a key first step toward expanding long-term Medicare coverage.

Another solution is to build in a stop loss. Most older Americans have some kind of supplemental policy to cover large co-payments, deductibles, and care not covered by Medicare (such as dental work). Few of these plans, however, provide stop-loss coverage. The government could require supplemental plans to adopt a stop loss measure that limits annual out-of-pocket expenditures. Then, if medical costs exceed a certain dollar value, say $3,000 a year, they would be covered. Cost estimates for this additional coverage are about $4.6 billion dollars a year. If the entire cost of this proposal were transferred to beneficiaries, premiums would cost an additional $9.50 a month (Maxwell, Moon, and Storeygard 2001). Opponents of a stop-loss measure argue that older people who receive relatively generous employee sponsored health insurance coverage would be opposed to this reform. As employer coverage of retirees plummets, however, such redundancy in coverage is less likely to be a problem. Only 36 percent of retirees had employer coverage in 2004 (MedPac 2005) and fully 20 percent of employers who now provide the supplemental retiree coverage report that they will eliminate it within three years (Kaiser Family Foundation 2003, 2005a, 2005b).

The Best Solution for Healthcare Inequality

Supporters of family-friendly policies point out that a national health insurance program, one that emphasizes prevention for all ages, would be more efficient, more effective, and more egalitarian. Medicare would be folded into a national health insurance program and Medicaid would be unnecessary. The United States spends the most money, and the most per capita, of any nation on health care and our spending continues to reach epic amounts (Quadagno 2005). Our system of dividing people into different risk pools, relying on employers, and shifting costs back to recipients is not working—that is, 44 million Americans lack insurance coverage, U.S. health care costs are higher than any other industrialized nation's, and our health outcomes rank near the bottom. The best way to finally turn our attention away from private medical care profits, and toward less expensive public health strategies, is to create a unified national risk pool in which we all benefit from unprecedented preventative efforts.

Short of that sort of transformation, supporters of family-friendly policies favor retaining and expanding the universal features of Medicare. That means opposing mean-testing, sliding scales, and privatization. We could curb growing out-of-pocket expenses by providing full coverage of the first 100 days of nursing home care and developing a mandatory stop loss clause in supplemental insurance plans. Given pronounced gender, race, and class differences in health and in health insurance coverage among those approaching old age, initiatives that would delay the age of eligibility beyond sixty-five are undesirable because they would lead to increased inequality in old age. Supporters of family-friendly policies favor keeping the age at sixty-five. Moreover, they favor revision of the prescription drug program to better fit the needs of the aged and permit negotiation of drug pricing. These reforms would reduce inequality in old age by improving coverage for groups that most need it, shoring up the universality of the program, and constraining costs. Other countries have improved health and contained costs without resorting to privatization, means-testing, or excessive cost sharing; we can do the same.

An Early Life Course Agenda

Thus far we have analyzed proposals that would expand our universal old age welfare state to reduce gender, race, class, and marital status inequality among older people. Much of old age inequality, however, originates with inequalities earlier in the life course. Imagine how universal, reliable, and safe day care would affect the earnings and work histories, and consequently the pensions and Social Security benefits, of poor single mothers. Here we assess the two most important family-friendly interventions, universal day care and paid family leave, which when added to universal health insurance would positively affect women's financial security throughout the life course. The key to all of these proposals, however, is that they be universal, and thus unrelated to gender, race, class, or marital status.

Universal Day Care

One family-friendly policy missing from the U.S. welfare state that has great potential to soften gender, race, class, and marital status stratification before old age is universal child care. A universal child care policy could provide a substantial boost to women's participation in the labor force and in particular ease the burdens poor and single women face. For many women, given the high price and relatively inadequate supply of quality day care for their children, it does not make financial sense to work (Crittenden 2001). Currently, middle-income families receive tax subsidies and low-income families can receive subsidized child care. The availability of high quality day care for poor women is consistently limited, however. In many states, only about 15 percent of women who qualify for these benefits actually receive any help with day care costs. This is disquieting given evidence that the cost of day care limits women's employment, particularly for new mothers (Michalopoulos and Robins 2002). Studies show that women in western European countries that have universal day care systems, such as Sweden, have very high labor force participation rates, a significantly smaller gendered wage gap, and lower poverty rates among women at all ages (Crittenden 2001; Gornick, Meyers, and Ross 1997).

Though few in the United States favor universal day care, many support the expansion of public preschools to younger aged children (Quadagno 1994; Michel 1999). Providing accessible and affordable child care is the most important strategy for improving women's income security, and one successful strategy for meeting this goal has been to implement, largely at the state level, universal preschool programs. Currently, Georgia offers a universal Pre-K program. Every four-year-old may attend regardless of income. The programs must run six and a half hours a day, five days a week, for the 180-day school year. New York State is slated to have a similar universal Pre-K system, but funding has been a problem and the program has not yet been broadly implemented. Other states and communities have developed universal Pre-K programs based on progressive funding and sliding scale fees. One such plan, which covers four-year-olds, requires those earning $15,000 a year to pay $205 a year in additional taxes and those earning more than $87,500 a year to pay $800. In all, about forty-two states invest in some form of state Pre-K initiatives, but three-quarters of that spending is concentrated in ten states: California, Florida, Georgia, Illinois, Massachusetts, Michigan, New Jersey, New York, Ohio, and Texas (National Institute for Early Education Research 2005). In these states, resources are generally targeted toward the poorest children.

Advocates are quick to point out that Pre-K is cost effective for children. For example, the RAND Corporation, using an experimental design, showed that the investment of $12,000 per preschool student provided benefits of $25,000 over twenty years. They included probability of grade retention, high school graduation, need for special education, arrest rates, employment rates, and welfare use and earnings in their measures (Scrivner and Wolfe 2003). Pre-K may be cost effective for parents as well in that it would provide a form of high-quality, low-cost day care that frees parents to work. In other words, universal Pre-K would in the long run reduce old age inequality by shoring up the incomes of women, particularly lower-income single mothers. How much would it cost to implement a program like Georgia's across the entire country? One estimate is that it would cost between $40 and $50 billion dollars annually if we expanded the program to cover three- and four-year-olds (Century Foundation 2000).

Paid Family Leave

Another family-friendly policy missing from the U.S. welfare state that also has great potential for reducing inequality throughout the life course is paid family leave. Paid workers often need time from work to have a baby, care for a child, respond to an acute or chronic health problem for a family member, or care for a frail or dying older relative. Given that the United States has no paid universal leave, many women stop or limit paid work when the demands of unpaid care work mount. Some limited family leave policies can be found at the state level. Five states, including New York, New Jersey, Hawaii, California, and Rhode Island, currently provide paid leave through their disability programs for an average of about six weeks. In these cases, disability is defined as being pregnant. It appears that take-up rates are fairly good. One study found that almost all women earning less than $20,000 a year in Rhode Island took six weeks of maternity leave, whereas in states without this leave 20 percent of similar women took less than six weeks (Bond et al. 1991). California was the first state to pass a paid family leave law, which went into effect in 2004. Under this program, workers are eligible for six weeks to care for a seriously ill family member or a newborn at a rate of 55 percent of their wages up to $728 per week. Because responsibility for funding is spread across all workers, the cost of this program is quite low. The California family leave policy is paid for by a .08 percent tax on the first $68,829 that workers earn with a maximum of $55 a year (Appelbaum and Milkman 2004). Proposals to expand unemployment insurance to cover parental leave estimate that costs would range from $11 to $28 per worker, per year (Institute for Women's Policy Research 2000).

At the national level, a long-standing effort by some women's groups to implement paid family leave was nipped in the bud when Bill Clinton signed the 1993 Unpaid Family Leave Act. This legislation implemented a twelve-week family leave policy, but it was unpaid and applied only to larger companies. Studies show that few women are actually able to take advantage of it, mainly because they cannot afford to take unpaid leaves (Gerstel and McGonagle 1999; Waldfogel 2001). The act covers only about 60 percent of private sector workers and just under 50 percent were both covered and eligible (Waldfogel 2001). Most studies show it had little impact on increasing the number of individuals taking leaves (Han and Waldfogel 2003; Ruhm 1997). Moreover, it is clearly not linked to any improvements in women's labor force participation or increase in wages. By comparison, as shown in table 7.1, many industrialized countries provide up to a year of paid leave for parents. Because this leave was often predominantly used only by women, some countries require fathers take at least part of the leave, or parents lose some of it, to help reduce gender disparities in responsibility for unpaid care work (Gornick and Meyers 2003).[1]

In the absence of federal or state benefits, many women rely on corporate benefits for paid family leaves. The availability of these benefits is unregulated, however, and the differences among women with regard to who has access to paid family leave are enormous. Figure 7.5 shows trends in paid parental leave by educational attainment (Han and Waldfogel 2003). In the early 1960s, women with different educational attainment had virtually equal, albeit low, probabilities of receiving paid leave after the birth of a first child, just under 20 percent. By the 1990s, differences in who had access to such leave were dramatic. Where more than 60 percent of women with a college degree had paid leave, fewer than 20 percent

Table 7.1   **Paid Family Leave Policies in Industrialized Countries**

	Paid Maternity Leave	Paid and Unpaid Parental Leave
Denmark	18 Weeks (100%)	Paid 28 weeks (60%)
Finland	18 weeks (66%)	Paid 28 weeks (66%)
Norway	52 weeks (80%) or 42 weeks (100%)	
Sweden	15 months (80%)	
Belgium	16 weeks (76–82%)	Paid 3 months FT or 6 months PT (Low Flat Rate)
France	16 weeks (100%)	Unpaid for 3 years
Germany	14 weeks (100%)	3 years (Low Flat Rate)
Italy	5 months (80%)	43 weeks (30%)
Luxembourg	16 weeks (100%)	26 weeks (Low Flat Rate)
Netherlands	16 weeks (100%)	Unpaid for 26 weeks
Australia	No National Policy	52 weeks of Unpaid Leave
Canada	15 weeks (55%—up to $282 a week)	35 weeks (55%—up to $282 week)
United Kingdom	18 weeks at flat rate/ 6 weeks (90%)	13 weeks unpaid
United States	None	12 weeks unpaid

Sources: Authors' compilations; Gornick and Meyers 2003.

of women without high school degrees and fewer than 30 percent of women with them had paid leave through their employer. These statistics provide yet another example of how the provision of benefits, in this case paid parental leave, though the private market tends to increase, rather than decrease, inequality.

Beyond paid parental leaves, European nations also have more rigid controls over how much and what times individuals can work, which leaves more space for family life (Bosch, Dawkins, and Michon 1994). By contrast, workplaces in the United States are often incompatible with family life, prompting many women to choose between their work and their children rather than try to juggle both (Clarkberg and Moen 2001; Schor 1991). Women with less education who are employed in the service sector, which is increasingly open twenty-four hours and seven days a week, are often expected to work during hours in which no day care centers are open. Further, the U.S. tradition of just two weeks of paid vacation time leaves little flexibility for sick children, trips to the dentist, or even school field trips. Many low-income women lack any paid leave whatsoever, thus they talk about losing jobs because of their own child's illness (Edin and Lein 1997). As children get older, it often becomes even more difficult for parents to mesh the logistics of the children's assorted sports practices, games, and recitals with their own work schedules. In

Figure 7.5   Women Receiving Paid Leave for First Birth

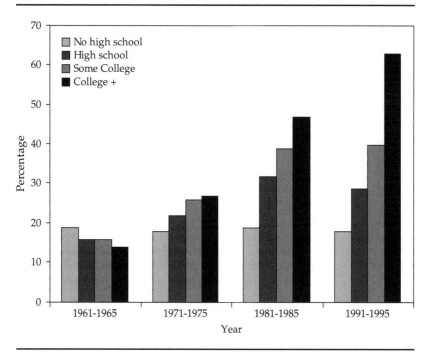

Source: Han and Waldfogel 2003.

contrast, Europeans average more than a month of vacation time and work 15 percent fewer hours per year, making it easier for parents to meet the dual demands of work and family (Rubery, Smith, and Fagan 1998).

Other Early Life Course Programs

The United States already has some programs in place for younger people and their families, but virtually all are means-tested rather than universal. As is traditionally the case, means-tested programs lack the popularity to guarantee adequate funding for generous benefits and are vulnerable to budget cuts during periods with economic downturns or conservative fiscal leadership (Korpi and Palme 1998). In this section, we briefly review the strengths and weaknesses of the three main programs already in place for younger families: EITC, TANF, and Medicaid. Although supporters of family-friendly policies clearly favor the universal reforms just discussed, here we attend to more modest suggestions for reforms that could make the existing means-tested programs more family friendly.

Of all the means-tested programs, EITC is certainly the most successful at reducing inequality by redistributing resources to those with lower earnings. The program provides a lump sum payment, in the form of a tax rebate, for low-income workers. In the past ten years, EITC benefits have risen significantly. In 1993, they lifted 11 percent of working single mothers above the poverty line, and by 1999, 27 percent (Porter and Dupree 2001). The EITC has some limitations, however. First, because it is a lump sum payment, women do not use it to meet daily needs, but instead spend it on larger purchases, such as a car or a deposit on an apartment (Smeeding et al. 2000). Second, the EITC may suffer the same fate of other means-tested policies, which are constantly undermined by attacks questioning whether recipients deserve benefits. Because the main critique of welfare beneficiaries throughout the 1980s and 1990s was that they were not employed, many thought the EITC, which requires recipients to work, was shielded from the deserving question. For a while, this seemed to be true because Congress funneled increasing sums of money to the program. The tide now may have turned. A January 20, 2003, editorial in the *Wall Street Journal* argued that EITC recipients are "lucky duckies." The tax system is in fact too progressive, creating "two different tax-paying classes: those who pay a lot and those who pay very little" ("Lucky Duckies Again: Look at Who Won't Pay Taxes under Bush's Plan," http://www.opinionjournal.com/editorial/feature.html?id=110002938).

These kinds of attacks often drive benefit and eligibility restrictions. Currently, the EITC is relatively easy to apply for and requires no special visit to the welfare office or interaction with case workers, which contributes to its unusually high participation rate. Close to 80 percent of those eligible receive benefits, versus nearly half that for other means-tested policies, such as Medicaid and TANF (Smeeding et al. 2000). There have been rumblings among Republicans in Congress about the ease of the eligibility process, however. Ernest J. Istook, Jr. (R-Okla.), chairman of the House Appropriations Committee subcommittee on transportation, Treasury, and independent agencies, argued that the EITC eligibility process should more closely resemble that for food stamps where, as reporter Allen Crenshaw put it in a 2003 *Washington Post* article, "a certain amount of bureaucracy" is involved ("Cracktown on Tax Credit Put Off to Allow Comment," May 23, p. E01). The IRS is now targeting EITC recipients for audits after concerns that some recipients do not actually meet eligibility standards.

The EITC is an effective mechanism for reducing inequality at earlier stages in the life course with promising effects as these cohorts reach old age. This efficacy, though, depends on keeping the program streamlined, maximizing take up, and avoiding stigmatizing or punitive approaches to gatekeeping. To maintain it, the program will have to sustain enough political support and leverage to ensure adequate funding even during periods of fiscal constraint.

Although EITC provides modest support to working women, there is little in the U.S. welfare state to support women who provide care for children, the aged, and those with chronic illnesses. The only economic support for women who need time out of the labor force to meet family obligations is TANF. In 1996, the means-tested Aid to Families with Dependent Children (AFDC), which guaranteed poor single mothers a modest income so they could stay at home and raise their children or get back on their feet after a marriage dissolved, was replaced by TANF as part of the Personal Responsibility and Work Opportunity Reconciliation Act (Mink 1998). TANF limits eligibility for benefits to a maximum of three years per episode and five years per lifetime. Increasingly, women receiving TANF benefits are required to work and are not permitted to further their education. Thus, many women, particularly those with chronically ill family members who need intensive care, have lost an important safety net (Oliker 2000).

Other industrialized countries provide much more generous supplements to those who care for older people, children, and the chronically ill. In Germany, Japan, Sweden, and many other countries with universal long-term care policies, those caring for chronically ill family members receive payments for their work (Karlsson et al. 2004). Moreover, in the Scandinavian countries, single parents need not worry about delinquent child support payments. The state actually pays women their child support awards and then in turn collects this money from the noncustodial parent (Gornick and Meyers 2003). Indeed, most western European citizens receive annual subsidies for raising their children. Finally, Scandinavian countries have a broad array of universal benefits, including national health insurance, that insure against a host of potential knocks to people's financial well-being by guaranteeing all citizens a base level of protection. Given that we provide none of these benefits to women juggling work and family, and that we are thus far unwilling to provide either universal paid parental leave or universal day care, it is imperative that we develop better provisions for poor women who need some time out of the work force to attend to family members.

Medicaid is another important safety net for poor younger women and children because it provides free and comprehensive health coverage. Throughout the book, we have emphasized Medicaid for people age sixty-five and older. Here we want to highlight the way Medicaid affects poor women and children. Many poor and pregnant women, as well as lower-income children, rely on Medicaid for their access to health care. Women are twice as likely as men to be covered by Medicaid, a means-tested public health insurance program for the poor (Mills and Bhandari 2003). Among women, blacks and Hispanics are significantly more likely than whites to be covered by it. The program reimburses physicians at such low levels that many beneficiaries have tremendous difficulty actually finding physicians willing to treat them. Moreover, many who need Medicaid do not receive it because of strict eligibility guidelines and processes (Ellwood 1999). Throughout the 1980s and 1990s, the federal government has shifted much of the costs of Medicaid to states. Then, as many state economies weakened and tax revenues declined, states responded by making cuts to Medicaid. Means-tested programs like Medicaid are inherently unstable because they are so vulnerable to budget cuts. The program lacks a powerful constituency, making it an easy place to target benefit cuts during budget crises (Korpi and Palme 1998). Given that it is unlikely that the United States will move toward a national health insurance plan, it will be imperative that the federal government and states ensure that Medicaid coverage for poor families is not on the chopping block. Moreover, access to health care for poor Americans on Medicaid would be greatly improved by increasing reimbursements to health care providers so that they have less incentive to discriminate against patients based on payment source.

The extent to which children have access to health insurance is an issue for parents, more often mothers, because they are responsible for their children's health care costs. In the late 1990s, the federal government instituted SCHIP, which expanded coverage to children just above the poverty level and in a few states to their parents (Kaiser Family Foundation 2000). The results of this expansion have generally been positive (Dubay, Hill, and Kenney 2002; Hill and Lutzky 2003). The percentage of uninsured near-poor children dropped from 23.3 percent to 14.7 percent from 1996 to 2003 (Cohen, Hao, and Coriaty-Nelson 2004; Dubay, Hill, and Kenney 2002). It is difficult to gauge, however, how much of this drop is attributable to the economy and how much to SCHIP. The percentage of poor children has dropped from about 22 percent to 15.4 percent over the same period (Cohen, Hao, and Coriaty-Nelson 2004). The program had a mixed impact on the ease of accessing coverage and care. Many states simplified eligibility processes for Medicaid by reducing paperwork and even eliminating asset tests to bring the program in line with SCHIP (Hill and Lutzky 2003). Other states, however, have more difficult eligibility processes for Medicaid than for SCHIP (Hill and Lutzky 2003). In these states, children just below the poverty line have had more difficulty accessing public health insurance than those just above it. The extent to which SCHIP will be a successful expansion of public insurance is yet to be determined. With the economic downturn in the early twenty-first century, SCHIP, like Medicaid, is facing program retrenchment in light of budget crises in state and local governments (Dubay, Hill, and Kenney 2002).

Although TANF and Medicaid provide important safety nets for many, we find that these programs, which are politically unpopular and at risk of budgetary cuts, do too little to help families juggle paid and unpaid work and prepare for the economic and health hardships associated with old age. In the end, a limited and mainly poverty-based welfare state means that many women go throughout most of their lives with very limited public policy supports to soften the blows associated with labor force discrimination and disproportionate responsibility for unpaid care work for children, the aged, and the chronically ill. The shortfalls in our public policies hit hardest those women with the fewest resources. Wealthier women are more likely to be able to afford the cost of high-quality child or parent care and to hold jobs that guarantee paid leave and extensive health insurance coverage, whereas most lower-income women do without these important supports. Ultimately, the targeted support programs currently in place for the early- and mid-life course families lack the political and economic backing necessary to provide substantial and meaningful support to many lower-income women. The story is dramatically different in western European countries that provide paid leave and child care for all women, regardless of income or marital status. It is in those countries that lower-income women actually fare best. Economic disadvantages among women and children is substantially lower in these countries. In the United States these disadvantages only build as women age. Social Security and Medicare help soften the consequences of a lifetime of gender, race, and class inequality, but they cannot undo a lifetime of damage resulting from inadequate policy supports.

Discussion

Supporters of family-friendly policies call for minor tinkering with Social Security to make it more responsive to changing family structures, and major tinkering with Medicare to make it more comprehensive and less costly. Ultimately, family-friendly policies, including national health insurance, universal child care, and paid family leave, do a better job than market-friendly policies of reducing inequality in old age. These are effective welfare programs aimed at reducing gender, race, class, and marital status inequality throughout the life course and, particularly, in old age.

Some, perhaps many, might dismiss these proposals as economically infeasible. We find, however, that many of the reforms are either budget neutral or in fact cost saving. Others may dismiss the proposals as politically infeasible (Myles and Quadagno 2000; Gilbert 2002; Hacker 2002). Polls showing that people want the government to do more, not less, for older Americans suggest otherwise (AARP 2005; Pew Research Center 2005; Public Agenda 2005; Quadagno 2005; Street and Sittig Cossman 2006). With respect to health care, the issue is to install a national health insurance program for all ages. It has been attempted many times in our history. It is becoming increasingly clear that individuals, big business, and health care providers are weary of excessive costs and excessive red tape. Time and time again, however, efforts to implement national health insurance are blocked by those who gain significantly under the current system and are most likely to lose if we move to a single-payer source (Quadagno 2005). With respect to Social Security, the most equitable program is already installed. As a universal program, it has been successful at reducing poverty in old age and, despite repeated attacks, remains popular. The issue here is to preserve it and to tweak it, slightly, to make it more responsive to sociodemographic changes, particularly among women.

It seems clear that lack of support for, or progress on, a family-friendly reform agenda is not due to high cost or lack of public support. Rather, the problem is lack of leadership to take on the corporate interests that gain from privatization, including investment firms, insurance companies, and pharmaceuticals. Promoters of market-friendly welfare state policies have taken the time and the money to develop and promote and implement pro-market solutions. Discussions of privatization, which were unthinkable in the 1980s, had become commonplace by 2005. Market-friendly forces have created and pumped funds into conservative think tanks that lay out policy agendas and then figure out how to sell them. By contrast, liberals have long dismissed both new ideas and old ideas that could take on a new currency based on the premise that they are politically infeasible. They shy away from ever laying out a real reform agenda. There are precious few liberal think tanks, and the ones that we have, such as the Center for Budget and Policy Priorities, mainly focus on middle-of-the-road solutions or critiques of the conservative agenda. If family-friendly policies are to make any serious inroads, supporters need to develop a liberal counterpart to the Cato or American Enterprise Institute.

Among supporters of family-friendly policies, feminist organizations do the best job of focusing on reforms that reduce gender, race, and class inequality. Historically, they have not placed enough importance on universal eligibility at older ages. For example, over the years, feminist organizations have spent millions attacking proposals that support marriage through TANF, but have failed to challenge marriage-based eligibility through Social Security (National Council of Women's Organizations 1999; Pollack 2003). This is odd given that the economic consequences of the latter eclipse those of the former (Social Security Administration 2006). In fact, the National Council of Women's Organization's Task Force on Women and Social Security supports more generous widow benefits for women, even though the only way to access those benefits is through marriage (National Council of Women's Organizations 1999). Recently, however, activists at the Institute for Women's Policy Research and elsewhere have begun to argue against benefits based on marital status at any age. They now prioritize universal and redistributive benefits at all ages.

Supporters of family-friendly policies favor universal, redistributive, and federal, rather than targeted or privatized, welfare programs. They do so while taking cost into account. Cost containment is imperative, but it must be accomplished in ways that reduce rather than increase inequality in old age. Many reform policies aim to reduce poverty through means-tested programs but there is little evidence that these programs work to reduce poverty, and substantial evidence that they increase inequality. Other reform policies aim to provide welfare through privatization and there is a great deal of evidence they neither reduce inequality nor increase savings. Moreover, they take public discussions and decisions out of the public arena. They also mimic inequalities generated in the market along gender, class, race, and marital status lines.

For decades, the market has been widely regarded as one of the main sources of inequality in the United States. To now regard it as one of the main solutions is untenable. Only family-friendly public, universal, redistributive welfare policies adequately place the social welfare of individuals over the welfare of the private market. Given that every market system in the world has high levels of inequality, strong government interventions are needed to effectively soften the blows of a capitalist system and reduce inequality linked to gender, race, class, and marital status. The question is one of will: Do we want to entrench inequality or equality?

= Endnotes =

Chapter 1

1. The concept of market friendly policies has been widely used in discussions of World Bank policies in dealing with debtor nations, but has not been adopted by U.S. and European social welfare state scholars. In restructuring debts, the World Bank often requires that debtor nations make welfare policies more market friendly by cutting welfare expenditures, deregulating, privatizing social provision, and shifting costs and responsibilities back to individuals and their families (see, for example, Rogoff 2003). The concept of family-friendly policies has been widely used in discussions of corporate policies aimed at helping families juggle paid and unpaid responsibilities, but has not been adopted by U.S. and European social welfare state scholars. In trying to attract and retain workers with families, many companies provide such options as paid leaves, flex time, job sharing, child-care facilities, and other arrangements aimed at helping families manage competing responsibilities for work and children (see, for example, Nielsen, Simonsen, and Verner 2006).

2. In using the term family friendly, we are not in any way promoting a particular form of family. Families come in many shapes and sizes and our intent here is to differentiate policies that help support people—whether single, married, cohabiting, gay, straight, with child, childless, and so on— from policies that help support the market.

3. For example, European pension designs have long included substantial minimum income guarantees, which the United States does not. It has only been in recent years that European pensions have included as many years as the United States does (thirty-five years) in calculating old-age pension benefits.

Chapter 7

1. To be clear, we are not favoring paid care leaves that are somewhat common now in Western Europe. Kimberly Morgan and Kathrin Zippel's (2003) evaluation of these two- to three-year leaves paid at relative low and flat rates reveals that they tend to reinforce a traditional gendered division of labor, entrench women in lower paid jobs, and increase inequality between women.

References

Aaron, Henry J., and Robert D. Reischauer. 1995. "The Medicare Reform Debate: What Is the Next Step?" *Health Affairs* 14(4): 8–30. http://content.healthaffairs.org/contents-by-date.0.shtml.

———. 1998a. " 'Rethinking Medicare Reform' Needs Rethinking." *Health Affairs* 17(1): 69–71.

———. 1998b. *Countdown to Reform: The Great Social Security Debate.* New York: Century Foundation Press.

AARP. 2005. *Public Attitudes Toward Social Security and Private Accounts.* Washington: AARP Knowledge Management.

Abel, Emily K., and Margaret K. Nelson, editors. 1990. *Circles of Care: Work and Identity in Women's Lives.* Albany, N.Y.: State University of New York Press.

Abramovitz, Mimi. 1988. *Regulating the Lives of Women: Social Welfare Policy from Colonial Times to the Present.* Boston, Mass.: South End Press.

Acemoglu, Daron, and Joshua D. Angrist. 2001. "Consequences of Employment Protection? The Case of the Americans with Disabilities Act." *The Journal of Political Economy* 109(5): 915–57.

Acker, Joan. 1988. "Class, Gender, and the Relations of Distribution." *Signs* 13(3): 473–97.

———. 1990. "Hierarchies, Jobs, Bodies: A Theory of Gendered Organizations." *Gender and Society* 4(2): 139–58.

———. 2006. *Class Questions: Feminist Answers.* Lanham, Md.: Rowman & Littlefield.

Adam, Emma K. 1999. "The Effects of Relationship Style, Hours of Paid Work and Division of Child-Rearing Labor on Emotional and Physiological Stress in Working Mothers." Unpublished manuscript.

Alecxih, Lisa Maria B., Steven Lutzky, Purvi Sevak, and Gary Claxton. 1997. *Key Issues Affecting Access to Medigap Insurance.* New York: Commonwealth Fund.

Allen, Susan M. 1994. "Gender Differences in Spousal Caregiving and Unmet Need for Care." *Journals of Gerontology* 49(4): S187–95.

Alliance for Board Diversity. 2005. *Women and Minorities on Fortune 100 Boards.* New York: Catalyst, The Prout Group, The Executive Leadership Council, and the Hispanic Association on Corporate Responsibility.

Anderson, Bridget. 2000. *Doing the Dirty Work? The Global Politics of Domestic Labour.* London: Zed Books.

Anderson, Deborah, Melissa Binder, and Kate Krause. 2002. "Women, Children, and the Labor Market—The Motherhood Wage Penalty: Which Mothers Pay It and Why?" *American Economic Review* 92(2): 354–8.

Anderson, Gerard, Jeremy Hurst, Peter Sotir Hussey, and Melissa Jee-Hughes. 2000. "Health Spending and Outcomes: Trends in OECD Countries, 1960–1998." *Health Affairs* 19(3): 150–7.

Angel, Ronald, and Jacqueline Lowe Angel. 1997. *Who Will Care for Us? Aging and Long–Term Care in Multicultural America*. New York: New York University Press.

Appelbaum, Eileen, and Ruth Milkman. 2004. "Paid Family Leave in California: New Research Findings." *The State of California Labor* 4(November): 45–67. http://repositories.cdlib.org/ile/scl2004/02/.

Arendell, Terry, editor. 1997. *Contemporary Parenting: Challenges and Issues*. Vol. 9 of *Understanding Families*. Thousand Oaks, Calif.: Sage Publications.

Arno, Peter S., Carol Levine, and Margaret M. Memmott. 1999. "The Economic Value of Informal Caregiving." *Health Affairs* 18(2): 182–8.

Aura, Saku. 2001. "Does the Balance of Power Within a Family Matter? The Case of the Retirement Equity Act." *IGIER* Working Paper 202. Milano, Italy: Innocenzo Gasparini Institute for Economic Research, Università Bocconi.

Avellar, Sarah, and Pamela J. Smock. 2006. "Has the Price of Motherhood Declined Over Time? A Cross-Cohort Comparison of the Motherhood Wage Penalty." *Journal of Marriage and the Family* 65(3): 597–607.

Baca Zinn, Maxine, and Bonnie Thornton Dill. 2005. "What Is Multiracial Feminism?" In *Gender Inequality: Feminist Theories and Politics*, 3rd ed., edited by Judith Lorber. Los Angeles, Calif.: Roxbury Publishing.

Bajtelsmit, Vickie L., and Nancy A. Jianakoplos. 2000. "Women and Pensions: A Decade of Progress?" *EBRI* Issue Brief no. 227. Washington: Employee Benefit Research Institute.

Baker, Dean, and Mark Weisbrot. 1999. *Social Security: The Phony Crisis*. Chicago, Ill.: University of Chicago Press.

Barker, Judith C. 2002. "Neighbors, Friends, and Other Nonkin Caregivers of Community–Living Dependent Elders." *Journals of Gerontology Series B–Psychological Sciences and Social Sciences* 57(3): S158–67.

Barlett, Donald L., and James B. Steele. 1992. *America: What Went Wrong?* Kansas City, Mo.: Andrews and McMeel.

———. 2006. *Critical Condition: How Health Care in America Became Big Business—and Bad Medicine*. New York: Broadway Books.

Baumgarten, Mona, R. N. Battista, C. Infante-Rivard, J. A. Hanley, R. Becker, and S. Gauthier. 1992. "The Psychological and Physical Health of Family Members Caring for an Elderly Person with Dementia." *Journal of Clinical Epidemiology* 45(1): 61–70.

Becker, Gary S. 1981. *A Treatise on the Family*. Cambridge, Mass.: Harvard University Press.

———. 1985. "Human Capital, Effort, and the Sexual Division of Labor." *Journal of Labor Economics* 3(1): S33–58.

———. 2005. "A Political Case for Social Security Reform." *Wall Street Journal*, February 15, 2005, p. A-18.

Bengston, Vern L., Tonya M. Parrott, and Elisabeth O. Burgess. 1996. "Progress and Pitfalls in Gerontological Theorizing." *Gerontologist* 36(6): 768–72.

Bergmann, Barbara. 1982. "The Housewife and Social Security Reform: A Feminist Perspective." In *A Challenge to Social Security: The Changing Roles of Women and Men in American Society,* edited by Richard V. Burkhauser and Karen C. Holden. New York: Academic Press.

Bianchi, Suzanne M., Melissa A. Milkie, and Liana C. Sayer. 2000. "Is Anyone Doing the Housework? Trends in the Gender Division of Household Labor." *Social Forces* 79(1): 191–228.

Bianchi, Suzanne M., John P. Robinson, and Melissa A. Milkie. 2006. *Changing Rhythms of American Family Life.* New York: Russell Sage Foundation.

Bianchi, Suzanne M., Lekha Subaiya, and Joan R. Kahn. 1999. "The Gender Gap in the Economic Well-Being of Nonresident Fathers and Custodial Mothers." *Demography* 36(2): 195–203.

Bielby, William T., and James N. Baron. 1986. "Men and Women at Work: Sex Segregation and Statistical Discrimination." *American Journal of Sociology* 91(4): 759–99.

Biles, Brian, Lauren Hersch Nicholas, and Barbara S. Cooper. 2004. "The Cost of Privatization: Extra Payments to Medicare Advantage Plans." Issue Brief 750. Washington: Commonwealth Fund. http://www.cmwf.org/usr_doc/750_Biles_costofprivatization_update_ib.pdf.

Biles, Brian, Lauren Hersch Nicholas, and Stuart Guterman. 2006. "Medicare Beneficiary Out-of-Pocket Costs: Are Medicare Advantage Plans a Better Deal?" Issue Brief 927. New York: The Commonwealth Fund. http://www.cmwf.org/usr_doc/927_Biles_MedicarebeneOOPcosts_MA_ib.pdf.

Binney, Elizabeth A., and Carroll L. Estes. 1988. "The Retreat of the State and Its Transfer of Responsibility: The Intergenerational War." *International Journal of Health Services* 18(1): 83–96.

Bird, Chloe E. 1999. "Gender, Household Labor, and Psychological Distress: The Impact of the Amount and Division of Housework." *Journal of Health and Social Behavior* 40(1): 32–45.

Black, Dan, Amelia Haviland, Seth Sanders, and Lowell Taylor. 2004. "Gender Wage Disparities Among the Highly Educated." Presented at the Microeconomics Workshop on Labor and Population at Yale University. New Haven, Conn., May 14, 2004.

Black, Sir Douglas, J. N. Morris, Cyril Smith, Peter Townsend, Stuart Blume, A. J. Forsdick, and Nicky Hart. 1982. *Inequalities in Health: The Black Report.* New York: Penguin Books.

Blair-Loy, Mary, and Amy S. Wharton. 2004. "Organizational Commitment and Constraints on Work-Family Policy Use: Corporate Flexibility Policies in a Global Firm." *Sociological Perspectives* 47(3): 243–67.

Blau, Francine D., and John W. Graham. 1990. "Black-White Differences in Wealth and Asset Composition." *Quarterly Journal of Economics* 105(2): 321–39.

Blau, Francine D., and Lawrence M. Kahn. 1997. "Swimming Upstream: Trends in the Gender Wage Differential in the 1980s." *Journal of Labor Economics* 15(1): 1–42.

Blau, Francine D., Mary C. Brinton, and David B. Grusky. 2006. *The Declining Significance of Gender?* New York: Russell Sage Foundation.

Blau, Francine D., Patricia Simpson, and Deborah Anderson. 1998. "Continuing Progress? Trends in Occupational Segregation in the United States over the 1970's and 1980's." *NBER* Working Paper 6716. Cambridge, Mass.: National Bureau of Economics Research.

Block, Fred L. 1987. *The Mean Season: The Attack on the Welfare State.* New York: Pantheon Books.

Boccuti, Cristina, and Marilyn Moon. 2003. "Comparing Medicare and Private Insurers: Growth Rates in Spending over Three Decades." *Health Affairs* 22(2): 230–7.

Bond, James T., Ellen Galinsky, M. Lord, G. L. Staines, and K. R. Brown. 1991. *Beyond the Parental Leave Debate: The Impact of Laws in Four States.* New York: Families and Work Institute.

Bosch, Gerhard, Peter Dawkins, and François Michon. 1994. *Times Are Changing: Working Time in 14 Industrialised Countries.* Geneva: International Institute for Labour Studies.

Bowler, Mary. 1999. "Women's Earnings: An Overview." *Monthly Labor Review* 122(12): 13–21.

Brenner, Johanna. 1987. "Feminist Political Discourses: Radical vs. Liberal Approaches to the Feminization of Poverty and Comparable Worth." *Gender and Society* 1(4): 447–65.

Brines, Julie. 1994. "Economic Dependency, Gender, and the Division of Labor at Home." *American Journal of Sociology* 100(3): 652–88.

Britt, Russ. 2004. "Insurers Get Bigger Health Dollar Cut: Profits Up, Premiums Up, But Medical Spending Lags." *CBS Market Watch.com,* October 15, 2004. http://www.marketwatch.com/News/Story/Story.aspx?guid=%7BFB8AFAC9-E146-4B00-9022-EFB4D38D6E7B%7D.

Brody, Elaine M. 1990. *Women in the Middle: Their Parent-Care Years.* New York: Springer Publishing.

———. 2004. *Women in the Middle: Their Parent Care Years,* 2nd ed. New York: Springer Publishing.

Brown-Waite, Ginny. 2005. "Women and Social Security: Unfair, Biased and Outdated." http://brown-waite.house.gov/News/DocumentPrint.aspx?DocumentID=35998.

Browne, Irene, and Joya Misra. 2003. "The Intersection of Gender and Race in the Labor Market." *Annual Review of Sociology* 29: 487–513.

Brubaker, E., and T. H. Brubaker. 1993. "Caring for Adult Children with Developmental Disabilities." In *Older Adults with Developmental Disabilities: Optimizing Choice and Change,* edited by Evelyn Sutton. Baltimore, Md.: Paul H. Brookes Publishing.

Budig, Michelle J., and Paula England. 2001. "The Wage Penalty for Motherhood." *American Sociological Review* 66(2): 204–25.

Bullard, Robert D. 1993. *Confronting Environmental Racism: Voices from the Grassroots.* Boston, Mass.: South End Press.

———. 1994. *Unequal Protection: Environmental Justice and Communities of Color.* San Francisco, Calif.: Sierra Club Books.

Burkhauser, Richard V., and Karen C. Holden, eds. 1982. *A Challenge to Social Security: The Changing Roles of Women and Men in American Society.* New York: Academic Press.

Burkhauser, Richard V., and Timothy M. Smeeding. 1994. "Social Security Reform: A Budget Neutral Approach to Reducing Older Women's Disproportionate Risk of Poverty." Center for Policy Research Policy Brief No. 2. Syracuse, N.Y.: Syracuse University.

Burkhauser, Richard V., Greg J. Duncan, Richard Hauser, and Roland Berntsen. 1991. "Wife or Frau, Women Do Worse: A Comparison of Men and Women in the United States and Germany after Marital Dissolution." *Demography* 28(3): 353–60.

Burkins, Glenn. 1998. "CoreStates Will Pay Nearly 1.5 Million to Its Minority and Female Managers." *Charlotte (N.C.) Observer*, April 20, 1998: 1.

Butrica, Barbara A., and Howard Iams. 2000. "Divorced Women at Retirement: Projections of Economic Well-being in the Near Future." *Social Security Bulletin* 63(3): 3–12.

Calasanti, Toni M., and Kathleen F. Slevin. 2001. *Gender, Social Inequalities, and Aging*. Walnut Creek, Calif.: AltaMira Press.

Cancian, Francesca M., and Stacey J. Oliker. 2000. *Caring and Gender*. Thousand Oaks, Calif.: Pine Forge Press.

Cancian, Maria., and Dan R. Meyer. 2004. "Fathers of Children Receiving Welfare: Can They Provide More Child Support?" *Social Service Review* 78(2): 179–206.

Cantor, Marjorie H. 1989. "Social Care: Family and Community Support Systems." *The Annals of the American Academy of Political and Social Science* 503: 99–112.

Carlson, Marcia J. 2006. "Family Structure, Father Involvement, and Adolescent Behavioral Outcomes." *Journal of Marriage and the Family* 68(1): 137–54.

Case, Anne, Darren Lubotsky, and Christina Paxson. 2002. "Economic Status and Health in Childhood: The Origins of the Gradient." *American Economic Review* 92(5): 1308–34.

Castro, Ida L. 1998. *Equal Pay: A Thirty–Five Year Perspective*. Washington: U.S. Department of Labor, Women's Bureau.

Catalyst. 1999. *Women of Color in Corporate Management: Opportunities and Barriers.* New York: Catalyst.

———. 2002. *2002 Catalyst Census of Women Corporate Officers and Top Earners in the Fortune 500*. New York: Catalyst.

———. 2006. " 'Blending In' vs. 'Sticking Together': Women of Color Using Differing Strategies for Informal Networking." Press Release, May 31, 2006. New York: Catalyst. http://www.catalystwomen.org/pressroom/press_releases/5_31_06%20-%20WoC%20Networks.pdf.

Centers for Medicare and Medicaid Services. 2005a. "Your Medicare Coverage." Washington: U.S. Department of Health and Human Services. September 16, 2005. http://www.medicare.gov/Coverage/Home.asp.

———. 2005b. "Medicare Enrollment, 1966–2003." Baltimore, Md.: U.S. Department of Health and Human Services. September 16, 2005. http://www.cms.hhs.gov/MedicareEnRpts.

Century Foundation. 1998. *The Basics: Social Security Reform*. New York: The Century Foundation.

———. 2000. "Universal Preschool." New Ideas for a New Century. Idea Brief No. 5. New York: Century Foundation. http://www.tcf.org/Publications/Education/UniversalPreschool.pdf.

Chang, Cyril F., and Shelley I. White-Means. 1991. "The Men Who Care: An Analysis of Male Primary Caregivers Who Care for Frail Elderly at Home." *Journal of Applied Gerontology* 10(3): 343–58.

Charles, Kerwin Kofi, and Erik Hurst. 2002. "The Transition to Home Ownership and the Black–White Wealth Gap." *Review of Economics and Statistics* 84(2): 281–97.

Choudhury, Sharmila, and Michael V. Leonesio. 1997. "Life-Cycle Aspects of Poverty Among Older Women." *Social Security Bulletin* 60(2): 17–36.

Clarkberg, Marin, and Phyllis Moen. 2001. "Understanding the Time-Squeeze: Married Couples' Preferred and Actual Work-Hour Strategies." *The American Behavioral Scientist* 44(7): 1115–36.

Cockburn, Iain M. 2004. "The Changing Structure of the Pharmaceutical Industry." *Health Affairs* 23(1): 10–22.

Cohen, Robin A., Cathy Hao, and Zakia Coriaty-Nelson. 2004. "Health Insurance Coverage: Estimates from the National Health Interview Survey, 2003." Atlanta, Ga.: Centers for Disease Control. September 2004. http://www.cdc. gov/nchs/data/nhis/earlyrelease/insur200409.pdf.

Cokkinides, Vilme E., and Ann L. Coker. 1998. "Experiencing Physical Violence During Pregnancy: Prevalence and Correlates." *Family and Community Health* 20(4): 19–37.

Collins, Karen Scott, Cathy Schoen, and Susan Joseph. 1999. "Informal Caregiving." *1998 Survey of Women's Health* Data Brief. New York: Commonwealth Fund. http://www.cmwf.org/publications/publications_show.htm?doc_id= 235577.

Collins, Patricia Hill. 1991. *Black Feminist Thought: Knowledge, Consciousness, and the Politics of Empowerment.* New York: Routledge.

Commonwealth Fund. 2006. "Is Social Security Progressive?" Economic and Budget Issue Brief. Washington: Congressional Budget Office.

———. 2004a. *The Outlook for Social Security.* Washington: Congressional Budget Office. http://www.cbo.gov/showdoc.cfm?index=5530&sequence=0.

———. 2004b. *Administrative Costs of Private Accounts in Social Security.* Washington: Congressional Budget Office. http://www.cbo.gov/showdoc.cfm?index= 5277&sequence=0.

———. 2005. *The Long-Term Budget Outlook.* Washington: Congressional Budget Office. http://www.cbo.gov/showdoc.cfm?index=6982&sequence=0.

Congressional Research Service. 2000. "Social Security: Summary of Major Changes in the Cash Benefits Program." RL30565. Washington: Social Security Administration. http://www.ssa.gov/history/reports/crsleghist2.html.

Conley, Dalton. 1999. *Being Black, Living in the Red: Race, Wealth, and Social Policy in America.* Berkeley, Calif.: University of California Press.

Connecticut Partnership for Long-Term Care. 2006. "Frequently Asked Questions about Long-Term Care Insurance." Hartford, Conn.: State of Connecticut, Office of Policy and Management. http://www.opm.state.ct.us/pdpd4/ltc/FAQ/ FAQ.htm.

Council of Economic Advisers. 1998. *Explaining Trends in the Gender Wage Gap.* Washington: Government Printing Office.

Cowan, Carolyn Pape, and Philip A. Cowan. 1992. *When Partners Become Parents: The Big Life Change for Couples.* New York: Basic Books.

Cowan, Robert S. 1991. "More Work for Mother: The Postwar Years." In *The Sociology of Gender: A Text–Reader,* edited by Laura Kramer. New York: St. Martin's Press.

Crimmins, Eileen M., and Yasuhiko Saito. 2001. "Trends in Healthy Life Expectancy in the United States, 1970–1990: Gender, Raciel, and Educational Differences." *Social Science and Medicine* 52(11): 1629–41.

Crittenden, Ann. 2001. *The Price of Motherhood: Why the Most Important Job in the World Is Still the Least Valued.* New York: Metropolitan Books.

Crystal, Stephen, Richard W. Johnson, Jeff Urey Harman, Usha Sambamoorthi, and Rizie Kumar. 2000. "Out-of-Pocket Health Care Costs Among Older Americans." *Journals of Gerontology* 55B(1): S51–62.

Cumming, Elaine, and William Earl Henry. 1961. *Growing Old: The Process of Disengagement.* New York: Basic Books.

Cutler, David M. 2004. *Your Money or Your Life: Strong Medicine for America's Health Care System.* Oxford: Oxford University Press.

Cutler, David M. and Mark McClellan. 2001. "Is Technological Change in Medicine Worth It?" *Health Affairs(Published by Project HOPE)* 20(5): 11–29.

Dalton, Conley. 1999. *Being Black, Living in the Red: Race, Wealth, and Social Policy in America.* Berkeley, Calif.: University of California Press.

Dannefer, Dale. 2003. "Cumulative Advantage/Disadvantage and the Life Course: Cross–Fertilizing Age and Social Science Theory." *Journals of Gerontology, Series B: Psychological Sciences and Social Sciences* 58B(6): S327–37.

Danziger, Sheldon, and Peter Gottschalk. 1994. *Uneven Tides: Rising Inequality in America.* New York: Russell Sage Foundation.

Danzon, Patricia M., and Michael F. Furukawa. 2003. "Prices and Availability of Pharmaceuticals: Evidence from Nine Countries." *Health Affairs* Supplemental Web Exclusives: W3(July–December): 521–36.

Davis, Karen, Cathy Schoen, Stephen Schoenbaum, Ann-Marie Audet, Michelle Doty, Alyssa Holmgren, and Jennifer Kriss. 2006. *Mirror, Mirror on the Wall: An Update on the Quality of American Health Care Through the Patient's Lens.* Pub. no. 915. New York: The Commonwealth Fund. http://www.cmwf.org/Publications/Publications_show.htm?doc_id=364436.

Davis, Margaret H., and Sally T. Burner. 1995. "Three Decades of Medicare: What the Numbers Tell Us." *Health Affairs* 14(4): 231–43.

de la Luz Ibarra, Maria. 2000. "Mexican Immigrant Women and the New Domestic Labor." *Human Organization* 59(4): 452–64. http://www.sfaa.net/ho/2000/winter2000.html.

DeNavas-Walt, Carmen, Bernadette D. Proctor, and Cheryl Hill Lee. 2005. "Income, Poverty, and Health Insurance Coverage in the United States: 2004." *Current Population Reports,* series P60, no. 229. Washington: U.S. Census Bureau. http://www.census.gov/prod/2005pubs/p60-229.pdf.

Derthick, Martha. 1979. *Policymaking for Social Security.* Washington: Brookings Institution Press.

DeVault, M. L. 1987. "Doing Housework: Feeding and Family Life." In *Families and Work,* edited by Naomi Gerstel and Harriet Engel Gross. Philadelphia, Pa.: Temple University Press.

Diamond, Peter A., and Peter R. Orszag. 2002. *"Reducing Benefits and Subsidizing Individual Accounts: An Analysis of the Plans Proposed by the President's Commission to Strengthen Social Security."* New York: Center on Budget and Policy Priorities and Century Foundation.

Ditsler, Elaine, Peter Fisher, and Colin Gordon. 2005. "On the Fringe: The Substandard Benefits of Workers in Part-Time, Temporary, and Contract Jobs." 879. New York: The Commonwealth Fund. http://www.cmwf.org/publications/publications_show.htm?doc_id=324095.

Drobnic, Sonja, and Immo Wittig. 1997. "Part-Time Work in the United States of America." In *Between Equalization and Marginalization: Women Working Part–Time in Europe and the United States of America*, edited by Hans-Peter Blossfeld and Catherine Hakim. New York: Oxford University Press.

Dubay, Lisa, Ian Hill, and Genevieve M. Kenney. 2002. "Five Things Everyone Should Know about SCHIP." *Assessing the New Federalism*, series A, no. A–55. Washington: Urban Institute Press.

Dutton, Donald G., and Susan Painter. 1993. "The Battered Woman Syndrome: Effects of Severity and Intermittency of Abuse." *American Journal of Orthopsychiatry* 63(4): 614–22.

The Economist. 2005. "Bush Campaigns for Social Security." *The Economist* 374(8417): 53.

Edin, Kathryn, and Laura Lein. 1997. "Work, Welfare, and Single Mothers' Economic Survival Strategies." *American Sociological Review* 62(2): 253–66.

Eitzen, D. Stanley, and Maxine Baca Zinn. 2003. *Social Problems*, 9th ed. Boston, Mass.: Allyn and Bacon.

Elder, Glen H., Jr. 1985. *Life Course Dynamics: Trajectories and Transitions, 1968–1980*. Ithaca, N.Y.: Cornell University Press.

———. 1998. "The Life Course as Developmental Theory." *Child Development* 69(1): 1–12.

Ellwood, Marilyn. 1999. "The Medicaid Eligibility Maze: Coverage Expands, but Problems Persist." *Assessing the New Federalism*, Occasional Paper No. 30. Washington: Urban Institute Press. http://www.urban.org/url.cfm?ID=309273.

Employee Benefit Research Institute (EBRI). 2004. "Health Insurance Coverage of Individuals Ages 55–64." *Notes* 25(3): 15. http://www.ebri.org/pdf/notespdf/0304notes.pdf.

———. 2005a. "Gender, Income, and Education Differences." In *Fact Sheet–1998 Health Confidence Survey*. Washington: Employee Benefit Research Institute.

———. 2005b. "EBRI Databook on Employee Benefits, Chapter 4: Participation in Employee Benefit Programs." Washington: Employee Benefit Research Institute. http://www.ebri.org/publications/books/index.cfm?fa=databook.

———. 2005c. "Sources of Health Insurance and Characteristics of the Uninsured: Analysis of the March 2005 Current Population Survey." EBRI Issue Brief no. 287. Washington: Employee Benefit Research Institute. http://www.ebri.org/publications/ib/index.cfm?fa=ibDisp&content_id=3597.

Engelhardt, Gary V., and Jonathan Gruber. 2004. "Social Security and the Evolution of Elderly Poverty." *NBER* Working Paper No. 10466. Cambridge, Mass.: National Bureau of Economic Research.

England, Paula, and Nancy Folbre. 1999. "The Cost of Caring." *The Annals of the American Academy of Political and Social Science* 561(1): 39–51.

———. 2005. "Gender and Economic Sociology." In *The Handbook of Economic Sociology*, edited by Neil Smelser and Richard Swedberg, 2nd edition. New York: Princeton University Press and Russell Sage Foundation.

———. 2006. "Toward Gender Equality: Progress and Bottlenecks." In *The Declining Significance of Gender?* edited by Francine D. Blau, Mary C. Brinton, and David B. Grusky. New York: Russell Sage Foundation.

England, Paula, Michelle Budig, and Nancy Folbre. 2002. "Wages of Virtue: The Relative Pay of Care Work." *Social Problems* 49(4): 455–73.

Epel, Elissa S., Elizabeth H. Blackburn, Jue Lin, Firdaus S. Dhabhar, Nancy E. Adler, Jason D. Morrow, and Richard M. Cawthon. 2004. "Accelerated Telomere Shortening in Response to Life Stress." *Proceedings of the National Academy of Sciences of the United States of America* 101(49): 17312–5.

Esping-Andersen, Gøsta. 1990. *The Three Worlds of Welfare Capitalism.* Cambridge: Polity Press.

Essex, Elizaveth L., and Jinkuk Hong. 2005. "Older Caregiving Parents: Division of Household Labor, Marital Satisfaction, and Caregiver Burden." *Family Relations* 54(3): 448–60.

Estes, Carroll L. 1989. "Aging, Health and Social Policy: The Crisis and the Crossroads." *Journal of Aging and Social Policy* 1(1–2): 17–32.

———. 2001. *Social Policy and Aging: A Critical Perspective.* Thousand Oaks, Calif.: Sage Publications.

Estes, Carroll L., and Ida Vsw Red. 1993. *The Long Term Care Crisis: Elders Trapped in the No-Care Zone.* Newbury Park, Calif.: Sage Publications.

Even, William E., and David A. Macpherson. 2000. "The Changing Distribution of Pension Coverage." *Industrial Relations* 39(2): 199–227.

———. 2004. "When Will the Gender Gap in Retirement Income Narrow?" *Southern Economic Journal* 71(1): 182–200.

Families USA. 2005a. "Gearing Up: The Holes in Part D: Gaps in the New Medicare Drug Benefit." Part 1 of 2. *Families USA* Publication no. 05-102. Washington: Families USA. http://www.familiesusa.org/assets/pdfs/Gearing-Up-2-Part-1-Filling-Holes.pdf.

———. 2005b. "Gearing Up: Filling the Holes in Part D: The Essential Role of State Pharmacy Assistance Programs." Part 2 of 2. *Families USA* Publication no. 05-103. Washington: Families USA. http://www.familiesusa.org/assets/pdfs/Gearing-Up-2-Part-2-SPAPs.pdf.

Farkas, Janice I., and Angela M. O'Rand. 1998. "The Pension Mix for Women in Middle and Late Life: The Changing Employment Relationship." *Social Forces* 76(3): 1007–32.

Favreault, Melissa M., Gordon B. T. Mermin, and C. Eugene Steuerle. 2006. "Minimum Benefits in Social Security." *AARP* Publication no. 2006–17. Washington: AARP Public Policy Institute. http://assets.aarp.org/rgcenter/econ/2006_17_socsec.pdf.

Favreault, Melissa M., Frank J. Sammartino, and C. Eugene Steuerle, eds. 2002. *Social Security and the Family.* Washington: Urban Institute Press.

Feagin, Joe R. 2000. *Racist America: Roots, Current Realities, and Future Reparations.* New York: Routledge.

Ferrara, Peter J. 1980. *Social Security: The Inherent Contradiction.* San Francisco, Calif.: Cato Institute.

Fessenden, Ford, Robert Fresco, Delthia Ricks, and Curtis L. Taylor. 1998. "The Health Divide: A Difference of Life and Death." *Newsday,* November 29, 30, December 4, 1998.

Fields, Jason. 2003. "Children's Living Arrangements and Characteristics: March 2002." *Current Population Reports,* series P20, no. 547. Washington: U.S. Census Bureau.

Fischer, Mary J., and Douglas S. Massey. 2004. "The Ecology of Racial Discrimination." *City and Community* 3(3): 221–41.

Fitzpatrick, Kevin, and Mark La Gory. 2000. *Unhealthy Places: The Ecology of Risk in the Urban Landscape.* New York: Routledge.

Folbre, Nancy. 1994. *Who Pays for the Kids? Gender and the Structures of Constraint.* New York: Routledge.

Fossett, James W., Janet D. Perloff, Phillip R. Kletke, and John A. Peterson. 1992. "Medicaid and Access to Child Health Care in Chicago." *Journal of Health Politics, Policy and Law* 17(2): 273–98.

Fraser, Nancy. 2005. "Redistribution, Recognition, and Cross Re–dressing." In *Gender Inequality: Feminist Theories and Politics,* edited by Judith Lorber. 3rd edition. Los Angeles, Calif.: Roxbury Publishing.

Freund, Peter E. S., Meredith B. McGuire, and Linda S. Podhurst. 2003. *Health, Illness, and the Social Body: A Critical Sociology,* 4th ed. Upper Saddle River, N.J.: Prentice Hall.

Friedman, Milton, Richard K. Armey, Steve Forbes, Phil Gramm, Virginia Postrel, Jennifer Roback, Judy Shelton, and Fred L. Smith, Jr. 1994. "Serfdom USA: How Far Have We Traveled Down Hayek's 'Road'?" *Policy Review* 69(14): 14–21.

———. 2002. *Capitalism and Freedom,* 40th anniversary ed. Chicago, Ill.: Chicago University Press.

Fuchs, Victor R. 1988. *Women's Quest for Economic Equality.* Cambridge, Mass.: Harvard University Press.

Gazmararian, J. A., R. Petersen, A. M. Spitz, M. M. Goodwin, L. E. Saltzman, and J. S. Marks. 2000. "Violence and Reproductive Health: Current Knowledge and Future Research Directions." *Maternal and Child Health Journal* 4(2): 79–84.

Geiger, H. Jack. 1996. "Race and Health Care—An American Dilemma?" *New England Journal of Medicine* 335(11): 815–6.

Gennetian, Lisa A., Greg Duncan, Virginia Knox, Wanda Vargas, Elizabeth Clark-Kauffman, and Andrew S. London. 2004. "How Welfare Policies Affect Adolescents' School Outcomes: A Synthesis of Evidence from Experimental Studies." *Journal of Research on Adolescence* 14(4): 399–423.

Gerstel, Naomi, and Katherine McGonagle. 1999. "Job Leaves and the Limits of the Family and Medical Leave Act: The Effects of Gender, Race, and Family." *Work and Occupations* 26(4): 510–34.

Gilbert, Neil. 2002. *Transformation of the Welfare State: The Silent Surrender of Public Responsibility.* New York: Oxford University Press.

Gilder, George F. 1981. *Wealth and Poverty.* New York: Basic Books.

Gittleman, Maury, and Edward N. Wolff. 2000. "Racial Wealth Disparities: Is the Gap Closing?" Working Paper no. 311. Annandale-on-Hudson, N.Y.: Levy Economics Institute of Bard College.

Glass, Jennifer L. 2004. "Blessing or Curse? Work–Family Policies and Mother's Wage Growth Over Time." *Work and Occupations* 31(3): 367–94.

Glass, Jennifer L., and Sarah Beth Estes. 1997. "The Family Responsive Workplace." *Annual Review of Sociology* 23: 289–313.

Glazer, Nona Y. 1990. "The Home as Workshop: Women as Amateur Nurses and Medical Care Providers." *Gender and Society* 4(4): 479–99.

Gleason, W. J. 1993. "Mental Disorders in Battered Women: An Empirical Study." *Violence and Victims* 8(1)(Spring): 53–68.

Goldin, Claudia D. 1977. "Female Labor Force Participation: The Origin of Black and White Differences, 1870 and 1880." *Journal of Economic History* 37(1): 87–108.

———. 1992. *Understanding the Gender Gap: An Economic History of American Women*. New York: Oxford University Press.

———. 1995. "Career and Family: College Women Look to the Past." *NBER* Working Paper no. 5188. Cambridge, Mass.: National Bureau of Economic Research.

———. 2006. "The Rising(and Then Declining) Significance of Gender." In *The Declining Significance of Gender?* edited by Francine D. Blau, Mary C. Brinton, and David B. Grusky. New York: Russell Sage Foundation.

Goldin, Claudia D., and Solomon Polachek. 1987. "Residual Differences by Sex: Perspectives on the Gender Gap in Earnings." *American Economic Review* 77(2): 143–51.

Goldstein, Arthur, and Bonnie Damon. 1993. "We the American Elderly." Report WE-9. Washington: U.S. Department of Commerce, Bureau of the Census.

Goldstein, Joshua R., and Catherine T. Kenney. 2001. "Marriage Delayed or Marriage Forgone? New Cohort Forecasts of First Marriage for U.S. Women." *American Sociological Review* 66(4): 509–19.

Gordon, Linda. 1994. *Pitied But Not Entitled: Single Mothers and the History of Welfare, 1890–1935*. New York: Free Press.

Gornick, Janet C., and Jerry A. Jacobs. 1998. "Gender, the Welfare State, and Public Employment: A Comparative Study of Seven Industrialized Countries." *American Sociological Review* 63(5): 688–710.

Gornick, Janet C., and Marcia Meyers. 2003. *Families that Work: Policies for Reconciling Parenthood and Employment*. New York: Russell Sage Foundation.

Gornick, Janet C., Marcia K. Meyers, and Katherin E. Ross. 1997. "Supporting the Employment of Mothers: Policy Variation Across Fourteen Welfare States." *Journal of European Social Policy* 7(1): 45–70.

Gornick, Marian E., Paul W. Eggers, Thomas W. Reilly, Renee M. Mentnech, Leslye K. Fitterman, Lawrence E. Kucken, and Bruce C. Vladeck. 1996. "Effects of Race and Income on Mortality and Use of Services among Medicare Beneficiaries." *New England Journal of Medicine* 335(11): 791–9.

Grall, Timothy S. 2005. "Support Providers: 2002, Household Economic Studies." *Current Population Reports,* series P70, no. 99. Washington: U.S. Census Bureau.

Green, Cynthia. 2003. "Something Smells at Wal-Mart: Sex Discrimination Charges Underscore Stubborn Anti-Union Culture." New York: Labor Research Association. http://www.laborresearch.org/story.php?id=303.

Grogan, C., and E. Patashnik. 2003. "Between Welfare Medicine and Mainstream Entitlement: Medicaid at the Political Crossroads." *Journal of Health Politics, Policy and Law* 28(5): 821–58.

Gupta, Sanjiv. 1999. "The Effects of Transitions in Marital Status on Men's Performance of Housework." *Journal of Marriage and the Family* 61(3): 700–11.

Gutmann, Amy, ed. 1988. *Democracy and the Welfare State*. Princeton, N.J.: Princeton University Press.

Hacker, Jacob S. 2002. *The Divided Welfare State: The Battle Over Public and Private Social Benefits in the United States*. New York: Cambridge University Press.

———. 2006. *The Great Risk Shift: The Assault on American Jobs, Families, Health Care, and Retirement and How You Can Fight Back*. New York: Oxford University Press.

Hadley, Jack, and John Holahan. 2003. "Covering the Uninsured: How Much Would It Cost?" *Health Affairs* Supplementary Web Exclusives W3(January–June): 250–65.

Haider, Steven J., Alison Jacknowitz, and Robert F. Schoeni. 2003. "The Economic Status of Elderly Divorced Women." Working Paper 2003–046. Ann Arbor, Mich.: Michigan Retirement Research Center.

Halfon, Neal, and Miles Hochstein. 2002. "Life Course Health Development: An Integrated Framework for Developing Health, Policy, and Research." *Milbank Quarterly* 80(3): 433–79.

Han, Wen-Jui, and Jane Waldfogel. 2003. "Parental Leave: The Impact of Recent Legislation on Parents' Leave Taking." *Demography* 40(1): 191–200.

Harrell, Jules P., Sadiki Hall, and James Taliaferro. 2003. "Physiological Responses to Racism and Discrimination: An Assessment of the Evidence." *American Journal of Public Health* 93(2): 243–8.

Harrington, Michael. 1984. *The New American Poverty.* New York: Holt, Rinehart, and Winston.

Harrington Meyer, Madonna. 1990. "Family Status and Poverty among Older Women: The Gendered Distribution of Retirement Income in the United States." *Social Problems* 37(4): 551–63.

———. 1996. "Making Claims as Workers or Wives: The Distribution of Social Security Benefits." *American Sociological Review* 61(3): 449–65.

———. 2005. "Decreasing Welfare, Increasing Old Age Inequality: Whose Responsibility Is It?" In *The New Politics of Old Age Policy*, edited by Robert B. Hudson. Baltimore, Md.: Johns Hopkins University Press.

———, editor. 2000. *Care Work: Gender, Labor, and the Welfare State.* New York: Routledge.

Harrington Meyer, Madonna, and Marcia Bellas. 1995. "U.S. Old Age Policy and the Family." In *Handbook of Aging and the Family*, edited by Rosemary H. Blieszner and Victoria H. Bedford. Westport, Conn.: Greenwood Press.

Harrington Meyer, Madonna, and Pamela Herd. 2001. "Aging and Aging Policy in the U.S." In *The Blackwell Companion to Sociology*, edited by Judith R. Blau. Malden, Mass.: Blackwell Publishing.

Harrington Meyer, Madonna, and Michelle Kesterke-Storbakken. 2000. "Shifting the Burden Back to Families? How Medicaid Cost-Containment Reshapes Access to Long Term Care in the United States." In *Care Work: Gender, Labor, and the Welfare State*, edited by Madonna Harrington Meyer. New York: Routledge.

Harrington Meyer, Madonna, and Eliza K. Pavalko. 1996. "Family, Work, and Access to Health Insurance among Mature Women." *Journal of Health and Social Behavior* 37(4): 311–25.

Harrington Meyer, Madonna, Douglas Wolf, and Christine Himes. 2006. "Declining Eligibility for Social Security Spouse and Widow Benefits in the United States?" *Research on Aging* 28(2): 240–60.

Hartmann, Heidi, and Sunhwa Lee. 2003. *Social Security: The Largest Source of Income for Both Women and Men in Retirement.* IWPR Publication no. D455. Washington: Institute for Women's Policy Research.

Hartmann, Heidi, Stephen J. Rose, and Vicky Lovell. 2006. "How Much Progress in Closing the Long-Term Earnings Gap?" In *The Declining Significance of Gender?* edited by Francine D. Blau, Mary C. Brinton, and David B. Grusky. New York: Russell Sage Foundation.

Haug, Marie R., and Steven J. Folmar. 1986. "Longevity, Gender, and Life Quality." *Journal of Health and Social Behavior* 27(4): 332–45.

Hayek, Friedrich A. 1994. *The Road to Serfdom,* 50th anniversary ed. Chicago, Ill.: University of Chicago Press.

Hayek, Friedrich A., Stephen Kresge, and Leif Wenar. 1994. *Hayek on Hayek: An Autobiographical Dialogue.* Chicago, Ill.: University of Chicago Press.

Hayward, Mark D., and Melonie Heron. 1999. "Racial Inequality in Active Life among Adult Americans." *Demography* 36(1): 77–91.

Hayward, Mark D., Eileen M. Crimmins, and Toni P. Miles. 2000. "The Significance of Socioeconomic Status in Explaining the Gap in Chronic Health Conditions." *American Sociological Review* 65(6): 910–30.

Hayward, Mark D., Amy M. Pienta, and Diane K. McLaughlin. 1997. "Inequality in Men's Mortality: The Socioeconomic Status Gradient and Geographic Context." *Journal of Health and Social Behavior* 38(4): 313–30.

He, Wan, Manisha Sengupta, Victoria A. Velkoff, and Kimberly A. Debaros. 2005. "65+ in the United States." *Current Population Reports,* Special Studies series P23, no. 209. Washington: U.S. Census Bureau. http://www.census.gov/prod/2006pubs/p23-209.pdf.

Herd, Pamela. 2005a. "Ensuring a Minimum: Social Security Reform and Women." *The Gerontologist* 45(1): 12–25.

———. 2005b. "Reforming a Breadwinner Welfare State: Gender, Race, Class and Social Security Reform." *Social Forces* 83(4): 1365–94.

———. 2005c. "Universalism Without the Targeting: Privatizing the Old–Age Welfare State." *The Gerontologist* 45(3): 292–8.

———. 2006a. "Crediting Care or Marriage? Reforming Social Security Family Benefits." *Journals of Gerontology: Series B: Psychological Sciences and Social Sciences* 61B(1): S24–34.

———. 2006b. "Do Functional Health Inequalities Decrease in Old Age? Educational Status and Functional Decline among the 1931–1941 Birth Cohort." *Research on Aging* 28(3): 375–92.

———. 2006c. "Understanding the Options: Big Choices and Medicare Reform." In *Big Choices: The Future of Health Insurance for Older Americans: Proceedings of a Conference Held on April 22–23, 2004,* edited by Kenneth S. Apfel and Betty Sue Flowers. Austin, Tx.: Center for Health and Social Policy, Lyndon B. Johnson School of Public Affairs, University of Texas at Austin. http://www.utexas.edu/lbj/pubs/pdf/big_choices2006.pdf.

Herd, Pamela, and Madonna Harrington Meyer. 2002. "Carework: Invisible Civic Engagement." *Gender and Society* 16(5): 665–88.

Herd, Pamela, and Eric R. Kingson. 2005. "Selling Social Security." In *The New Politics of Old Age Policy,* edited by Robert B. Hudson. Baltimore, Md.: Johns Hopkins University Press.

Herd, Pamela, Brian Goesling, and James House. Forthcoming. "Unpacking the Relationship between Socioeconomic Position and Health." *Journal of Health and Social Behavior.*

Herd, Pamela, Robert Schoeni, and James House. Forthcoming. "Does Income Supports Affect Health?" In *The Health Effects of Nonhealth Policies,* edited by James House, Robert Schoeni, Harold Pollack, and George Kaplan. New York: Russell Sage Foundation.

Hernes, Helga Maria. 1987. "Women and the Welfare State: The Transition from Private to Public Dependence." In *Women and the State: The Shifting Boundaries of Public and Private,* edited by Anne Showstack Sassoon. London: Hutchingson.

Hewlett, Sylvia Ann. 1986. *A Lesser Life: The Myth of Women's Liberation in America.* New York: William Morrow.

Hill, Ian, and Amy Westpfahl Lutzky. 2003. "Getting In, Not Getting In, and Why: Understanding SCHIP Enrollment." *Assessing the New Federalism.* Occasional Paper no. 66. Washington: Urban Institute.

Himes, Christine L. 2000a. "Obesity, Disease, and Functional Limitation in Later Life." *Demography* 37(1): 73–82.

———. 2000b. "Association between Body Size and Mortality in Later Life." Presented at the annual meeting of the Population Association of America, March 2000, Syracuse, N.Y.

———. 2001. "Elderly Americans." *Population Bulletin* 56(4): 3–40.

Hoadley, Jack. 2006. *Medicare's New Adventure: The Part D Drug Benefit.* Pub. no. 911. New York: The Commonwealth Fund. http://www.cmwf.org/publications/publications_show.htm?doc_id=362249.

Hobson, Barbara. 2000. *Gender and Citizenship in Transition.* New York: Routledge.

Hochschild, Arlie Russell. 1997. *The Time Bind: When Work Becomes Home and Home Becomes Work.* New York: Metropolitan Books.

Hochschild, Arlie Russell, and Anne Machung. 1989. *The Second Shift: Working Parents and the Revolution at Home.* New York: Viking.

Holden, Karen C. 1979. "The Inequitable Distribution of OASI Benefits Among Homemakers." *The Gerontologist* 19(3): 250–6.

Holden, Karen C., and Ksiang-hui Daphne Kuo. 1996. "Complex Marital Histories and Economic Well-Being: The Continuing Legacy of Divorce and Widowhood as the HRS Cohort Approaches Retirement." *The Gerontologist* 36(3): 383–90.

Holden, Karen C., and Sean Nicholson. 1998. "Selection of a Joint-and-Survivor Pension." Discussion paper 1175–98. Madison, Wisc.: University of Wisconsin, Institute for Research on Poverty.

Holden, Karen C., and Pamela J. Smock. 1991. "The Economic Costs of Marital Dissolution: Why Do Women Bear a Disproportionate Cost?" *Annual Review of Sociology* 17: 51–78.

Holtz-Eakin, Douglas. 2004. "Health Care Spending and the Uninsured." Statement of the Director before the Committee on Health, Education, Labor, and Pensions United States Senate. January 28, 2004. Washington: Congressional Budget Office. http://www.cbo.gov/showdoc.cfm?index=6316&sequence=0.

———. 2005. "The Cost and Financing of Long–Term Care Services." Statement of Douglas Holtz-Eakin, Director, before the Subcommittee on Health Committee on Ways and Means U.S. House of Representatives. April 27, 2005. Washington: Congressional Budget Office. http://www.cbo.gov/showdoc.cfm? index=6316&sequence=0.

Hondagneu-Sotelo, Pierrette. 2000. "The International Division of Caring and Cleaning Work: Transnational Connections or Apartheid Exclusions?" In *Care Work: Gender, Labor, and the Welfare State,* edited by Madonna Harrington Meyer. New York: Routledge.

Hooyman, Nancy R., and Judith Gonyea. 1995. *Feminist Perspectives on Family Care: Policies for Gender Justice.* Vol. 6, *Family Caregivers Application Series.* Thousand Oaks, Calif.: Sage Publications.

House, James S. 2002. "Understanding Social Factors and Inequalities in Health: 20th Century Progress and 21st Century Prospects." *Journal of Health and Social Behavior* 43(2): 125–53.

House, James S., Karl R. Landis, and Debra Umberson. 1988. "Social Relationships and Health." *Science* 241(4865): 540–5.

House, James S., Ronald C. Kessler, A. Regula Herzog, Richard P. Mero, Ann M. Kinney, and Martha J. Breslow. 1990. "Age, Socioeconomic Status, and Health." *Milbank Quarterly* 68(3): 383–411.

House, James S., James M. Lepkowski, Ann M. Kinney, Richard P. Mero, Ronald C. Kessler, and A. Regula Herzog. 1994. "The Social Stratification of Aging and Health." *Journal of Health and Social Behavior* 35(3): 213–34.

Hoyert, Donna L., and Marsha Mailick Seltzer. 1992. "Factors Related to the Well–Being and Life Activities of Family Caregivers." *Family Relations* 41(1): 74–81.

Hoynes, Hilary, Marianne Page, and Ann Stevens. 2005. "Poverty in America: Trends and Explanations." *NBER* Working Paper 11681. National Bureau of Economic Research. http://papers.nber.org/papers/w11681.

Institute for Women's Policy Research. 2000. "Paid Family and Medical Leave: Essential Support for Working Women and Men." IWPR Publication no. A124. Washington: Institute for Women's Policy Research. http://www.iwpr.org/pdf/famlve2.pdf.

———. 2006. "Memo to John Roberts: The Gender Wage Gap is Real." IWPR Publication no. C362. Washington: Institute for Women's Policy Research. http://www.iwpr.org/pdf/C362.pdf.

Institute of Medicine. Committee on the Consequences of Uninsurance. 2002. *Care Without Coverage? Too Little Too Late?* Washington: National Academy Press. http://www.iom.edu/CMS/3809/4660/4333.aspx.

Jacobs, Jerry A., and Kathleen Gerson. 2004. *The Time Divide: Work, Family, and Gender Inequality.* Cambridge, Mass.: Harvard University Press.

Jette, Alan M. 1996. "Disability Trends and Transitions." In *Handbook of Aging and the Social Sciences*, 4th ed., edited by Robert H. Binstock and Linda K. George. San Diego, Calif.: Academic Press.

Johnson, Richard W. 1999. *The Gender Gap in Pension Wealth: Is Women's Progress in the Labor Market Equalizing Retirement Benefits?* Pub. ID 310238. Washington: Urban Institute.

Johnson, Richard W., and Melissa M. Favreault. 2004. "Economic Status in Later Life among Women Who Raised Children Outside of Marriage." *Journals of Gerontology: Series B: Psychological Sciences and Social Sciences* 59B(6): S315–23.

Johnson, Richard W., and Rudolph G. Penner. 2004. "Will Health Care Costs Erode Retirement Security?" Issue in Brief no. 23. Chestnut Hill, Mass.: Center for Retirement Research, Boston College. http://www.urban.org/uploadedPDF/1000699_retirement_security.pdf.

Johnson, Richard W., Usha Sambamoorthi, and Stephen Crystal. 1999. "Gender Differences in Pension Wealth: Estimates Using Provider Data." *The Gerontologist* 39(3): 320–33.

Johnson, Richard W., Cori E. Uccello, and Joshua H. Goldwyn. 2003. *Single Life vs. Joint and Survivor Pension Payout Options: How Do Married Retirees Choose?*

Pub. no. 410877. Washington: Urban Institute. http://www.urban.org/ UploadedPDF/410877_survivor_pension_payouts.pdf.

Kaiser Family Foundation. 2001. "Women and Medicare." Fact Sheet 1638. Menlo Park, Calif.: The Henry J. Kaiser Family Foundation.

———. 2002. *The Wide Circle of Caregiving: Key Findings from a National Survey: Long-Term Care from the Caregiver's Perspective*. Menlo Park, Calif.: The Henry J. Kaiser Family Foundation. http://www.kff.org/kaiserpolls/loader.cfm? url=/commonspot/security/getfile.cfm&PageID=13990.

———. 2003a. "Dual Enrollees: Medicaid's Role for Low-Income Medicare Beneficiaries." Fact Sheet 4091. Menlo Park, Calif.: The Henry J. Kaiser Family Foundation. http://www.kff.org/medicaid/upload/Dual-Enrollees-Medicaid-s-Role-for-Low-Income-Medicare-Beneficiaries-Fact-Sheet.pdf.

———. 2003b. "Medicare + Choice." Fact Sheet 2052-06. Menlo Park, Calif.: The Henry J. Kaiser Family Foundation

———. 2004. *Summaries of the Medicare Prescription Drug Improvement and Modernization Act of 2003*. Publication nos. 6112 and 6120. Menlo Park, Calif.: The Henry J. Kaiser Family Foundation. http://www.kff.org/medicare/med011604pkg.cfm.

———. 2005. "Medicare Advantage." Fact Sheet 2052–08. Menlo Park, Calif.: The Henry J. Kaiser Family Foundation. April. http://www.kff.org/medicare/upload/Medicare-Advantage-April-2005-Fact-Sheet.pdf.

———. 2006. "Prescription Drug Trends." Fact Sheet 30570–05. Menlo Park, Calif.: The Henry J. Kaiser Family Foundation. June. http://www.kff.org/rxdrugs/upload/3057–05.pdf.

Kaplan, George A., and John W. Lynch. 2001. "Is Economic Policy Health Policy?" *American Journal of Public Health* 91(3): 351–3.

Karlsson, Martin, Les Mayhew, Robert Plumb, and Ben Rickayzen. 2004. *An International Comparison of Long-Term Care Arrangements*. London: Cass Business School. http://www.cass.city.ac.uk/media/stories/resources/Full_report_-_LTC.pdf.

Katz Olson, Laura. 2003. *The Not-So-Golden Years: Caregiving, the Frail Elderly, and the Long-Term Care Establishment*. Lanham, Md.: Rowman and Littlefield.

Katz, Michael B. 1986. *In the Shadow of the Poorhouse: A Social History of Welfare in America*. New York: Basic Books.

Kelly, Timothy B., and Nancy P. Kropf. 1995. "Stigmatized and Perpetual Parents: Older Parents Caring for Adult Children with Life-Long Disabilities." *Journal of Gerontological Social Work* 25(1–2): 3–16.

Kennelly, Ivy. 1999. " 'That Single-Mother Element': How White Employers Typify Black Women." *Gender & Society* 13(2): 168–92.

Kessler-Harris, Alice. 1995. "Designing Women and Old Fools: The Construction of the Social Security Amendments of 1939." In *U.S. History as Women's History: New Feminist Essays*, edited by Linda K. Kerber, Alice Kessler-Harris, and Kathryn Kish Sklar. Chapel Hill, N.C.: University of North Carolina Press.

Kiecolt-Glaser, Janice K., Jason R. Dura, Carl E. Speicher, O. Joseph Trask, and Ronald Glaser. 1991. "Spousal Caregivers of Dementia Victims: Longitudinal Changes in Immunity and Health." *Psychosomatic Medicine* 53(4): 345–62.

Kinsella, Kevin. 1988. "Aging in the Third World." *International Population Reports*, series P95, no. 79. Washington: Government Printing Office for the U.S. Census Bureau.

Knijn, Trudie, and Monique Kremer. 1997. "Gender and the Caring Dimension of Welfare States: Toward Inclusive Citizenship." *Social Politics* 4(3): 328–61.

Koitz, David Stuart. 1997. "The Entitlements Debate." 97–39 EPW (Updated January 28, 1998). Washington: Library of Congress, Congressional Research Service. http://countingcalifornia.cdlib.org/crs/pdf/97–39.pdf.

Kominski, Gerald F., and Christina Witsberger. 1993. "Trends in Length of Stay for Medicare Patients: 1979–87." *Health Care Financing Review* 15(2): 121–35.

Korpi, Walter. 2000. "Faces of Inequality: Gender, Class and Patterns of Inequalities in Different Types of Welfare States." *Luxembourg Income Study* Working Paper no. 224. Syracuse, N.Y.: Syracuse University.

Korpi, Walter, and Joakim Palme. 1998. "The Paradox of Distribution and Strategies of Equality: Welfare State Institutions, Inequality, and Poverty in the Western Nations." *American Sociological Review* 63(5): 661–87.

Krivo, Lauren J., and Robert L. Kaufman. 2004. "Housing and Wealth Inequality: Racial–Ethnic Differences in Home Equity in the United States." *Demography* 41(3): 585–605.

Ku, Leighton, and Matthew Broaddus. 2005. *Out-of-Pocket Medical Expenses for Medicaid Beneficiaries Are Substantial and Growing.* Washington: Center on Budget and Policy Priorities. http://www.cbpp.org/5-31-05health.pdf.

Landa, Kenneth C., and Stephen T. Russell. 1996. "Wealth Accumulation across the Adult Life Course: Stability and Change in Sociodemographic Covariate Structures of Net Worth Data in the Survey of Income and Program Participation, 1984–1991." *Social Science Research* 25(4): 423–62.

Lantz, Paula M., James S. House, Richard P. Mero, and David R. Williams. 2005. "Stress, Life Events, and Socioeconomic Disparities in Health: Results from the Americans' Changing Lives Study." *Journal of Health and Social Behavior* 46(3): 274–88.

Lantz, Paula M., James S. House, James M. Lepkowski, David R. Williams, Richard P. Mero, and Jieming Chen. 1998. "Socioeconomic Factors, Health Behaviors, and Mortality: Results from a Nationally Representative Prospective Study of US Adults." *Journal of the American Medical Association* 279(21): 1703–8.

Lee, Sunwha, and Lois Shaw. 2003. *Gender and Economic Security in Retirement.* IWPR Publication no. D456. Washington: Institute for Women's Policy Research.

Leete, Laura, and Juliet B. Schor. 1994. "Assessing the Time Squeeze Hypothesis: Hours Worked in the United States, 1969–1989." *Industrial Relations* 33(1): 24–43.

Leimer, Dean R. 1999. "Lifetime Redistribution under the Social Security Program: A Literature Synopsis." *Social Security Bulletin* 62(2): 43–51.

Leira, Arnlaug. 1992. *Welfare States and Working Mothers: The Scandinavian Experience.* New York: Cambridge University Press.

Lemieux, Jeff. 2003. "Explaining Premium Support: How Medicare Reform Could Work." Washington: Centrists.Org. http://www.centrists.org/pages/2003/10/26_lemieux_health.html.

Levine, Philip B., Olivia S. Mitchell, and John W.R. Phillips. 2000. "Benefit of One's Own: Older Women's Entitlement to Social Security Retirement." *Social Security Bulletin* 63(2): 47–53.

Link, Bruce G., and Jo C. Phelan. 1995. "Social Conditions As Fundamental Causes of Disease." *Journal of Health and Social Behavior* 35(Extra Issue): 80–94.

Link, Bruce G., Jo C. Phelan, and Allen M. Fremont. 2000. "Evaluating the Fundamental Cause Explanation for Social Disparities in Health." In *Handbook of Medical Sociology*, 5th ed., edited by Chloe E. Bird and Peter Conrad. Upper Saddle River, N.J.: Prentice Hall.

Lister, Ruth. 1997. *Citizenship: Feminist Perspectives.* New York: New York University Press.

Litt, Jacquelyn. 2004. "Women's Carework in Low–Income Households—The Special Case of Children with Attention Deficit Hyperactivity Disorder." *Gender & Society* 18(5): 625–44.

London, Andrew, and Nancy A. Myers. 2006. "Race, Incarceration, and Health: A Life-Course Approach." *Research on Aging* 28(3): 409–22.

Lorber, Judith. 2005. *Gender Inequality: Feminist Theories and Politics,* 3rd ed. Los Angeles, Calif.: Roxbury Publishing.

Luke, Douglas, Emily Esmundo, and Yael Bloom. 2000. "Smoke Signs: Patterns of Tobacco Billboard Advertising in a Metropolitan Region." *Tobacco Control* 9(1): 16–23.

Macintyre, Sally, Kate Hunt, and Helen Sweeting. 1996. "Gender Differences in Health: Are Things Really As Simple As They Seem?" *Social Science and Medicine* 42(4): 617–24.

Macpherson, David A., and Barry T. Hirsch. 1995. "Wages and Gender Composition: Why Do Women's Jobs Pay Less?" *Journal of Labor Economics* 13(3): 426–71.

Mandel, Hadas, and Moshe Semyonov. 2006. "A Welfare State Paradox: State Interventions and Women's Employment Opportunities in 22 Countries." *American Journal of Sociology* 111(6): 1910–49.

Manton, Kenneth G., and Eric Stallard. 1996. "Changes in Health, Mortality, and Disability and Their Impact on Long-Term Care Needs." *Journal of Aging and Social Policy* 7(3–4): 25–52.

Margolis, Richard J. 1990. *Risking Old Age in America.* Boulder, Colo.: Westview Press.

Marmor, Theodore R. 2000. *The Politics of Medicare,* 2nd ed. New York: Aldine de Gruyter.

Marmot, Michael G., H. Bosma, H. Hemingway, E. Brunner, and S. Stansfeld. 1997. "Contribution of Job Control and Other Risk Factors to Social Variations in Coronary Heart Disease Incidence." *Lancet* 350(9073): 235–9.

Marmot, Michael G., G. D. Smith, S. Stansfeld, C. Patel, F. North, J. Head, I. White, E. Brunner, and A. Feeney. 1991. "Health Inequalities Among British Civil Servants: The Whitehall II Study." *Lancet* 337(8754): 1387–93.

Marshall, Thomas Humphrey. 1950. *Citizenship and Social Class, and Other Essays.* Cambridge: Cambridge University Press.

Martinson, M., and J. Stone. 1993. "Small Scale Community Living Options Serving Three or Fewer Adults with Developmental Disabilities." In *Older Adults with Developmental Disabilities: Optimizing Choice and Change,* edited by Evelyn Sutton. Baltimore, Md.: Paul H. Brookes Publishing.

Massachusetts Institute of Technology. 1999. "A Study on the Status of Women Faculty in Science at MIT." *MIT Faculty Newsletter* XI(4), March 1999. http://web.mit.edu/fnl/women/women.pdf.

Mathers, Colin D., Ritu Sadana, Joshua A. Salomon, Christopher J. L. Murray, and Alan D. Lopez. 2001. "Healthy Life Expectancy in 191 Countries, 1999." *Lancet* 357(9269): 1685–91.

Maxwell, Stephanie, Marilyn Moon, and Misha Segal. 2001. *Growth in Medicare and Out–of–Pocket Spending: Impact on Vulnerable Beneficiaries.* New York and Washington: Commonwealth Fund and The Urban Institute.

Maxwell, Stephanie, Marilyn Moon, and Matthew Storeygard. 2001. *Reforming Medicare's Benefit Package: Impact on Beneficiary Expenditures.* Pub. no. 461. New York: Commonwealth Fund. http://www.cmwf.org/publications/publications_show.htm?doc_id=221299.

McCall, Leslie. 2001. *Complex Inequality: Gender, Class, and Race in the New Economy.* New York: Routledge.

McDonnell, Ken. 2005. "Retirement Annuity and Employment–Based Pension Income." *EBRI Notes* 26(2): 7–14.

McGinnis, Michael J., Pamela Williams-Russo, and James R. Knickman. 2002. "The Case for More Active Policy Attention to Health Promotion." *Health Affairs* 21(2): 78–93.

McManus, Patricia A., and Thomas A. DiPrete. 2001. "Losers and Winners: The Financial Consequences of Separation and Divorce for Men." *American Sociological Review* 66(2): 246–68.

McWilliams, J. Michael, Alan M. Zaslavsky, Ellen Meara, and John Z. Ayanian. 2004. "Health Insurance Coverage and Mortality among the Near-Elderly." *Health Affairs* 23(4): 223–33.

MedPac. 2005. *A Data Book: Health Care Spending and the Medicare Program.* Washington: Medicare Payment Advisory Commission. http://www.medpac.gov/publications/congressional_reports/Jun04dataBookTofC.pdf.

———. 2007. "The Medicare Advantage Program and MedPac Recommendations." April 11, 2007, testimony before the Committee on Finance, U.S. Senate. Washington.

Menchik, Paul L. 1993. "Economic Status as a Determinant of Mortality Among Black and White Older Men: Does Poverty Kill?" *Population Studies* 47(3): 427–36.

Menchik, Paul L., and Nancy Ammon Jianakoplos. 1997. "Black-White Wealth Inequality: Is Inheritance the Reason?" *Economic Inquiry* 35(2): 428–42.

MetLife Mature Market Institute. 1999. *The MetLife Juggling Act Study: Balancing Caregiving with Work and the Costs Involved.* New York: MetLife.

Michalopoulos, Charles, and Philip K. Robins. 2002. "Employment and Child–Care Choices of Single-Parent Families in Canada and the United States." *Journal of Population Economics* 15(3): 465–93.

Michel, Sonya. 1999. *Children's Interests/Mothers' Rights: The Shaping of America's Child Care Policy.* New Haven, Conn.: Yale University Press.

Mills, Robert J., and Shailesh Bhandari. 2003. "Health Insurance Coverage in the United States: 2002." *Current Population Reports*, series P60, no. 223. Washington: U.S. Census Bureau. http://www.census.gov/prod/2003pubs/p60-223.pdf.

Mink, Gwendolyn. 1998. *Welfare's End.* Ithaca, N.Y.: Cornell University Press.

Minkler, Meredith. 1986. " 'Generational Equity' and the New Victim Blaming: An Emerging Public Policy Issue." *International Journal of Health Services* 16(4): 539–51.

Mirowsky, John, and Catherine E. Ross. 2003a. *Education, Social Status, and Health.* Somerset, N.J.: Aldine Transaction.

———. 2003b. *Social Causes of Psychological Distress,* 2nd ed. New York: Aldine de Gruyter.

Mirowsky, John, Catherine E. Ross, and John Reynolds. 2000. "Links Between Social Status and Health Status." In *Handbook of Medical Sociology,* edited by Chloe E. Bird, Peter Conrad, and Allen M. Fremont. Upper Saddle River, N.J.: Prentice Hall.

Mishel, Lawrence R., Jared Bernstein, and Sylvia A. Allegretto. 2005. *The State of Working America, 2004/2005.* Ithaca, N.Y.: Cornell University Press.

Misra, Joya. 1998. "Mothers or Workers? The Value of Women's Labor: Women and the Emergency of Family Allowance Policy." *Gender and Society* 12(4): 376–99.

———. 2002. "Class, Race, and Gender and Theorizing Welfare States." *Research in Political Sociology* 11: 19–52.

Mitchell, J. B. 1991. "Physician Participation in Medicaid Revisited." *Medical Care* 29(7): 645–53.

Moen, Phyllis, and Elaine Wethington. 1999. "Midlife Development in a Life Course Context." In *Life in the Middle: Psychological and Social Development in Middle Age,* edited by Sherry L. Willis and James D. Reid. San Diego, Calif.: Academic Press.

Moen, Phyllis, Julie Robison, and Vivian Fields. 1994. "Women's Work and Caregiving Roles: A Life Course Approach." *Journals of Gerontology* 49(4): S176–86.

Moffit, Robert E. 2004. "What Federal Workers Are Doing Today That You Can't." WebMemo 604. Washington: Heritage Foundation.

Moody, Harry R. 2002. *Aging: Concepts and Controversies.* Newbury Park, Calif.: Pine Forge Press.

Moon, Marilyn, with Pamela Herd. 2002. *A Place at the Table: Women's Needs and Medicare Reform.* New York: Century Foundation.

Moon, Marilyn, Barbara Gage, and Alison Evans. 1997. *An Examination of Key Medicare Provisions in the Balanced Budget Act of 1997.* Washington: Urban Institute. http://www.urban.org/url.cfm?ID=410316.

Moore, James H., Jr. 2006. "Projected Pension Income: Equality or Disparity? Over Time, Both Eligibility for Pensions and Income from Employer-Sponsored Pension Plans will Increase for Baby Boomers." *Monthly Labor Review* 129(3): 58–68.

Morgan, Kimberly J., and Kathrin Zippel. 2003. "Paid to Care: The Origins and Effects of Care Leave Policies in Western Europe." *Social Politics* 10(1): 49–85.

Mui, Ada C. 1992. "Caregiver Strain Among Black and White Daughter Caregivers: A Role Theory Perspective." *The Gerontologist* 32(2): 203–12.

Munnell, Alicia H. 2005. "Mandatory Social Security Coverage of State and Local Workers: A Perennial Hot Button." Issue in Brief 32. Chestnut Hill, Mass.: Boston College, Center for Retirement Research.

Munnell, Alicia H., and Annika Sundén. 2003. "Suspending the Employer 401(k) Match." Issue in Brief 12. Chestnut Hill, Mass.: Boston College, Center for Retirement Research.

————. 2004. *Coming Up Short: The Challenge of 401(k) Plans.* Washington: Brookings Institution Press.

Munnell, Alicia H., Geoffrey M. B. Tootell, Lynn E. Browne, and James McEneaney. 1996. "Mortgage Lending in Boston: Interpreting HMDA Data." *American Economic Review* 86(1): 25–53.

Murray, Charles A. 1984. *Losing Ground: American Social Policy, 1950–1980.* New York: Basic Books.

Mutchler, Jan E., and Jeffrey A. Burr. 1991. "Racial Differences in Health and Health Care Service Utilization in Later Life: The Effect of Socioeconomic Status." *Journal of Health and Social Behavior* 32(4): 342–56.

Myles, John. 1996. "When Markets Fail: Social Welfare in Canada and the United States." In *Welfare States in Transition: National Adaptations in Global Economies,* edited by Gøsta Esping-Andersen. London: Sage.

Myles, John, and Jill Quadagno. 2000. "Envisioning a Third Way: The Welfare State in the Twenty-First Century." *Contemporary Sociology* 29(1): 156–67.

Nakano Glenn, Evelyn. 2005. "Gender, Race, and Citizenship." In *Gender Inequality: Feminist Theories and Politics,* 3rd ed., edited by Judith Lorber. Los Angeles, Calif.: Roxbury Publishing.

National Alliance for Caregiving and AARP. 1997. *Family Caregiving in the U.S.: Findings from a National Survey.* Washington: AARP and National Alliance for Caregiving.

————. 2004. *Caregiving in the U.S.* Washington: National Alliance for Caregiving and AARP. http://assets.aarp.org/rgcenter/il/us_caregiving.pdf.

National Center for Health Statistics (NCHS). 2004. "Table A. Expectation of Life by Age, Race, and Sex: United States, 2002." *National Vital Statistics Reports* 53(6): 3.

————. 2005a. "Table 4.2. Percent distributions of current cigarette smoking status for adults 18 years of age and over, and mean number of cigarettes smoked in a day among current smokers 18 years of age and over, by selected characteristics: United States, average annual, 1999–2001." *Health Behaviors of Adults: United States, 1999–2001.* series 10, no. 219. Hyattsville, Md.: U.S. Department of Health and Human Services, Centers for Disease Control and Prevention.

————. 2005b. *Health, United States, 2005, with Chartbook on Trends in the Health of Americans.* Hyattsville, Md.: U.S. Department of Health and Human Services, CDC, NCHS. http://www.cdc.gov/nchs/hus.htm.

National Commission on Civic Renewal. 1999. *Update to "A Nation of Spectators Report."* College Park, Md.: University of Maryland.

National Council of Women's Organizations. 1999. "Strengthening Social Security for Women." Presented at the Working Conference on Women and Social Security, Arlie House, July 19–22, 1999, Warrenton, Va. http://ncwo-online.org/data/images/AirlieHouseReport1.pdf.

National Institute for Early Education Research. 2005. *The State of Preschool Yearbook: 2005.* Rutgers, State University of New Jersey. http://nieer.org/yearbook/.

Navaie-Waliser, Maryam, Aubrey Spriggs, and Penny H. Feldman. 2002. "Informal Caregiving—Differential Experiences by Gender." *Medical Care* 40(12): 1249–59.

Navarro, Vicente. 1993. *Dangerous to Your Health: Capitalism in Health Care.* New York: Monthly Review Press.

Newacheck, Paul W., Michelle Pearl, Dana C. Hughes, and Neal Halfon. 1998. "The Role of Medicaid in Ensuring Children's Access to Care." *Journal of the American Medical Association* 280(20): 1789–93.

Newman, Katherine S. 2003. *A Different Shade of Gray: Midlife and Beyond in the Inner City.* New York: New Press.

NewsHour with Jim Lehrer. 2000. "Al Gore on Retirement Savings." PBS *Online NewsHour,* June 20, 2000. http://www.pbs.org/newshour/bb/social_security/social_security_6-20.html (accessed November 21, 2006).

Nielsen, Helena Skyt, Marianne Simonsen, and Mette Verner. 2006. "Does the Gap in Family-friendly Policies Drive the Family Gap?" *The Scandinavian Journal of Economics* 106(4): 721–44.

North, Finoa M., S. Leonard Syme, Amanda Feeney, Martin Shipley, and Michael Marmot. 1996. "Psychosocial Work Environment and Sickness Absence among British Civil Servants: The Whitehall II Study." *American Journal of Public Health* 86(3): 332–40.

Office of Management and Budget. 2005. "Table 8. Budget Summary by Category." Budget of the United States Government, FY 2004, MSR, Summary Tables. Washington: Executive Office of the President. http://www.whitehouse.gov/omb/budget/fy2004/summarytables.html.

Okamato, Dina, and Paula England. 1999. "Is There a Supply Side to Occupational Sex Segregation?" *Sociological Perspectives* 42(4): 557–82.

Oliker, Stacey J. 2000. "Examining Care at Welfare's End." In *Care Work: Gender, Labor, and the Welfare State,* edited by Madonna Harrington Meyer. New York: Routledge.

O'Neill, June. 2003. "The Gender Gap in Wages, Circa 2000." *American Economic Review* 93(2): 309–14.

O'Rand, Angela M. 1996. "The Cumulative Stratification of the Life Course." In *Handbook of Aging and the Social Sciences,* 4th ed., edited by Robert H. Binstock, Linda K. George, Victor W. Marshall, George C. Myers, and James H. Schulz. San Diego, Calif.: Academic Press.

O'Rand, Angela M., and John C. Henretta. 1999. *Age and Inequality: Diverse Pathways Through Later Life.* Boulder, Colo.: Westview Press.

Orava, Tamma A., Peter J. McLeod, and Donald Sharpe. 1996. "Perceptions of Control, Depressive Symptomatology and Self-Esteem of Women in Transition from Abusive Relationships." *Journal of Family Violence* 11(2): 167–86.

Organization for Economic Cooperation and Development (OECD). 2005. "Pensions at a Glance: Public Policies Across OECD Countries 2005 Edition." May 2, 2005. Paris: OECD. Organization for Economic Cooperation and Development. http://www.oecd.org/dataoecd/44/55/34816545.pdf.

Orloff, Ann Shola. 1993. "Gender and the Social Rights of Citizenship: The Comparative Analysis of Gender Relations and Welfare States." *American Sociological Review* 58(3): 303–28.

———. 1996. "Gender in the Welfare State." *Annual Review of Sociology* 22(1996): 51–78.

Orr, Amy J. 2003. "Black-White Differences in Achievement: The Importance of Wealth." *Sociology of Education* 76(4): 281–304.

Orszag, Peter R. 1999. "Individual Accounts in the United Kingdom: Lessons for the United States." Testimony before the House Committee on Ways and Means, Hearing on Social Security Reform Lessons Learned in Other Countries. February 11, 1999. Washington: U.S. House of Representatives.

Ozawa, Martha N. 1976. "Income Redistribution and Social Security." *Social Service Review* 50(2): 209–23.

Padavic, Irene, and Barbara F. Reskin. 2002. *Women and Men at Work,* 2nd ed. Newbury Park, Calif.: Pine Forge Press.

Palmer, Heather M., and Keith S. Dobson. 1994. "Self-Medication and Memory in an Elderly Canadian Sample." *The Gerontologist* 34(5): 658–64.

Palmer, John L. 2006. "Entitlement Programs for the Aged: The Long-Term Fiscal Context." *Research on Aging* 28(3): 289–302.

Park, Edwin, Melanie Nathanson, Robert Greenstein, and John Springer. 2003. "The Troubling Medicare Legislation." Washington: Center on Budget Priorities. http://www.cbpp.org/11-18-03health2.pdf.

Parreñas, Rhacel Salazar. 2000. "Migrant Filipina Domestic Workers and the International Division of Reproductive Labor." *Gender and Society* 14(4): 560–80.

Pascall, Gillian. 1986. *Social Policy: A Feminist Analysis.* London: Tavistock.

Pauly, Mark, Patricia Danzon, Paul Feldstein, and John Hoff. 1991. "A Plan For 'Responsible National Health Insurance.' " *Health Affairs* 10(1): 5–25.

Pavalko, Eliza K., and Brad Smith. 1999. "The Rhythm of Work: Health Effects of Women's Work Dynamics." *Social Forces* 77(3): 1141–62.

Pavalko, Eliza K., and Shari Woodbury. 2000. "Social Roles As Process: Caregiving Careers and Women's Health." *Journal of Health and Social Behavior* 41(1): 91–105.

Pavalko, Eliza K., Glen H. Elder, Jr., and Elizabeth C. Clipp. 1993. "Worklives and Longevity: Insights from a Life Course Perspective." *Journal of Health and Social Behavior* 34(4): 363–80.

Pavalko, Eliza K., Krysia N. Mossakowski, and Vanessa J. Hamilton. 2003. "Does Perceived Discrimination Affect Health? Longitudinal Relationships between Work Discrimination and Women's Physical and Emotional Health." *Journal of Health and Social Behavior* 44(1): 18–33.

Perkins, H. Wesley, and Debra K. DeMeis. 1996. "Gender and Family Effects on the 'Second-Shift' Domestic Activity of College-Educated Young Adults." *Gender and Society* 10(1): 78–93.

Pew Research Center. 2005. "AARP, Greenspan Most Trusted on Social Security. Bush Failing in Social Security Push." For The People and The Press. News Release, March 2, 2005. Washington: Pew Research Center. http://people-press.org/reports/pdf/238.pdf.

Pierson, Paul. 2001. *The New Politics of the Welfare State.* New York: Oxford University Press.

Piven, Frances Fox, and Richard A. Cloward. 1982. *The New Class War: Reagan's Attack on the Welfare State and Its Consequences.* New York: Pantheon Books.

Pollack, Wendy. 2003. "Marrying(Uncle) Sam? The Problem with the Bush Administration's 'Marriage Promotion' Agenda." National Organization for Women, Guest Commentary, October 7, 2003. http://www.now.org/issues/economic/welfare/100703marriage.html.

Porter, Kathryn H., and Allen Dupree. 2001. *Poverty Trends for Families Headed by Working Single Mothers, 1993–1999.* Washington: Center on Budget and Policy Priorities. http://www.cbpp.org/8-16-01wel.pdf.

Porter, Kathryn H., Kathy Larin, and Wendell Primus. 1999. *Social Security and Poverty Among the Elderly: A National and State Perspective.* Washington: Center on Budget and Policy Priorities. http://www.cbpp.org/4-8-99socsec.pdf.

Potter, John D. 1992. "Reconciling the Epidemiology, Physiology, and Molecular Biology of Colon Cancer." *Journal of American Medical Association* 268(12): 1573–7.

President's Commission to Strengthen Social Security. 2001. *Strengthening Social Security and Creating Personal Wealth for All Americans.* Final Report, December 21, 2001. Washington: President's Commission to Strengthen Social Security. http://www.csss.gov/reports/Final_report.pdf.

Proctor, Bernadette D., and Joseph Dalaker. 2002. "Poverty in the United States: 2001." *Current Population Reports,* series P60, no. 219. Washington: U.S. Census Bureau.

———. 2003. "Poverty in the United States: 2002." *Current Population Reports,* series P60, no. 222. Washington: U.S. Census Bureau. http://www.census.gov/prod/2003pubs/p60-222.pdf.

Public Agenda. 2005. "Medicare: Results of Survey Question re Federal Budget." PublicAgenda.org Issue Guides. April 18–22, 2005. http://www.publicagenda.org/issues/major_proposals_detail2.cfm?issue_type=medicare&proposal_graphic=majpropmedicarebudget.jpg.

Quadagno, Jill S. 1984. "Welfare Capitalism and the Social Security Act of 1935." *American Sociological Review* 49(5): 632–47.

———. 1987. "Theories of the Welfare State." *Annual Review of Sociology* 13(1987): 109–28.

———. 1988. "Women's Access to Pensions and the Structure of Eligibility Rules: Systems of Production and Reproduction." *Sociological Quarterly* 29(4): 541–58.

———. 1994. *The Color of Welfare: How Racism Undermined the War on Poverty.* New York: Oxford University Press.

———. 1996. "Social Security and the Myth of the Entitlement 'Crisis.' " *Gerontologist* 36(3): 391–99.

———. 1999. "Creating a Capital Investment Welfare State: The New American Exceptionalism." *American Sociological Review* 64(1): 1–11.

———. 2001. *Aging and the Life Course: An Introduction to Social Gerontology.* 2nd ed. Burr Ridge, Ill.: McGraw Hill College.

———. 2005. *One Nation, Uninsured: Why the U.S. Has No National Health Insurance.* New York: Oxford University Press.

Raabe, Phyllis H. 1990. "The Organizational Effects of Workplace Family Policies: Past Weaknesses and Recent Progress Toward Improved Research." *Journal of Family Issues* 11(4): 477–91.

Rawlston, Valerie A., and William E. Spriggs. 2001. "Pay Equity 2000: Are We There Yet?" Special Research Report 02–2001. Washington: National Urban League, Institute for Opportunity and Equality.

Reading, Richard. 1997. "Social Disadvantage and Infection in Childhood." *Sociology of Health and Illness* 19(4): 395–414.

Reich, Robert D. 1999. "We Are All Third Wayers Now." *The American Prospect* online edition, March 1.

Rennison, Callie Marie. 2003. "Intimate Partner Violence, 1993–2001." NCJ 197838. Washington: U.S. Department of Justice. http://www.ojp.usdoj.gov/bjs/pub/pdf/ipv01.pdf.

Rennison, Callie Marie, and Sarah Welchans. 2000. "Special Report: Intimate Partner Violence." NCJ 178247. Washington: Department of Justice, Bureau of Labor Statistics. May. http://www.ojp.usdoj.gov/bjs/pub/pdf/ipv.pdf.

Reskin, Barbara F. 1988. "Bringing the Men Back In: Sex Differentiation and the Devaluation of Women's Work. 1987 Cheryl Miller Lecture." *Gender & Society* 2(1): 58–81.

———. 1993. "Sex Segregation in the Workplace." *Annual Review of Sociology* 19: 241–70.

———. 1999. "Racial and Ethnic Segregation among Women." In *Latinas and African American Women at Work: Race, Gender and Economic Inequality,* edited by Irene Browne. New York: Russell Sage Foundation.

———. 2000. "The Proximate Causes of Employment Discrimination." *Contemporary Sociology* 29(2): 319–28.

Reskin, Barbara F., and Heidi I. Hartmann. 1987. *Women's Work, Men's Work: Sex Segregation on the Job.* Washington: National Academy Press.

Reskin, Barbara F., and Patricia A. Roos. 1990. *Job Queues, Gender Queues: Explaining Women's Inroads into Male Occupations.* Philadelphia, Pa.: Temple University Press.

Rice, Tom, and Kate Desmond. 2002. *An Analysis of Reforming Medicare Through a "Premium Support" Program.* Washington: Kaiser Family Foundation. http://www.kff.org/medicare/loader.cfm?url=/commonspot/security/getfile.cfm&PageID=14147.

Ridgeway, Cecilia. 2006. "Gender as an Organizing Force in Social Relations: Implications for the Future of Inequality." In *The Declining Significance of Gender?* edited by Francine D. Blau, Mary C. Brinton, and David B. Grusky. New York: Russell Sage Foundation.

Rieker, Patricia, and Chloe E. Bird. 2000. "Sociological Explanations of Gender Differences in Mental and Physical Health." In *Handbook of Medical Sociology,* 5th ed., edited by Chloe E. Bird, Peter Conrad, and Allen M. Fremont. Upper Saddle River, N.J.: Prentice Hall.

Rogoff, Kenneth. 2003. "The IMF Strikes Back." *Foreign Policy* 134: 39–46.

Rogowski, Jeannette, and Lynn Karoly. 2002. *Gender Differences in Access to Employer-Sponsored Retirement Benefits Among the Near Elderly.* RAND Corporation internal paper.

Rollins, Judith. 1985. *Between Women: Domestics and Their Employers.* Philadelphia, Pa.: Temple University Press.

Romero, Mary. 2002. *Maid in the U.S.A.,* 10th anniversary edition, with new introduction and afterword by Dorothy Smith. New York: Routledge.

Rose, Stephen J., and Heidi Hartmann. 2004. *Still a Man's Labor Market: The Long–Term Earnings Gap.* Washington: Institute for Women's Policy Research. http://www.iwpr.org/pdf/C355.pdf.

Ross, Catherine E., and Chloe E. Bird. 1994. "Sex Stratification and Health Lifestyle: Consequences for Men's and Women's Perceived Health." *Journal of Health and Social Behavior* 35(2): 161–78.

Ross, Catherine E., and John Mirowsky. 2001. "Neighborhood Disadvantage, Disorder, and Health." *Journal of Health and Social Behavior* 42(3): 258–76.

Ross, Catherine E., and Chia-Ling Wu. 1996. "Education, Age, and the Cumulative Advantage in Health." *Journal of Health and Social Behavior* 37(1): 104–20.

Ross, Stephen L., and Margery Austin Turner. 2005. "Housing Discrimination in Metropolitan America: Explaining Changes Between 1989 and 2000." *Social Problems* 52(2): 152–80.

Rothman, Kenneth J. 1986. *Modern Epidemiology*. Boston, Mass.: Little, Brown.

Rubery, Jill, Mark Smith, and Colette Fagan. 1998. "National Working-Time Regimes and Equal Opportunities." *Feminist Economics* 4(1): 71–101.

Ruggie, Mary. 1984. *The State and Working Women: A Comparative Study of Britain and Sweden*. Princeton, N.J.: Princeton University Press.

Ruhm, Christopher J. 1997. "Policy Watch: The Family and Medical Leave Act." *Journal of Economic Perspectives* 11(3): 175–86.

———. 1998. "The Economic Consequences of Parental Leave Mandates: Lessons from Europe." *Quarterly Journal of Economics* 113(1): 285–317.

Sahyoun, Nadine R., Laura A. Pratt, Harold Lentzner, Achintya Dey, and Kristen N. Robinson. 2001. "The Changing Profile of Nursing Home Residents: 1985–1997." *Aging Trends* No. 4. Hyattsville, Md.: National Center for Health Statistics. http://www.cdc.gov/nchs/data/ahcd/agingtrends/04nursin.pdf.

Sainsbury, Diane, editor. 1994. *Gendering Welfare States*. Thousand Oaks, Calif.: Sage Publications.

———. 1999. *Gender and Welfare State Regimes*. New York: Oxford University Press.

Satel, Sally. 2001. "The Indoctrinologists Are Coming." *Atlantic Monthly* 287(1): 59–64.

Sayer, Liana C. 2005. "Gender, Time and Inequality: Trends in Women's and Men's Paid Work, Unpaid Work and Free time." *Social Forces* 84(1): 285–303.

Scharlach, Andrew E. 1994. "Caregiving and Employment: Competing or Complementary Roles?" *The Gerontologist* 34(3): 378–85.

Schieber, George J., and Jean-Pierre Poullier. 1989. "International Health Care Expenditure Trends: 1987." *Health Affairs* 8(3): 169–77.

Schone, Pal. 2005. "The Effect of a Family Policy Reform on Mother's Pay: A Natural Experiment Approach." *Review of Economics and the Household* 3(2): 145–70.

Schor, Juliet. 1991. *The Overworked American: The Unexpected Decline of Leisure*. New York: Basic Books.

Schulman, Kevin A., Jesse A. Berlin, William Harless, Jon F. Kerner, Shryl Sistrunk, Bernard Gersh, R. Dubé, C. K. Taleghani, J. E. Burke, S. Williams, J. M. Eisenberg, and J. J. Escarce. 1999. "The Effect of Race and Sex on Physicians' Recommendations for Cardiac Catheterization." *New England Journal of Medicine* 340(8): 618–26.

Schwartz, Christine R., and Robert D. Mare. 2005. "Trends in Educational Assortative Marriage from 1940 to 2003." *Demography* 42(4): 621–46.

Schwartz, Roger A., and Charles P. Sabatino. 1994. "Medicaid Estate Recovery under OBRA '93: Picking the Bones of the Poor?" Washington: American Bar Association. Commission on Legal Problems of the Elderly.

Scrivner, Scott, and Barbara Wolfe. 2003. "Universal Preschool: Much to Gain But Who Will Pay?" IRP Discussion Paper no. 1271-03. Madison, Wisc.: Institute for Research on Poverty, University of Wisconsin–Madison. July. http://www.irp.wisc.edu/publications/dps/pdfs/dp127103.pdf.

Seccombe, Karen. 1999. *So You Think I Drive a Cadillac? Welfare Recipients' Perspectives on the System and its Reform*. Boston, Mass.: Allyn and Bacon.

Seccombe, Karen, and Cheryl Amey. 1995. "Playing by the Rules and Losing: Health Insurance and the Working Poor." *Journal of Health and Social Behavior* 36(2): 168–81.

Seccombe, Wally. 1974. "The Housewife and Her Labour Under Capitalism." *New Left Review* 83: 3–24.

Settersten, Richard A. 1999. *Lives in Time and Place: The Problems and Promises of Developmental Science.* Amityville, N.Y.: Baywood Publishing.

———. 2003. "Introduction." In *Invitation to the Life Course: Toward New Understandings of Later Life,* edited by Richard A. Settersten. Amityville, N.Y.: Baywood Publishing.

Shuey, Kim M., and Angela M. O'Rand. 2004. "New Risks for Workers: Pensions, Labor Markets, and Gender." *Annual Review of Sociology* 30(2004): 453–77.

———. 2006. "Changing Demographics and New Pension Risks." *Research on Aging* 28(3): 317–40.

Siaroff, Alan. 2000. "Women's Representation in Legislatures and Cabinets in Industrial Democracies." *International Political Science Review* 21(2): 197–215.

Simon, Robin W. 1998. "Assessing Sex Differences in Vulnerability among Employed Parents: The Importance of Marital Status." *Journal of Health and Social Behavior* 39(1): 38–54.

Skocpol, Theda. 1991. "Targeting Within Universalism: Politically Viable Policies to Combat." In *The Urban Underclass,* edited by Christopher Jencks and Paul E. Peterson. Washington: Brookings Institution Press.

———. 1992. *Protecting Soldiers and Mothers: The Political Origins of Social Policy in the United States.* Cambridge, Mass.: Belknap Press of Harvard University Press.

———. 1998. "Don't Blame Big Government: America's Voluntary Groups Thrive in a National Network." In *Community Works: The Revival of Civil Society in America,* edited by E. J. Dionne, Jr. Washington: Brookings Institution Press.

———. 1999. "Advocates without Members: The Recent Transformation of American Civic Life." In *Civic Engagement in American Democracy,* edited by Theda Skocpol and Morris P. Fiorina. Washington: Brookings Institution Press.

Skocpol, Theda, and Edwin Armenta. 1986. "States and Social Policies." *Annual Review of Sociology* 12(1986): 131–57.

Sloan, Frank, Janet Mitchell, and Jerry Cronwell. 1978. "Physician Participation in State Medicaid Programs." *Journal of Human Resources* 13(Supplement): 211–45.

Smeeding, Timothy M., and Susanna Sandström. 2005. "Poverty and Income Maintenance in Old Age: A Cross–National View of Low–Income Older Women." *Feminist Economics* 11(2): 163–74.

Smeeding, Timothy M., Carroll L. Estes, and Lou Glasse. 1999. "Social Security Reform and Older Women: Improving the System." Income Security Policy Series Paper no. 22. Syracuse, N.Y.: Center for Policy Research, Syracuse University. http://www-cpr.maxwell.syr.edu/incomsec/pdf/inc22.pdf.

Smeeding, Timothy M., Katherin Ross Phillips, and Michael O'Connor. 2000. "The EITC: Expectation, Knowledge, Use and Economic and Social Mobility." JCPR Working Paper 139. Evanston, Ill.: Joint Center for Poverty Research, Northwestern University.

Smith, James P. 1999. "Healthy Bodies and Thick Wallets: The Dual Relation between Health and Economic Status." *Journal of Economic Perspectives* 13(2): 145–66.

———. 2003. "Assimilation across the Latino Generations." *American Economic Review* 93(2): 315–19.

Smith, James P., and Raynard Kington. 1997. "Demographic and Economic Correlates of Health in Old Age: Asset and Health Dynamics among the Oldest Old (AHEAD)." *Demography* 34(1): 159–70.

Smith, Robin, and Michelle DeLair. 1999. "New Evidence from Lender Testing: Discrimination at the Pre-Application Stage." In *Mortgage Lending Discrimination: A Review of Existing Evidence,* edited by Margery Austin Turner and Felicity Skidmore. Washington: Urban Institute Press.

Smith, Shanna L., and Cathy Cloud. 1996. "The Role of Private, Nonprofit Fair Housing Enforcement Organizations in Lending Testing." In *Mortgage Lending, Racial Discrimination, and Federal Policy,* edited by John Goering and John Wienk. Washington: Urban Institute Press.

Smock, Pamela J., Wendy D. Manning, and Sanjiv Gupta. 1999. "The Effect of Marriage and Divorce on Women's Economic Well-Being." *American Sociological Review* 64(6): 794–812.

Social Security Administration (SSA). 1979. "Social Security Financing and Benefits: Report of the 1979 Advisory Council." Washington: U.S. Department of Health and Human Services.

———. 2002. "Fast Facts and Figures about Social Security, 2002." Washington: U.S. Department of Health and Human Services. http://www.ssa.gov/policy/docs/chartbooks/fast_facts/2002/index.html.

———. 2004. *Annual Statistical Supplement, 2002.* Washington: U.S. Department of Health and Human Services.

———. 2005a. "The 2005 OASDI Trustees Report." Washington: U.S. Department of Health and Human Services, Office of the Chief Actuary. April 5. http://www.ssa.gov/OACT/TR/TR05/index.html, http://www.ssa.gov/OACT/TR/TR05/tr05.pdf.

———. 2005b. "Fast Facts and Figures about Social Security 2004." Publication no. 13-11785. Washington: U.S. Department of Health and Human Services. http://www.ssa.gov/policy/docs/chartbooks/fast_facts/2004/.

———. 2006. *Annual Statistical Supplement 2005.* Social Security Bulletin. Washington: Department of Health and Human Services. http://www.ssa.gov/policy/docs/statcomps/supplement/2005/supplement05.pdf.

———. 2007. "OASDI Monthly Statistics, April 2007, Table 3." http://www.ssa.gov/policy/docs/statecomps/oasdi_monthly/2007-04/table03.pdf.

Sokoloff, Natalie J. 1992. *Black Women and White Women in the Professions: Occupational Segregation by Race and Gender, 1960–1980.* Perspectives on Gender. New York: Routledge.

Sorensen, Elaine, and Ariel Hill. 2004. "Single Mothers and Their Child-Support Receipt: How Well Is Child-Support Enforcement Doing?" *Journal of Human Resources* 39(1): 135–54.

Sorensen, Elaine, and Chava Zibman. 2000. "Child Support Offers Some Protection Against Poverty." New Federalism: National Survey of America's Families series, no. B–10. Washington: Urban Institute Press.

Stack, Carol B. 1974. *All Our Kin: Strategies for Survival in a Black Community.* New York: Harper and Row.

Starfield, Barbara. 2000. "Is US Health Really the Best in the World?" *Journal of the American Medical Association* 284(4): 483–5.

Stephens, Mary Ann Parris, and Melissa M. Franks. 1995. "Spillover between Daughters' Roles as Caregiver and Wife: Interference or Enhancement?" *Journals of Gerontology, Series B: Psychological Sciences and Social Sciences* 50B(1): 9–17.

Stewart, D. E., and A. Cecutti. 1993. "Physical Abuse in Pregnancy." *Canadian Medical Association Journal* 149(9): 1257–63.

Stone, Robyn I. 2000. "Long-Term Care for the Elderly with Disabilities: Current Policy, Emerging Trends, and Implications for the Twenty-First Century." Washington: Milbank Memorial Fund. http://www.milbank.org/reports/0008stone/LongTermCare_Mech5.pdf.

Stone, Robyn I., Gail Lee Cafferata, and Judith Sangl. 1987. "Caregivers of the Frail Elderly: A National Profile." *The Gerontologist* 27(5): 616–26.

Story, Louise. 2005. "Many Women at Elite Colleges Set Career Path to Motherhood." *New York Times*, September 20, 2005: A1.

Straus, Murray A., and Richard J. Gelles. 1990. "Gender Differences in Reporting of Marital Violence and Its Medical and Psychological Consequences." In *Physical Violence in American Families: Risk Factors and Adaptations to Violence in 8,145 Families*, edited by Murray A. Straus, Richard J. Gelles, and Christine Smith. New Brunswick, N.J.: Transaction Publishers.

Street, Debra, and Jeralynn Sittig Cossman. 2006. "Greatest Generation or Greedy Geezers? Social Spending Preferences and the Elderly." *Social Problems* 53(1): 75–96.

Street, Debra, and Janet Wilmoth. 2001. "Social Insecurity? Women and Pensions in the U.S." In *Women, Work, and Pensions: International Issues and Prospects*, edited by Jay Ginn, Debra Street, and Sara Arber. Philadelphia, Pa.: Taylor & Francis.

Svahn, J. A., and M. Ross. 1983. "Social Security Amendments of 1983: Legislative History and Summary of Provisions." *Social Security Bulletin* 46(7): 3–48.

Toder, Eric, Cori Uccello, John O'Hara, Melissa Favreault, Caroline Ratcliffe, Karen Smith, Gary Burtless, and Barry Bosworth. 1999. *Final Report: Modeling Income in the Near Term–Projections of Retirement Income Through 2020 for the 1931–60 Birth Cohorts.* Washington: Urban Institute Press. http://www.urban.org/UploadedPDF/410609_ModelingIncome.pdf.

Tong, Rosemarie. 1998. *Feminist Thought: A More Comprehensive Introduction.,* 2nd ed. Boulder, Colo.: Westview Press.

Torres-Gil, Fernando, Robert Greenstein, and David Kamin. 2005. "Hispanics' Large Stake in the Social Security Debate." Washington: Center on Budget and Policy Priorities. http://www.cbpp.org/6-28-05socsec.pdf.

Traustadóttir, Rannveig. 2000. "Disability Reform and Women's Caring Work." In *Care Work: Gender, Labor, and the Welfare State,* edited by Madonna Harrington Meyer. New York: Routledge.

Tuominen, Mary C. 2003. *We Are Not Babysitters: Family Childcare Providers Redefine Work and Care.* New Brunswick, N.J.: Rutgers University Press.

Turner, Heather A., and R. Jay Turner. 1999. "Gender, Social Status, and Emotional Reliance." *Journal of Health and Social Behavior* 40(4): 360–73.

Turner, Margery Austin, Stephen L. Ross, George Galster, and John Yinger. 2002. "Discrimination in Metropolitan Housing Markets: National Results from Phase I of HDS2000." Washington: Urban Institute Press. http://www.urban.org/publications/410821.html.

Turner, R. Jay, and F. Marino. 1994. "Social Support and Social Structure: A Descriptive Epidemiology." *Journal of Health and Social Behavior* 35(3): 193–212.

Turner, R. Jay, and Samuel Noh. 1988. "Physical Disability and Depression: A Longitudinal Analysis." *Journal of Health and Social Behavior* 29(1): 23–37.

U.S. Bureau of Labor Statistics. 2006. "Usual Weekly Earnings of Wage and Salary Workers: Second Quarter 2006." August 2, 2006. Washington: U.S. Department of Labor, Bureau of Labor Statistics. http://www.bls.gov/news.release/wkyeng.t02.htm.

U.S. Census Bureau. 1971. "Characteristics of the Low-Income Population:1970." *Current Population Reports,* series P60, no. 81. Washington: U.S. Census Bureau. http://www.census.gov/hhes/www/poverty/prevcps/p60-81.pdf.

———. 1979. "Characteristics of the Population Below the Poverty Level: 1977." *Current Population Reports,* series P60, no. 119. Washington: U.S. Census Bureau. http://www.census.gov/hhes/www/poverty/prevcps/p60-119.pdf.

———. 2004. "Age and Sex of All People, Family Members and Unrelated Individuals Iterated by Income-to-Poverty Ratio and Race in Annual Social and Economic Supplement." *CPS Annual Demographic Survey, March Supplement,* Table POV01. Washington: Bureau of Labor Statistics and U.S. Census Bureau. http://pubdb3.census.gov/macro/032004/pov/toc.htm.

———. 2005a. "Age–People (All Races) by Median Income and Sex: 1947 to 2001." *Historical Income Tables, People,* Table P-8. September 16, 2005. Washington: U.S. Census Bureau http://www.census.gov/hhes/www/income/histinc/p08ar.html.

———. 2005b. "America's Family and Living Arrangements: 2005." August 2, 2006. Washington: U.S. Census Bureau. http://www.census.gov/population/www/socdemo/hh-fam/cps2005.html.

———. 2006a. "Educational Attainment–People 25 Years Old and Over, by Total Money Earnings in 2005, Work Experience in 2005, Age, Race, Hispanic Origin and Sex." *CPS Annual Social and Economic Supplement,* Table PINC-03. December 7, 2006. Washington: Bureau of Labor Statistics and U.S. Census. Bureau. http://pubdb3.census.gov/macro/032006/perinc/new03_000.htm.

———. 2006b. "Poverty Status, by Type of Family, Presence of Related Children, Race and Hispanic Origin." *Historical Poverty Tables,* Table 4. August 2, 2006. Washington: U.S. Census Bureau, Housing and Household Economic Statistics Division. http://www.census.gov/hhes/www/poverty/histpov/famindex.html.

U.S. Congress. House Committee on Ways and Means. 2004. "Green Book: Background Material and Data on Programs within the Jurisdiction of the Committee on Ways and Means." Committee Report WMCP 108–6. Washington: U.S. Government Printing Office. http://waysandmeans.house.gov/Documents.asp?section=813.

U.S. Department of Labor. 1995. "Employment, Hours, and Earnings, United States, 1990–1995." Bulletin 2465. Washington: U.S. Department of Labor, Bureau of Labor Statistics.

U.S. General Accounting Office (GAO). 1979. *Minimum Social Security Benefit: A Windfall That Should Be Eliminated: Report to the Congress.* HRD-80-29. Washington: General Accounting Office. http://archive.gao.gov/f0202/111057.pdf.

———. 2001. *Retiree Health Benefits: Employer–Sponsored Benefits May Be Vulnerable to Further Erosion.* GAO-01-374. Washington: Government Printing Office. http://www.gao.gov/new.items/d01374.pdf.

———. 2003. *Retirement Income: Intergenerational Comparisons of Wealth and Future Income: Report to the Ranking Minority Member, Subcommittee on Employer-*

Employee Relations, Committee on Education and the Workforce, House of Representatives. GAO-03-429. Washington: General Accounting Office. http://www.gao.gov/new.items/d03429.pdf.

Umberson, Debra, Kristin Anderson, Jennifer Glick, and Adam Shapiro. 1998. "Domestic Violence, Personal Control, and Gender." *Journal of Marriage and the Family* 60(2): 442–52.

Venti, Steven F., and David A. Wise. 2001. "Aging and Housing Equity: Another Look." *NBER* Working Paper no. 8608. Cambridge, Mass.: National Bureau of Economic Research.

Verma, Satyendra. 2003. "Retirement Coverage of Women and Minorities: Analysis from SIPP 1998 Data." Report DD92. Washington: AARP Public Policy Institute. http://www.aarp.org/research/financial/pensions/aresearch-import-350-DD92.html.

Vernez, Georges. 1999. *Immigrant Women in the U.S. Workforce: Who Struggles? Who Succeeds?* Lanham, Md.: Lexington Books.

Voydanoff, Patricia, and Brenda W. Donnelly. 1999. "The Intersection of Time in Activities and Perceived Unfairness in Relation to Psychological Distress and Marital Quality." *Journal of Marriage and the Family* 61(3): 739–51.

Waidmann, Timothy A. 1998. "Potential Effects of Raising Medicare's Eligibility Age." *Health Affairs* 17(2): 156–64.

Waldfogel, Jane. 1998. "Understanding the 'Family Gap' in Pay for Women with Children." *Journal of Economic Perspectives* 12(1): 137–56.

———. 2001. "Family and Medical Leave: Evidence from the 2000 Surveys." *Monthly Labor Review* 124(9): 17–23.

Waldfogel, Jane, and Susan Mayer. 1999. "Differences between Men and Women in the Low–Wage Labor Market." *Focus* 20(1): 11–13.

Waldron, Ingrid, Christopher C. Weiss, and Mary Elizabeth Hughes. 1998. "Interacting Effects of Multiple Roles on Women's Health." *Journal of Health and Social Behavior* 39(3): 216–36.

Walker, David. 2006. "Tax Compliance: Challenges to Corporate Tax Enforcement and Options to Improve Securities Basis Reporting." Testimony before the Committee on Finance, U.S. Senate. GAO-06-851T. Washington: United States Government Accountability Office. http://www.gao.gov/new.items/d06851t.pdf.

Wallace, Michael, and Chin-fen Chang. 1990. "Barriers to Women's Employment: Economic Segmentation in American Manufacturing, 1950–1980." *Research in Social Stratification and Mobility* 9: 337–61.

Wallace, Steven P., Lene Levy-Storms, Raynard S. Kington, and Ronald M. Andersen. 1998. "The Persistence of Race and Ethnicity in the Use of Long-Term Care." *Journals of Gerontology* 53B(2): S104–12.

Walzer, Michael. 1988. "Socializing the Welfare State." In *Democracy and the Welfare State*, edited by Amy Gutmann. Princeton, N.J.: Princeton University Press.

Wasow, Bernard. 2004. "A New Minimum Benefit for Social Security." Idea Brief. New York: Century Foundation. http://www.socsec.org/publications.asp?pubid=463.

Waxman, Henry, A. 2006. "Pharmaceutical Industry Profits Increase by Over $8 Billion after Medicare Drug Plan Goes into Effect." Washington: U.S. Congress Committee on Oversight and Government Reform. http://oversight.house.gov/story.asp?

Waxman, Judith. 1992. "Testimony before the Joint Hearing of the Select Committee on Aging and the Congressional Black Caucus." U.S. House of Representatives. 102nd Cong., 1st session, September 13, 1991. Aging Commission, Publication no. 102–846. Washington: Government Printing Office.

Weir, Margaret. 1998. "Political Parties and Social Policy Making." In *The Social Divide: Political Parties and the Future of Activist Government,* edited by Margaret Weir. Washington: Brookings Institution Press.

Weitz, Rose. 2007. *The Sociology of Health, Illness and Health Care,* 4th ed. Belmont, Calif.: Wadsworth Publishing.

Weller, Christian E., and Laura Singleton. 2002. "The Scandal Beyond Enron: Pension Coverage Is Shaky and Dwindling. Will Congress Act?" *The American Prospect* 13(17): Online edition. http://www.prospect.org/print/V13/17/weller-c.html.

Wharton, Amy S. 1989. "Gender Segregation in Private–Sector, Public–Sector, and Self–Employed Occupations, 1950–1981." *Social Science Quarterly* 70(4): 923–40.

Whittle, Jeff, Joseph Conigliaro, C. B. Good, and Richard P. Lofgren. 1993. "Racial Differences in the Use of Invasive Cardiovascular Procedures in the Department of Veterans Affairs Medical System." *New England Journal of Medicine* 329(9): 621–7.

Wiener, Joshua M., and David G. Stevenson. 1998. "Long-Term Care for the Elderly: Profiles of Thirteen States." *Assessing the New Federalism* Occasional Paper no. 12. Washington: Urban Institute Press.

Williams, David R. 1997. "Race and Health: Basic Questions, Emerging Directions." *Annals of Epidemiology* 7(5): 322–33.

———. 2000. "Effects of the Social Environment—Race, Socioeconomic Status, and Health: The Added Effects of Racism and Discrimination." *Annals of the New York Academy of Sciences* 896(2000): 173–88.

Williams, David R., and Chiquita Collins. 1995. "US Socioeconomic and Racial Differences in Health: Patterns and Explanations." *Annual Review of Sociology* 21(1995): 349–86.

Williams, S. W., and P. Dilworth-Anderson. 2002. "Systems of Social Support in Families Who Care for Dependent African American Elders." *Gerontologist* 42(2): 224–36.

Williamson, John B., and Sara E. Rix. 1999. "Social Security Reform: Implications for Women." *Center for Retirement Research* Working Paper 1999-07. Chestnut Hill, Mass.: Boston College. http://www.bc.edu/centers/crr/papers/wp_1999-07.pdf.

Wilmoth, Janet, and Gregor Koso. 2002. "Does Marital History Matter? Marital Status and Wealth Outcomes Among Preretirement Adults." *Journal of Marriage and the Family* 64(1): 254–68.

Wilson, Theresa M. 1999. "Opting Out: The Galveston Plan and Social Security." *Pension Research Council* Working Paper 99-22. Philadelphia, Pa.: Wharton School, University of Pennsylvania. http://rider.wharton.upenn.edu/~prc/PRC/WP/wp99-22.pdf.

Wolf, Douglas A., Vicki Freedman, and Beth J. Soldo. 1997. "Division of Family Labor: Care for Elderly Parents." *Journals of Gerontology: Psychological and Social Sciences* 52B(Special Issue): 102–9.

Wolff, Edward N. 2002. "Asset Poverty in the United States, 1984–1999: Evidence from the Panel Study of Income Dynamics." Working Paper no. 356. Annandale-on-Hudson, N.Y.: Levy Economics Institute of Bard College.

———. 2004. "Changes in Household Wealth in the 1980s and 1990s in the U.S." Working Paper no. 407. Annandale-on-Hudson, N.Y.: Levy Economics Institute of Bard College.

Wood, Erica F., and Charles P. Sabatino. 1996. "Medicaid Estate Recovery and the Poor: Restitution or Retribution?" *Generations* 20(3): 84–7.

Wray, L. Randall. 2005. "The Ownership Society: Social Security Is Only the Beginning." Public Policy Brief no. 82. Annandale-on-Hudson, N.Y.: Levy Economics Institute of Bard College.

Wu, Ke Bin. 2004. "African Americans Age 65 and Older: Their Sources of Income." Fact Sheet FS 100. Washington: AARP Public Policy Institute.

Yabiku, Scott T. 2000. "Family History and Pensions: The Relationships between Marriage, Divorce, Children, and Private Pension Coverage." *Journal of Aging Studies* 14(3): 293–312.

Yamokoski, Alexis, and Lisa Keister. 2006. "The Wealth of Single Women: Marital Status and Parenthood in the Asset Accumulation of Young Baby Boomers in the United States." *Feminist Economics* 12(1–2): 167–94.

Yergin, Daniel, and Joseph Stanislaw. 1998. *The Commanding Heights: The Battle Between Government and the Marketplace that is Remaking the Modern World.* New York: Simon & Schuster.

Yinger, John. 2001. "Housing Discrimination and Residential Segregation as Causes of Poverty." In *Understanding Poverty,* edited by Sheldon Danziger and Robert H. Haveman. New York: Russell Sage Foundation.

Zimmerman, Mary K. 1993. "Caregiving in the Welfare State: Mothers' Informal Health Care Work in Finland." *Research in the Sociology of Health Care* 10: 193–211.

═ Index ═

Boldface numbers refer to figures and tables.